ultimate
beading
bible

ultimate
beading
bible

A Complete Reference with Step-by-Step Techniques

Edited by
Marie Clayton

COLLINS & BROWN

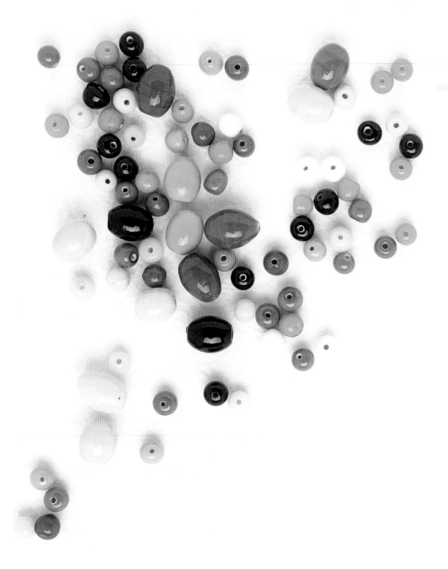

First published in the United Kingdom in 2014 by
Collins & Brown
10 Southcombe Street
London
W14 0RA

An imprint of Anova Books Company Ltd

Copyright © Collins & Brown 2014

Distributed in the United States and Canada by
Sterling Publishing Co, 387 Park Avenue South,
New York, NY 10016, USA.

ISBN 978-1-90939-718-7

A CIP catalogue for this book is available from the British Library.

10 9 8 7 6 5 4 3 2 1

Reproduction by Rival Colour Ltd, UK
Printed by Craft Print International Ltd, Singapore

This book can be ordered direct from the publisher at
www.anovabooks.com

contents

introduction

Throughout the ages, many people have loved beads. Lumps of honey-like Baltic amber were drilled to form large irregular beads by prehistoric man and all kinds of shells were used as decoration as early as 50,000 BC. In ancient Egypt a type of rough glass called faience was used to create small tubular and round beads, often with different colours and patterns – these were used in conjunction with beads made from precious stones and gold to fashion incredibly complex and detailed pieces. In ancient China and Japan, jade and bone were carved into exquisitely detailed beads, while porcelain and cinnabar were made as far back as 1300 BC by unknown technologically advanced processes.

Beading is a craft that has many different aspects – you can make your own beads, use them to create wonderful pieces of jewellery or unusual wirework, they can be loomed or woven into bead fabric, knotted or braided in strands, incorporated into knitting or crochet as you work the stitches, or stitched onto fabric using embroidery techniques. In this book we cover all these different ways of using beads, detailing the tools and materials required and explaining the techniques needed.

The first chapter looks at all the basic tools and materials that are used across many types of beading, with information on what they are used for and how to choose the right one for your needs. The second chapter moves on to beadmaking, covering how to make beads from a very wide range of materials and how to add further decoration to finished beads if required. Following this, bead jewellery making looks at threading in alternative ways, as well as using different threading materials and findings. Wirework covers both wire and bead jewellery and using these materials in other ways to make larger items.

Looming and weaving beaded fabric are both ancient crafts that are easy to work when you have learned the basic techniques. If you want to take these further, there are many traditional patterns to try or you can design your own. This chapter also covers some simple braiding and knotting techniques, which can be a very fast and effective way to use beads. The knitting and crochet chapter begins with the basic techniques and then shows how to incorporate beads as you work, either in simple rows or by following a chart. The last chapter covers beaded embroidery, explaining how to work a range of stitches with added beads.

Beading is a craft for everyone – it can be simple or complex and once you begin it can be very addictive! One of the nicest things about beads is their longevity – a beaded item will last and if you become bored with it you can take it apart and use the beads again, in a different way if you choose. Enjoy!

materials and tools

This first chapter begins by covering the basic materials that will be used for most types of beadwork throughout the book. Following this the tools required are arranged by type of beadwork, since most of them are specific to the technique being used. Some of the more general tools – such as pliers and wire cutters – you may already have but if not it's usually best to buy things as you need them.

beads

There are so many different types of beads, in so many shapes, colours and sizes, that it would be impossible to cover all types here – but this section will give you a flavour of what is available. Check out the following chapter on pages 42–77 too – this shows you how to make your own beads using different materials.

Seed beads

These tiny rounded beads are used for the majority of bead-weaving and embroidery projects and can be used for multi-strand jewellery. They come in a vast variety of colours, finishes and sizes, but the best quality are uniform in size and shape. When buying seed beads note that the higher the size number the smaller the bead, because the size number refers to the number of beads that can fit along an inch.

Bead colour and finish

The primary colour of a glass seed bead is the colour of the glass from which the cane was made; different mineral additions, such as gold and copper, change the colours of the glass creating rich hues. The finish of a bead refers to the final coating, which can make it iridescent, metallic, matte, pearlized or silver-lined.

Miyuki delicas

A more tubular version of a seed bead, these come from Japan and are almost perfectly identical in shape and size. They knit together to form a practically seamless piece of beaded cloth when used in bead looming (see page 158) or peyote stitch (see page 166).

Bugle beads

Bugle beads are long thin tubes, which may also be made of glass and come in many of the same finishes and colours as seed beads. If they are being used for embroidery check the edges because they are sometimes sharp enough to cut through thread. You may be able to resolve this by adding a seed bead at each end of the bugle bead to protect the thread.

Crystal beads

Real crystal beads are made from glass with a high lead content, which increases the sparkle when the facets are cut. This adds to their price but the obvious quality makes them worth using where possible. Cheaper 'crystal' beads are often pressed glass – glass pressed into moulds – so do not have as much sparkle but are more cost effective in many cases.

Pressed glass flower beads

One advantage of pressed glass is that it's easy to create more interesting shapes, such as flowers or butterflies. These flower-shape beads are available in sizes from 6mm up to 16mm.

Pressed glass

Pressed glass is made by pressing molten glass into a mould; a long rod of glass cane is heated in a furnace until it is red hot and then placed into a machine that presses it into shape and simultaneously inserts a needle to make a hole. Beads made in this way are very uniform in size and fast to make, so they are very cost effective. The beads can be finished in different ways, such as with a lustre or a matte effect, and are a popular choice for most types of beading.

Wood beads

Wood beads are cheap and lightweight even when quite large so they are good for chunky designs. They are also popular in jewellery for men, in casual bead designs and combined with other natural materials. The wood can be cut and polished into many shapes and may be left natural, stained or painted. Wooden beads often have larger threading holes than other beads, giving you a wider choice of stringing materials.

Wooden beads come in lots of different shapes and colours.

Metal beads

These can be pure metal or plated. Pure silver or gold beads are often sold by weight, with the price varying according to the current price of gold or silver. Metal beads come in different shapes and can have quite intricate surface patterns. They are often used as spacers between more colourful beads to add a different texture or just a glint of metal.

Decorative glass beads

Glass beads come in many other sizes and do not have to be round – they can be oval, pendant, even cubes. Transparent beads may have their hole silver-lined – coated with a reflective lining to catch the light – or colour-lined so the colour shows in a line through the centre of the bead. Glass beads may also have a thin film of metal fused to the surface to create a metallic sheen that changes colour at different angles. Lampwork beads are handmade and are very labour-intensive so tend to be expensive: a cane of glass is melted over a hot torch and rolled around a thin metal rod to create the bead, which is then further decorated with fine strings of glass, or gold or silver leaf.

Ceramic beads

Ceramic beads are made of clay and can be manufactured in a uniform shape and colour or may be handmade or hand painted so each one is slightly different. Because clay is malleable it's also easy to model quite complex or unique shapes. The finished beads are fired, then painted and glazed before final firing to add a colour and a protective finish. A range of art clays and polymer clays are available, which means clay beads can also be made at home, see pages 51 and 55.

Cloisonné beads

To make these beads, outlines in decorative wire are soldered onto a metal base bead and then the different areas of the design are filled with coloured glass enamel. Because of the materials used these beads can be quite heavy.

Acrylic and plastic beads

These are ideal to make items for children because they are inexpensive, hard-wearing and often colourful. They are also lightweight so you can use much larger beads without worrying about pulling threads – particularly in beaded knitting or crochet – although you will have to take care if the item needs to be pressed because a hot iron can melt plastic. They come in many of the same shapes and finishes as glass beads, so if you want to experiment they are a cheaper option than buying the same thing in glass.

Semi-precious stone beads

Beads made from semi-precious stones can be surprisingly cheap, although some will be very expensive. The choice is huge, the stones come in different qualities and may also vary enormously in colour or shade – amethyst, for instance, can be anything from pale lavender to deep purple. Some semi-precious stones need special care, so check with the dealer before buying. Also check the size of the drilled hole – sometimes it can be very small, which limits the type of threading material you can use.

Pearls

Pearls are created when a small piece of sand or a similar irritant gets inside the shell of an oyster; to get rid of the irritation the oyster coats it in layers of mother-of-pearl. Most pearls are now created by artificially inserting an irritant into farmed oysters. Since they are formed by a natural process, real pearls vary in size, shape and colour – the most precious are perfectly round – and can be expensive. Imitation pearls – which may be glass, acrylic or plastic beads with a pearlized coating – are much more affordable and are great for fun fashion projects, although the pearlized coating may not be very durable on the cheaper types.

Crystal beads combined with knotted fringing.

Amber

Amber is fossilized tree resin and because it was originally soft and sticky it sometimes contains insects or plant material as inclusions. Although it is traditionally a rich orange-brown, it is also available in other colours from pale lemon yellow to almost black. The most expensive type is transparent, but it is more often cloudy or opaque. Amber is fairly soft so it can easily be cut or polished.

Coral

Coral is a calcium carbonate material secreted by a marine animal to form an exoskeleton – it is most frequently red, but also can be found in pink, white, black and blue. The black is very rare and is protected. Coral beads can be round but may be in the form of long chips or branches, or carved into flowers or other shapes and the surface may be polished or have a coarse texture. The beads are easily scratched or chipped and are damaged by many chemicals so should be looked after carefully.

Reconstituted beads

If a natural bead seems to be really inexpensive, it may be made of reconstituted material; the dust and chips from expensive stone have been glued together with resin and reshaped. There is nothing wrong with these beads and they can be as attractive as the real thing – but be sure you know what you are getting.

Shells

Shells can make the most beautiful natural 'beads' and can often be found for free on a local beach. They can be very delicate so should not be used in items that will be subject to a great deal of wear and tear.

Slate and pebbles

Small, smooth, sea-worn slates or attractive small pebbles are another fabulous natural material. The main issue with using them is that they can be hard to drill and can be quite heavy in comparison to the same size bead.

threading materials

Choosing the right thread is key to achieving a successful project. There are many different types and even more brands of each type, but you will soon find your personal favourite that is most suited to your creations. But don't be afraid to try new types – you may become a convert.

Nylon beading thread

This type of thread is strong and is used both for straightforward stringing and for looming projects. Light and flexible, it comes in many different colours. Fine beading thread is used in bead weaving projects when the thread has to pass through tiny seed beads or delicas several times. It is stronger than sewing thread and easily threaded on a sharp needle.

Conditioners

These come in a little pot like lip-gloss, or you can use traditional beeswax, and are used to strengthen threads and help them to resist tangles. Run the thread along the conditioner from end to end, holding it firmly against the surface with your finger, so every bit is coated. Beeswax can make the thread quite stiff, so use it with caution.

Ribbon

Very narrow ribbons can be used instead of nylon thread or cord and threaded with beads. Wider ribbons can be used in different ways, such as using pleating or stitching – see page 112. Organza ribbons are particularly good to combine with beads because they are lightweight and colourful, but experiment with other types of ribbon to achieve different effects.

Monofilament, nylon bead wire and fishing wire

These are all-plastic threads mainly used for intricate Japanese crystal weave projects and illusion necklaces, where tiny beads hang in swathes with no apparent thread to hold them. It is not suitable for basic threading but is often used on cheaper bracelets or necklaces sold to tourists. If you buy beads abroad, re-thread them as soon as possible to avoid breakages.

Plastic-coated metal wire

Also known as tiger tail, this is extremely strong but can kink and bend in long lengths, so it is only suitable for straightforward stringing projects. Most types are too stiff to knot but can be crimped to secure clasps. There are many thicknesses and colours of plastic-coated wire available. Snip it with wire snippers or an old pair of scissors.

Natural fibre cords

Natural fibre cords are an obvious choice for large natural beads and pendants. Thick cotton, hemp, silk and leather all give a defined shape and can be knotted or braided to give texture. There are faux versions of suede and leather, if you prefer. Cords may also be braided or embellished with Chinese knots for extra texture.

Wire

Wire is available in solid silver and gold, as well as brass, copper, surgical steel and plated metals. The gauge of a wire refers to its thickness in diameter – the most versatile is 0.5mm (24 gauge). Memory wire has been treated by heat so that it returns to its original rounded coil even when pulled out of shape. It is available in several different sizes for necklaces, rings and bracelets. Wire can also be used to create your own findings, such as jump rings or eye pins. Very fine wire can be used for crocheted jewellery (see page 108).

Coloured metallic wire

This type of wire comes in a wide selection of bright colours and is usually either copper or aluminium. Coloured copper wire has a surface coating of several coats of coloured enamel. Anodized aluminium wire has had the surface altered by the anodizing process, which allows it to be dyed.

Chains

Chains are made by joining small links of wire together; different styles of joining the links result in assorted patterns such as 'trace' and 'rope' chains. Most beading suppliers sell it by the inch for use in projects, or you buy a longer length and just add a clasp to use the finished neck chain to hang a special pendant.

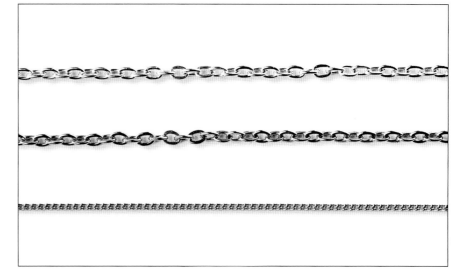

findings

Findings is the general term used for all the odds and ends that finish off a piece of jewellery – many of them can also be used in other ways. Some findings are very elaborate while others are simple classic shapes. Findings can be found in sterling silver and pure gold, as well as plated metals and some coloured steels.

▲ Jump rings

These are tiny circles of wire used to join components together. They are available in different metals and sizes, or you can make your own – see page 88. See page 80 for the correct technique to open and close jump rings.

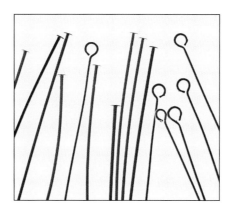

▲ Head pins and eye pins

Head pins and eye pins are essential for earrings and can also be used to make useful components for necklaces. You can make eye pins very easily by making a loop at the end of a length of 0.6mm (22 gauge) wire using round-nosed pliers, but head pins are best purchased ready-made. They look like dressmaking pins with no point and can be bought in an assortment of thicknesses and lengths, as well as assorted metals; some even have decorative heads.

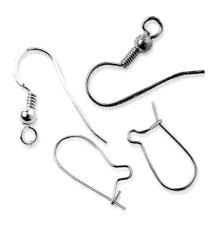

▲ Earring wires

For pierced ears, use these fishhook shape wires that hook through the ear. The twisted wire section and ball with a ring sits at the front – the beaded decorative part is hung from the ring. An alternative type is just a simple wire U-shape that goes through the ear with the front bent back to catch the end – the decorative part is hung from the kink in the wire at the front.

▲ Ear studs

Also for pierced ears, studs may have a flat disk at the front to bead or just a simple ball, in which case the beading can be hung behind the ball on the stud itself. Behind the ear the stud may be held securely with a push-on plastic disk or a metal butterfly shape. More expensive stud earrings have a screw-on end so they cannot be pulled out of the ear without unscrewing.

Choosing findings

Most findings are functional rather than decorative, so they are generally inconspicuous in pieces of jewellery. However, in some cases the findings can be more of a focal point, such as when using a very decorative clasp, an eye pin with a decorative top or textured silver spacer beads. In these cases, make sure that the finding does not draw too much attention from the rest of the design.

▲ Clip-on earring backs

For unpierced ears, earrings will need a clip-on back – the beads can be glued on to the disk at the front, or you can bead a perforated disk (see page 114) and then add the clip back to this.

▲ Ear clips

Ear clips are similar to clip-on earring backs but they have a small ring at the front instead of a disk to accommodate hung beads.

▲ Decorative clasps

The T-bar clasp is definitely a favourite for bracelets because it is easy to fasten with one hand. For the best security, it's hard to beat a simple lobster clasp. Multi-hole clasps are nice ways to combine multiple strands of a necklace down to one point for fastening. The S-hook is combined with a large jump ring on necklaces and is quick and easy to put on and take off.

▲ Spring ring clasps

As the name implies, this clasp is a ring with a spring inside; one section of the ring can be pulled open to slide a jump ring in and then springs back to hold it securely. Spring ring clasps come in silver or gold colour and in a range of sizes.

Metal for earrings

Because some people are allergic to base metal and can only wear pure gold or sterling silver through their ears, and others don't have pierced ears, it is just as well there are plenty of different types of earring wire available.
The basic shape is that of a fishhook that goes through the ear. The bottom ring can be twisted open and shut to add a beaded head pin. There are many variations, including types for non-pierced ears, so find the ones that you think are most comfortable.

▲ Barrel clasp

A barrel clasp has two sections that screw together, each with a ring at the other end so it can be fastened to a necklace with a jump ring. It comes in different metals and different sizes.

▲ Bolt ring clasp

Bolt rings fasten onto a jump ring, split ring or a tag – a flat rectangular metal finding with a drilled hole.

▲ Spacer bars

Spacer bars keep different rows of beads separate from each other around a multi-strand necklace or bracelet. There are huge chunky bars that make bold statements and tiny thin ones you'd hardly know were there; some have holes placed far apart for big beads, and some are quite close. Check the distance between holes with the size of the beads to make sure your beads will sit in neat rows.

Recycling findings

Look for old or broken necklaces with lovely clasps or spacers; you can give a vintage finding a whole new lease of life with some fresh new beads, or a gorgeous clasp may finish off a great new design with style.

▲ Calotte crimps

These consist of two small hinged cups with a loop attached. The thread or wire end is enclosed and held between the cups (see page 85) and the loop is attached to the clasp.

▲ Cord ends

Also known as end clamps, these finish off the end of leather cord or ribbon so it's possible to attach a clasp – see page 86.

▲ Bell caps

Also known as end caps, these sit over the knot to conceal it at the end of necklaces, bracelets or earrings.

▶ **Pendant holders**

Also known as bail clips or loops, these have claws to hold a pendant bead secure – see page 81.

▲ **Cuff links**

Cuff link findings have a flat disk on one side to add beading and come in gold or silver – although they may be plated rather than solid metal.

▲ **Perforated disks**

Perforated disks can be beaded (see page 114) and attached to brooches, cuff links or ring backs.

▲ **Ring backs**

Ring back findings have a flat disk on one side to add beads and are usually plated rather than solid metal.

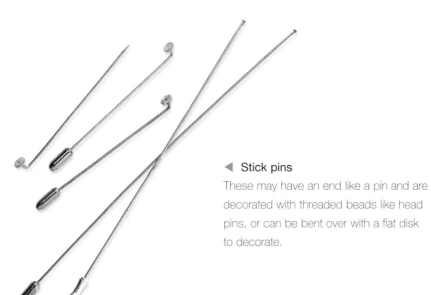

◀ **Stick pins**

These may have an end like a pin and are decorated with threaded beads like head pins, or can be bent over with a flat disk to decorate.

Using stick pins

These can be used to make lapel decorations instead of adding a brooch back, or to make hat decorations. They often have a removeable cap on the pin end, which is pushed back on after the pin has been put in place to keep it secure.

beadmaking tools

Some of the beads in this section can be made without any special tools, other techniques will need one or two tools – which may be the same or similar to those used in other chapters.

Formers

Base beads to decorate can be purchased in many different materials, but you can also make your own from suitable scraps left over from other beadmaking projects – or use failed beads as formers for other projects.

◀ Stamps for embossing

Rubber stamps are available in an enormous range of sizes, designs and shapes. Its best to buy what you need only when you need it and build up a collection over time.

▲ Needle tool

The sharp tip of a needle tool is useful to draw fine designs on soft materials, to sculpt with and to make holes in beads.

Craft blade

Blades are used to cut and slice many different materials and they should be very sharp – so be careful when using them. Always check which is the sharp side when picking up a blade without a handle.

▲ Moulds

There are lots of different craft moulds available, but you also might be able to use small sweet or ice cube moulds for some beads.

▶ Fabric dye pens

Similar to ordinary felt-tip pens, these
contain fabric dye instead of ink and are
used to draw on fabric or felt. Be careful
not to get the dye on your clothes.

◀ Brushes

A good selection of fine-tipped
and chisel-end brushes, in a
range of sizes, will be useful
for applying paint and ink.

▲ Ink

Craft inks are widely available in a
good assortment of colours. Some are
permanent, others are water-soluble.

Craft supplies

Most beading shops will not carry beadmaking supplies but many of
these will be available from craft supply shops, art shops or on the
Internet. Try cardmaking and scrapbooking sections for stamps, craft
blades and inks, the art section for brushes and the modelling section
for moulds and other shaping tools.

bead jewellery tools

You will find it much easier to make jewellery that looks well finished and professional if you have the proper tools – although there is no need to rush out and buy all of them immediately. After a couple of projects you will soon find out which ones you really need and which you can manage without.

Pliers

Small jewellery work pliers are essential for the neat finishing of jewellery pieces. There are several different types, and each fulfils a specific purpose. You can also buy three-in-one sets of pliers that incorporate the three main types in one tool. They are not as sturdy as separate tools, but they can be very handy if you like to travel with an in-progress project but don't want to carry everything with you.

◀ Needle-nosed pliers

Also known as snipe-nosed or chain-nosed pliers (top) these are similar to flat-nosed pliers but have long, pointed jaws with rounded sides. If you only want to buy one pair of pliers, these are the most versatile.

◀ Flat-nosed pliers

Half-round-nosed pliers (centre) have a flat gripping surface for holding small pieces while you work on them. They are essential for getting a firm hold when closing jump rings, and they make neat right-angle bends in wire.

◀ Round-nosed pliers

Round-nosed pliers (bottom) are used to create perfect circular wire loops. The jaws are tapered so you can make tiny loops or large ones.

◀ Wire cutters

These are the only things that should be used to snip any gauge of wire; even wire that seems as fine as thread will totally destroy your scissors. But don't use regular wire cutters on memory wire because it will chip the blades.

▲ Tweezers

Pick up tiny beads and findings with tweezers. They can also be used for holding pieces with one hand while manipulating or gluing with the other.

Beading mats and scoops

Small beads roll around – you can buy special beading mats but as an alternative a piece of towelling on the worktop will keep them in place until you need them. And although you can buy special bead scoops to pick up tiny beads, a small plastic spoon will often work just as well.

▲ Bead spinner

This is an excellent tool to string seed beads onto thread quickly and easily. See page 100 for how to use it.

▲ Beading board

This is useful when designing stringing patterns, especially when working with multiple strand designs. It will give you an idea of what the finished design will look like so that you can make changes before stringing.

▲ Beading needle

Needles are another workbox essential. Flexible, large-eyed ones made from twisted wire are great for threading normal bead thread and thicker cords through medium and large beads. For seed beads, embroidery, looming and weaving you will need a stiff, sharp needle (see page 40).

Needles

Beading needles start at a fine size 15 through to a thicker size 10. Collapsible eye and curved needles also available – collapsible eye needles are particularly flexible and are useful for stringing beads that have very small holes, while curved beading needles are used for beading hard shapes such as boxes and for restoration work.

◄ Glue

Glue is important for securing knots and attaching some findings. Cyanoacrylate dries fast and strong but also dries white, so don't get any on your beads! Specific branded bead glue takes a little longer to dry but is usually clear and strong. A dab of either of these glues is good for securing a knot – but at a pinch, a drop of clear nail polish will also do it. Two-part epoxy glue is incredibly strong, dries clear and is used to attach larger components together. It takes a little while to set after mixing, so you need to arrange the pieces to stay in position until then – try a bit of masking tape to hold them together. Two-part epoxy glue will hold metal, glass, crystal and wood, as well as other materials.

wireworking tools

To incorporate beads and wires you will need similar tools to those needed for jewellery making, although for some types of wire you may need some special tools.

Pliers and wire cutters

Small pliers and general-purpose wire cutters are essential for working with wire. You may be able to bend finer wire with your fingers but you will achieve crisper shapes with pliers, and to cut most wire you will need wire cutters rather than scissors.

◀ Needle-nosed or flat-nosed pliers

Needle-nosed pliers are known as snipe-nosed or chain-nosed pliers (top) – they are similar to flat-nosed pliers but have long, pointed jaws with rounded sides. If you only want to buy one pair of pliers, these are the most versatile.

◀ Round-nosed pliers

Round-nosed pliers (bottom) are used to create perfect circular wire loops and rings. The jaws are tapered so you can make tiny loops or large ones.

◀ Wire cutters

You may be able to cut very fine soft wire with scissors but wire cutters (middle) should be used to snip thicker gauges of wire. However, don't use regular wire cutters on memory wire because it will chip the blades.

◀ Memory-wire cutters

Memory-wire cutters are made from even stronger metal to cope with the added strength of this particular type of wire. Don't cut memory wire with ordinary wire cutters because it will quickly ruin them.

bead looming, weaving and knotting

For bead looming you will use a beading loom, but for weaving and knotting you will not need any tools other than beading thread and needles.

Bead loom

There are many different types of loom so do some research before buying one. Better looms can accommodate both large and small beads – be sure to check for this feature if you want to use more than one size bead. Many looms come with everything you need for your first project, including a basic selection of beads and threads.

Choosing a loom

Make sure you buy a loom that is wide enough and will hold enough strands of thread for the size and type of projects you want to make. Think ahead – you can always work with fewer strands on a wider loom to make smaller projects, but not the other way around.

knitting and crochet tools

You don't need any special tools to add beads to knitting or crochet – but you will need the basic tools to work the stitches.

Knitting needles

There is a huge choice of knitting needles available in different materials. Good needles are flexible, smooth and have well-shaped points. The two most common types are wooden and metal needles.

Needle sizes

There are three systems of sizing knitting needles and this table gives you the equivalent sizes across all three systems.

Metric	US	old UK and Canadian
25	50	–
19	35	–
15	19	–
10	15	000
9	13	00
8	11	0
7.5	11	1
7	10½	2
6.5	10½	3
6	10	4
5.5	9	5
5	8	6
4.5	7	7
4	6	8
3.75	5	9
3.5	4	–
3.25	3	10
3	2/3	11
2.75	2	12
2.25	1	13
2	0	14
1.75	00	–
1.5	000	–

Crochet hooks

Crochet hooks come in many shapes and sizes; some have thick handles and others are very fine. Some are made from metal, others from plastic or bamboo. The hook should be comfortable to hold and should not slip in your hand whilst you are working your stitches, so try out a few different ones to find out which one is the most suitable.

▶ **Plastic and aluminium hooks**
These are perhaps most common – both types allow the yarn to slip well through stitches, but can be a bit uncomfortable to use on large projects.

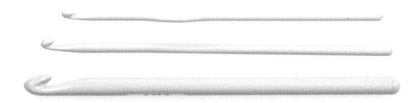

▶ **Steel hooks**
Tiny hooks are used to make very fine lace weight fabrics and are often made from steel because it is harder than aluminium and so less likely to break.

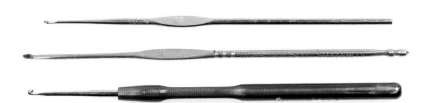

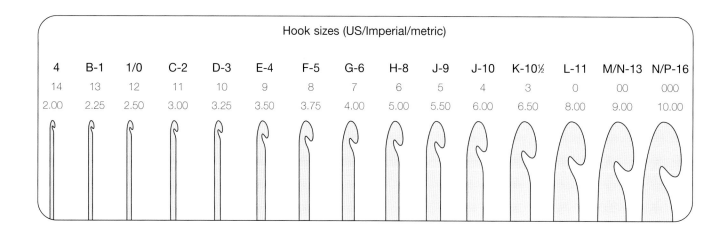

Hook sizes (US/Imperial/metric)														
4	B-1	1/0	C-2	D-3	E-4	F-5	G-6	H-8	J-9	J-10	K-10½	L-11	M/N-13	N/P-16
14	13	12	11	10	9	8	7	6	5	4	3	0	00	000
2.00	2.25	2.50	3.00	3.25	3.50	3.75	4.00	5.00	5.50	6.00	6.50	8.00	9.00	10.00

Anatomy of a hook

tip *throat* *shank* *grip* *handle*

Yarn needle

Use a blunt-tipped tapestry or yarn sewing needle to sew up the seams of knitted and crochet projects. You may find the type with a bent tip easier to use because you can see where it is coming up through the stitches.

Yarns

'Wool' is often used as a generic term for yarn, but knitting and crochet yarns can be made of many different materials. Fibres have varying properties so not all of them will be suitable for beading – you will need a smooth yarn so the beads will show up well, and one that is not too thick or it may not fit through the needle.

Wool yarn

Wool yarns are generally easy to work with and the fibre's elasticity will be forgiving if your tension is slightly uneven.

Cotton yarn

Cotton yarn is smooth and crisp and shows stitch detail well – although this also means that any unevenness in your knitting will show.

embroidery tools

For beaded embroidery you only need ordinary sewing tools, although you may find special beading needles a bit easier to use than ordinary needles if you plan to do a lot of beading.

▲ **Beading needles**

Beading needles for embroidery are very fine with a sharp tip to pierce the fabric. The eye is small, so only fine thread can be used with it. A needle threader won't go through either, so you may also need a handy magnifying glass.

◀ **Needle threader**

A needle threader will make threading most types of needles much easier and faster, although you will only be able to use it with medium to fine threads.

◀ **Thimble**

Many people find a thimble hard to use, but if you plan to do a lot of sewing it will save damaged fingertips.

▶ **Scissors**

Small sharp scissors are ideal to cut threads, ribbon and fabric.

▲ **Embroidery thread**

Stranded embroidery thread comes in a wide range of colours and can be used as it is or two or more strands can be separated out for a finer embroidered line or if the beads only have a small hole.

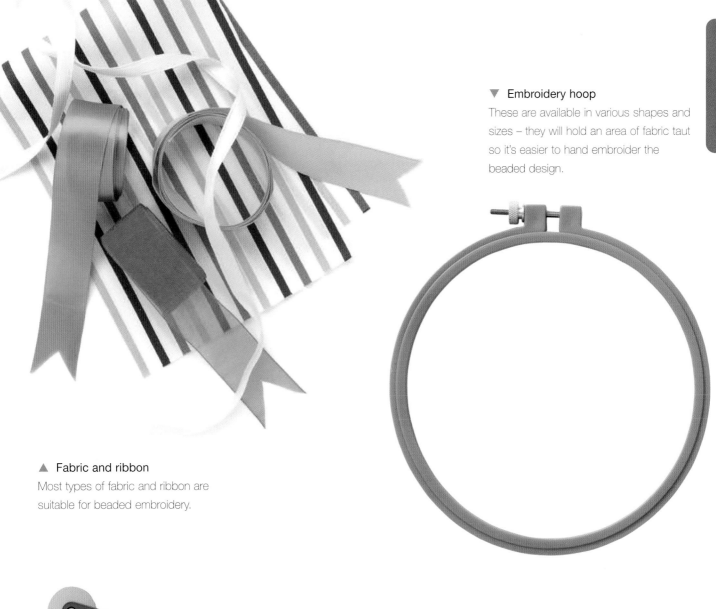

▼ Embroidery hoop

These are available in various shapes and sizes – they will hold an area of fabric taut so it's easier to hand embroider the beaded design.

▲ Fabric and ribbon

Most types of fabric and ribbon are suitable for beaded embroidery.

▲ Tracing wheel

This is great for making perforations to transfer designs from paper to fabric. It's usually used with dressmaker's carbon so it makes a row of little dots along each line.

▲ Pencils

Ordinary pencils are used to draw designs, carbon transfer pencils and silver marking pencils are used to transfer designs to fabric. Silver marking pencils show up on many fabrics but can be washed away.

◀ Tailor's chalk

Used to mark designs onto fabric, this can be a traditional triangular block of chalk or may be chalk powder in a dispenser. The marks can easily be brushed away when no longer needed.

▲ Water-soluble and air-soluble pens

Marks made by these pens are semi-permanent – water-soluble ink can be dabbed away with a damp cloth, while air-soluble ink fades over time on exposure to the air.

making beads

Fabulous and unusual beads can be made using many different materials and techniques. For some of these beads you will need to buy a few basic materials, but this chapter also includes beads made using seeds, aromatics and found natural materials.

beadmaking materials

Although there is an impossibly wide selection of ready-made beads, making your own beads can be quite simple and gives you the opportunity to make what you want in the exact colour needed. The beads in this section are made using different materials that are readily available from good craft stores or online, and are mostly inexpensive. A few of the beads are made using found materials that will cost nothing at all.

Air-dry clay

Air-dry or self-hardening clay is available in white, grey and terracotta colours. It is inexpensive and easy to mould but will dry hard after being left in the air for the time specified in the instructions.

Polymer clay

This is a synthetic material made from PVC plastic that is pliable and easy to work and is hardened by baking in an oven. It comes in a very wide range of colours and can also be mixed to make marbled colours or new shades. Knead it well to soften it prior to use.

Modelling materials

Check out your local craft shop for other materials that could be used to create different beads. Don't be afraid to experiment – sometimes a happy accident creates a wonderfully unusual bead.

Friendly plastic®

A decorative plastic that melts at a low temperature, which comes in strips in a variety of colours and patterns. It can be cut with scissors and moulded easily, and scraps can be melted into each other to create unique designs and colours.

Wool fleece

Also referred to as wool tops or roving, this is 100% wool yarn that has been cleaned and carded but not spun. It comes in a very wide range of colours and is used to make felt. If you don't use all of it immediately it should be stored away from moisture.

Paper

Use shredded newspaper or recycled shredded paper pulp to make papier mâché beads, or you can buy pre-prepared papier mâché pulp from many good craft shops or online.

Seeds and pips

Seeds and pips come in many different shapes and sizes but if you want to thread them the larger ones are generally easiest to pierce or drill. Most seeds and pips are naturally shades of beige or brown but you can always paint them in brighter colours if you prefer.

Seeds/spices

Many seeds, pips, nuts and spices are suitable as natural beads – they just need to be solid enough not to break apart when drilled for threading. Aromatic spices will create wonderfully scented beads.

Found objects

Many different shells, stones and buttons can be made into beads. Make sure shells and stones are not too fragile or too large and heavy. Buttons already have holes for threading – look out for unusual shapes, colours or designs.

Slate

Slate stones have been rubbed smooth by the sea and are flat and angular but with rounded edges. Slate is a fairly soft material so can be drilled with care, or used in other ways, see page 74.

Acrylic paint

This type of paint can be used on most surfaces so it's a great all-purpose option. Although it is not water-based paint it can be diluted with water to achieve different effects, but is water-resistant when dry.

Alcohol ink

Alcohol-based inks are also useful for colouring since they can be used on many materials, dry quickly and are transparent.

Metallic powder

Made from powdered mica, these non-toxic pigments will never rust or tarnish and are very colourfast and stable. The powder will cling to any sticky surface to add a metallic gleam.

Gold and silver leaf

Real gold and silver leaf is very expensive, but craft stores sell imitation versions that looks just as effective as the real thing. For some techniques you will also need size (a type of glue) to apply it and may also need varnish to protect it on the bead.

using formers

Formers are plain base beads that can be embellished in many different ways. Ready-made formers can be bought from craft stores, but you can also make your own using several different materials – including scraps left over from clay or polymer clay beadmaking.

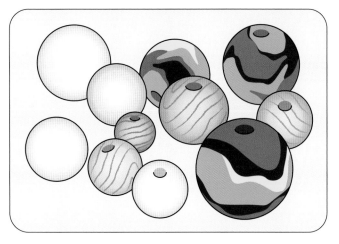

1 Formers or base beads are available in many different materials, including Styrofoam, paper, acrylic and wood. They can be bought unpainted or in various colours, or made from surplus clay or polymer clay.

2 Roll a piece of air-drying modelling clay or polymer clay between your palms to the required bead size. Pierce through the centre with a darning needle, and then thread the former onto a wooden skewer.

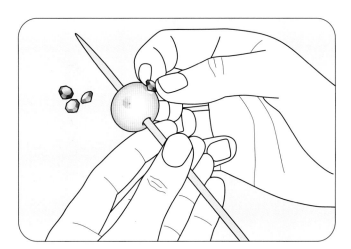

3 Before the clay has dried, you can press seed beads or gems into the surface at regular intervals to make an indentation. Remove the bead or gem and allow the former to dry. When it has hardened, fix the beads or gems into place using a two-part epoxy glue and allow to dry.

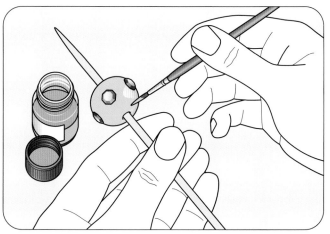

4 The former can be painted to a suitable base colour using a fine artist's brush and waterproof ink or dilute acrylic paint. You can match the base colour to the seed beads or gems that will encrust the final bead, which will disguise any small gaps in the decoration.

Formers covered with strings of transparent seed beads.

Encrusting formers with seed beads

The basic former bead is surface decorated or covered in a more decorative material to make the finished bead. See also pages 60–63.

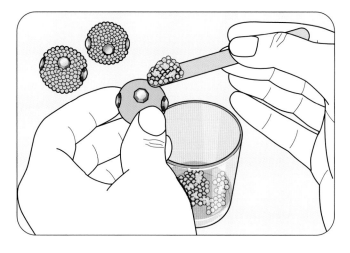

1 To encrust a former completely with seed beads, allow around 1 tsp of seed beads per former. Mix 1 tsp of waterproof craft glue with each 2 tsp of seed beads and smooth the mixture over a small area of the former at a time using a lolly stick. Allow to dry a little before moving on to the next area. When the bead is completely covered, set aside to dry fully.

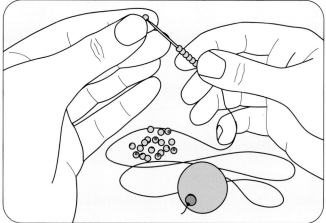

2 Alternatively you can wrap the former with strings of seed beads. Thread a needle with around 100cm (40in) of thread. Tie a seed bead that is slightly larger than the hole in the former onto the end of the thread, and then insert the needle through the former hole so the bead acts as an anchor. Thread lots of seed beads onto the needle.

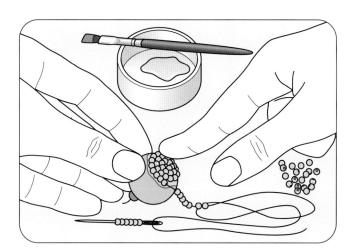

3 Spread fast-drying glue over the top quarter of the former (at the opposite end to the anchor bead), and then wrap the beaded thread in a spiral around the hole in the former. Press to make sure the beads are in contact with the glue. Allow to dry. Repeat until you reach halfway down the former.

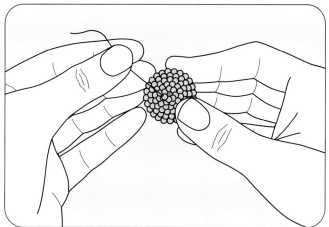

4 Cut off the anchor bead. Repeat the gluing and spiralling process over the other half of the former until it is completely covered. Set aside and allow to dry completely. Cut off the remaining thread and tuck any thread ends inside the embellished former.

clay beads

Self-hardening clay is available from craft stores in white, grey and terracotta colours. It does not need to be baked in a kiln or oven so it is inexpensive and very easy to use.

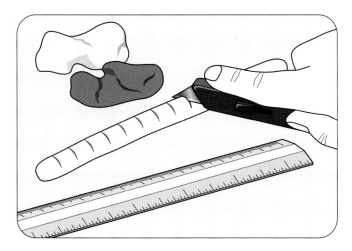

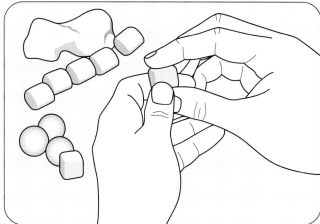

1 To achieve a batch of evenly sized beads, roll out the clay into a sausage shape of the same diameter as the desired bead. Use a ruler and craft knife to cut the sausage neatly into equal sections.

2 Create round beads by rolling each section of the clay into a ball between your palms in turn. To make cube shape beads, squash the ball between your fingers and thumbs, working round the shape.

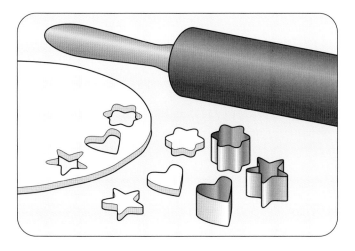

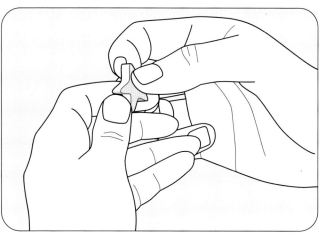

3 For flat beads, roll out the clay to the require thickness and use aspic or tiny sweet cutters to cut out different shapes, or cut shapes freehand with a craft knife.

4 Self-hardening clay is fibrous so it will not have a smooth edge when cut. To smooth the edge, rub over the surface with a wet finger and then allow to dry before proceeding.

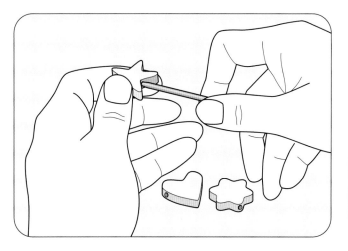

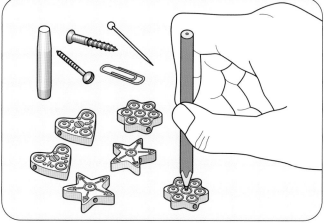

5 To pierce a threading hole, carefully push a sharp wooden skewer into the bead. Choose the neatest place for the hole and pierce from both directions into the middle for a neat hole at each end.

6 You can decorate clay beads before they dry by embossing them with different designs. Use craft stamps or experiment with different implements such as paperclips, buttons, screws and pen casings.

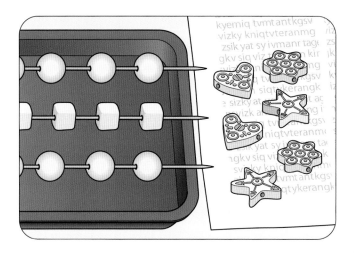

7 Suspend round and cube beads on wooden skewers to dry to prevent them from becoming distorted. Lay flat beads out on newsprint, turning them regularly.

Threading holes

Be careful when piercing the threading hole not to distort the shape of the bead. It may be easier to let it dry slightly so it is fairly stable before attempting to make the hole. If distortion is still a problem, make the initial piercing with a sharper tool such as a darning needle and then make the hole big enough for threading using the skewer.

A selection of handmade clay beads.

Embellishing clay beads

Clay beads can be decorated with colour after they are dry instead of embossing, or you can combine colour with the embossed design.

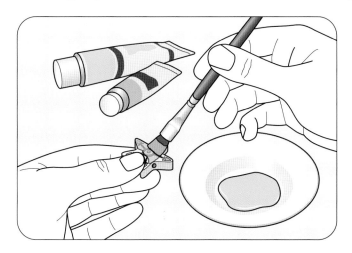

1 To colour the beads, use artist's acrylic paints and allow each colour or surface to dry before moving on to the next. Experiment with different colour combinations and effects.

2 Embossed beads can have a patina effect by painting in a colour and allowing to dry. Paint over the top in white making sure all embossed recesses are filled with white.

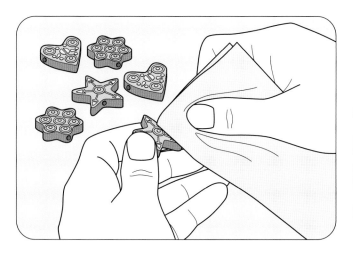

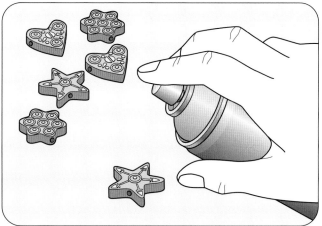

3 While it is still wet, wipe away the excess white paint on the surface using a soft cloth or paper tissue. The base colour will be revealed on the flat surfaces of the design, but the embossed areas will retain the white, highlighting the pattern.

4 When all the paint is dry, coat the beads with matte or gloss varnish – a spray varnish will give the most even coverage and a matte type is usually the most natural finish. Keep round and cube beads on their skewers while varnishing. Allow the varnish to dry thoroughly before using the beads.

polymer clay beads

Polymer clay is available in an exciting range of colours, which can be mixed to create new colours and different effects, or coloured with metallic powder or acrylic paint. Knead the clay well prior to use and bake the finished beads in the oven to harden them.

Modelling

Polymer clay is very easy to mould so it can be shaped into novelty beads, or cut and embossed in the same way as ordinary clay. You can make round beads or flat disk beads as described here.

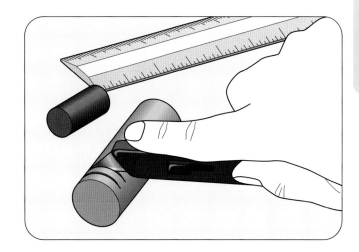

1 To achieve a batch of evenly sized beads, roll out the polymer clay into a sausage shape. Use a ruler and craft knife to cut the sausage neatly into equal sections.

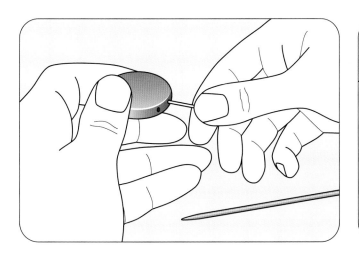

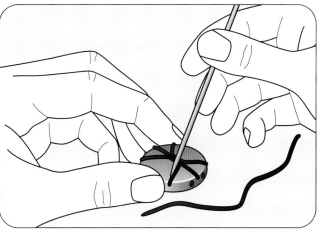

2 Smooth the cut disk into a pleasing shape, then carefully pierce a threading hole through the side by pushing a darning needle and then wooden skewer through the bead. Pierce from both directions into the middle for a neat hole at each end. Very large, flat beads may need two parallel threading holes.

3 To add further line detail to a modelled clay bead, roll very thin strands of polymer clay in a contrasting colour and use the tip of a wooden skewer to press them gently into the surface to attach them to the bead.

Polymer clay beads can be very colourful.

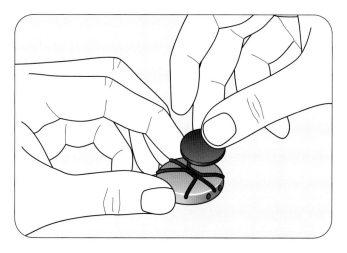

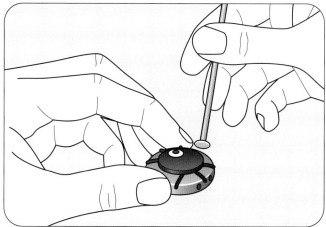

4 You can add extra layers for a more three-dimensional effect by placing further sections of clay on top, but be careful not to squash the threading holes when putting them in place. If a lot of modelled decoration is to be added, it is safer to leave the skewer in place for the moment.

5 For dots of colour – such as the eyes here – roll small balls of clay between your palms and then squash them flat. Use the tip of a wooden skewer to attach them to the bead. You can also use the tip of the skewer to draw patterns into the surface of the clay.

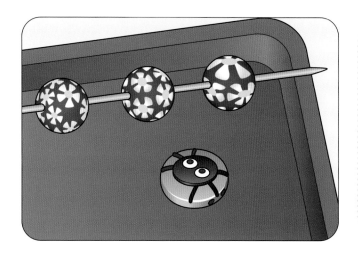

Smooth rolls

To make the surface of the initial sausage shape smooth and consistent, roll it out on a hard flat surface using a small piece of acrylic sheet in the same way as a rolling pin.

6 When you have finished modelling and decorating, bake the beads in an oven according to the polymer clay manufacturer's instructions. Place flat beads on a baking sheet and thread round ones onto skewers or wires so they do not become distorted during the hardening process.

Colouring with metallic powder

Although polymer clay comes in a good range of colours, you may want to colour the finished bead to achieve a special effect.

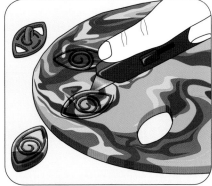

1 If the finished bead will be painted, you can use leftover scraps to create the initial shape. Knead the clay and roll it out 6mm (¼in) thick. Emboss the required design into the clay leaving space around it to cut out.

2 Place the clay on a suitable cutting surface and cut out the bead shapes neatly around the embossed design, using a sharp craft knife.

3 To smooth the edge, rub over the surface with a wet finger. Pierce a threading hole with a darning needle and then push a wooden skewer through the bead – pierce from both directions into the middle for a neat hole at each end.

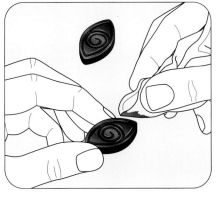

4 Wearing a dust mask, apply metallic powder across the bead using a soft paintbrush – the powder will stick readily to the tacky surface of the clay. Use several colours for a variegated finish.

5 Shake off the excess powder, then use a soft cloth to smooth over the surface and remove excess powder – this will also blend the colours if you have used more than one.

6 When you have finished modelling and decorating, bake the beads in an oven according to the polymer clay manufacturer's instructions. Coat the finished bead with varnish to protect the coloured finish.

Millefiori

Millefiori is a combination of the Italian words 'mille' (thousand) and 'fiori' (flowers) and is a glasswork technique that has become associated with Venice. More recently, the millefiori technique has been applied to polymer clays and similar materials. Because polymer clay is quite pliable and does not need to be heated and then reheated to fuse it, it is a much easier medium in which to produce millefiori beads than glass.

1 Roll the clay out into sausages 1cm (½in) in diameter and 6cm (2½in) long. Pinch evenly along one side of the alternate colours to form petal shapes and arrange these into a flower.

2 Squeeze the flower cylinder to fix the shape, then roll out a thin piece of clay and wrap it around the flower. Trim to fit and smooth the edges with your thumb to seal them.

3 Reduce the size of the basic flower shape by rolling it gently with a piece of acrylic sheet, intermittently squeezing along the cane and stretching it gently to prevent it splitting.

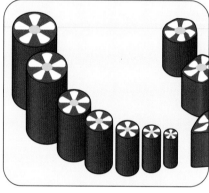

4 Continue reducing the cane to the desired size. You can leave it round or reshape it by pressing the cane lengthways on a smooth surface to make faceted sides.

5 You can make more complex canes by cutting several to the same length and packing them together. Wrap with a thin layer of clay as in step 2, then roll out again as in step 3.

A collection of millefiori beads.

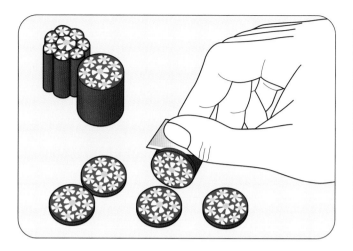

6 Roll the complex cane to bring it down to the required size and then cut off very thin slices using a craft knife or a very sharp blade.

7 Apply the slices of millefiori cane to a former or base bead, filling any gaps with slices from different size canes. Roll the finished bead between your palms until it is smooth.

Formers or base beads

Use the surplus clay left over from the trimming process to make formers or base beads (see page 48). It doesn't matter if these are strange colours, since the former will be decorated.

8 Use a darning needle to pierce a hole through the bead, first from one side and then the other. Bake in an oven according to the manufacturer's instructions.

A selection of imitation turquoise beads.

Imitating natural stones

Polymer clay is ideal to make very realistic copies of semi-precious natural stones. Study the markings on a variety of natural stones to come up with your own variations.

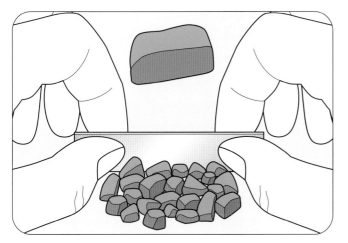

1 Mix equal parts of your base colour and translucent polymer clay roughly together – the translucent clay will give the bead a more natural look than using just a flat colour. Chop the prepared clay into small pieces with a blade – the pieces should be random sizes, not all even.

2 Paint all over the clay chunks with black acrylic paint and then set aside until the paint is completely dry – this may take at least an hour.

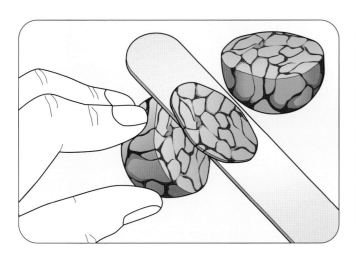

3 Roll the clay chunks into a rough ball and then slice the ball in half – you will now have streaks of black veining running through the base colour. Use the blade to slice off thin layers of the clay.

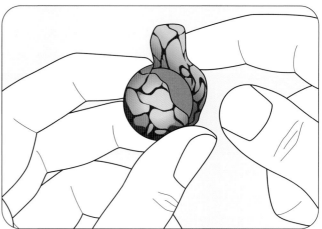

4 Apply the slices of clay to a polymer clay base bead. You can cover the base bead completely, or just some areas – study natural stones for information on different effects. Bake the polymer clay bead following the manufacturer's instructions.

Mokume' gane'

This is an ancient Japanese technique for working metal that is ideal for use with polymer clay.

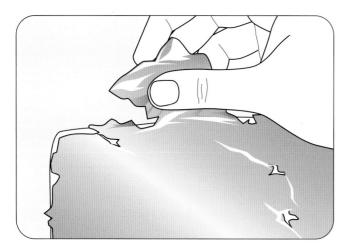

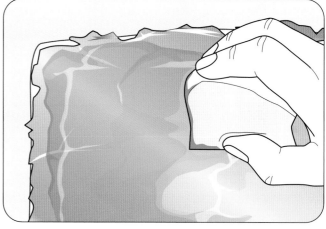

1 Roll out a vary thin sheet of translucent polymer clay and then apply a sheet of gold or sliver leaf on top.

2 Using a sponge, apply random areas of alcohol ink over the top of the metal leaf. The colours will blend into new shades where they overlap.

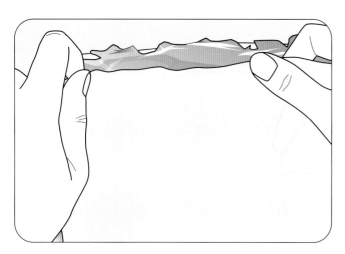

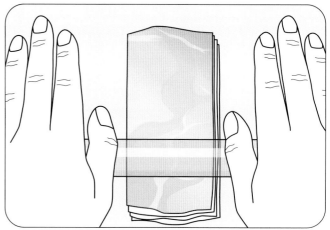

3 Add another very thin sheet of translucent clay on top of the alcohol ink layer. Roll this into place gently, then cut the layered clay into four equal pieces and stack these one on top of the other.

4 Roll the stacked clay out into a thin layer again, cut in half and stack again. The idea is to achieve many very thin separate layers of material – the different layers should not mix into one another to form one mass.

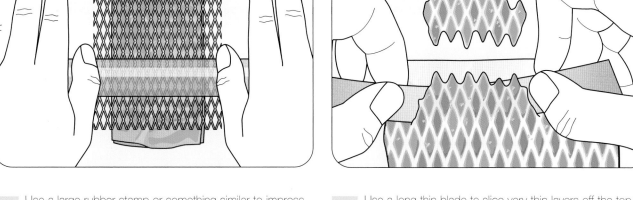

5 Use a large rubber stamp or something similar to impress a design into the clay – the pattern doesn't matter, you are just pressing the layers into one another in a random way.

6 Use a long thin blade to slice very thin layers off the top of the clay. Don't make the slices too thick.

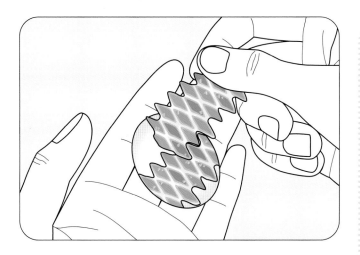

7 Apply the slices of clay to a base bead. Bake the bead as normal – the final bead will be beautifully coloured with random swirls of colour with metallic flecks.

Rolling clay

A fast way to roll out clay into an even and equal thickness sheet is to use a pasta roller. These have settings for different thicknesses, so you can work your way down by stages to the sheet thickness you need. Keep the pasta roller just for crafts – don't use it for food again afterwards.

Mokume' gane' beads can have unusual textures and colours.

plastic beads

Friendly Plastic® is a type of crafting plastic that comes in strips and can be cut with scissors or melted with a low heat to mould pieces together. It comes in many colours and patterns as standard, but it can also be used to create your own designs.

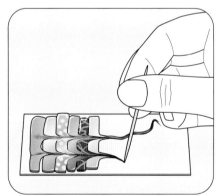

1 To create a unique colour and design, cut a small piece of Friendly Plastic® and dab a little oil-based paint over the surface.

2 Draw your design into the paint with a blunt pencil or a stylus. Set the design into the material by applying a little heat using a heat gun.

3 While the Friendly Plastic® is soft you can also cut out shapes with a cookie or aspic cutter, or cut them freehand with a craft knife. Make a piercing hole with a hot needle.

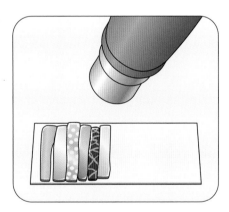

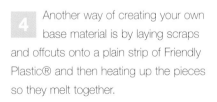

4 Another way of creating your own base material is by laying scraps and offcuts onto a plain strip of Friendly Plastic® and then heating up the pieces so they melt together.

5 To create a different effect, draw a wooden cocktail stick horizontally across the strips while they are still soft and semi-liquid to pull them into each other. Try experimenting with a series of lines in opposite directions.

felt

All you need to create brightly coloured felt beads is some wool fleece (unspun wool yarn) and either hot, soapy water or a felting needle. Felt beads can be quite large and eye-catching without being too heavy.

Felt beads

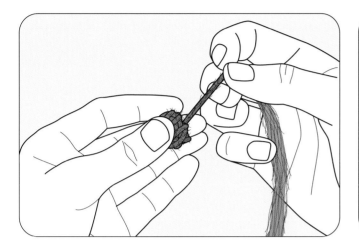

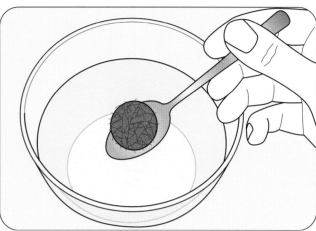

1 Tie a knot at the end of a length of fleece and wrap the fleece around it to form a tight, even ball. Make the initial ball about twice as big as the final bead because it will shrink considerably in the felting process.

2 Dip the ball into hot, soapy water. Squeeze it and dip it a couple of times to make sure that the water has penetrated right to the heart of the ball.

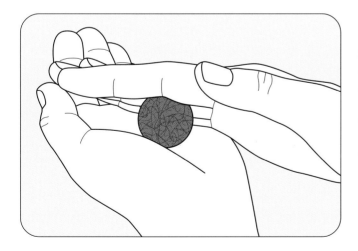

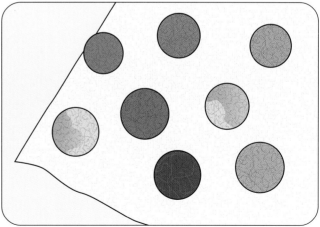

3 Roll the ball between your palms, gently at first but increasing the pressure as the fibres begin to mat together. Repeat the dipping and rolling process until you achieve the required size of bead, which should be quite firm and solid. Rinse out the soap.

4 Lay the wet beads out on paper towels or a similar absorbent material. Allow them to dry thoroughly, turning them regularly. They will take quite a while to dry completely – speed up the process by putting them in a warm linen closet or near a radiator.

Needle-felt beads

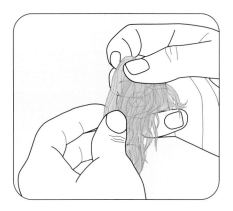

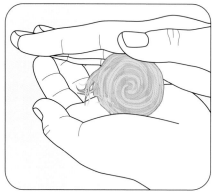

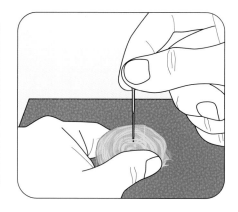

1 Pinch a small amount of fleece from the mass of wool and fluff it up by pulling a few strands apart with your finger and thumb. Repeat a few times so that the wool piece loosely measures about 4.5cm (1¾in) square.

2 Once the piece of wool is the correct size and the fibres are sufficiently separated, roll the wool into a very loose ball between your fingers, trying not to exert any pressure or compress it at this stage.

3 Pinch the wool together into a small ball and place it on a foam or polystyrene felting mat. Hold it by one side and very carefully begin to felt the wool by poking the fluff with the felting needle. Push the felting needle far enough through the wool so that the barbs on the needle are coming into contact with the foam mat. Roll the wool around on the mat as you felt, so that the felt takes on a ball shape and you work on all sides.

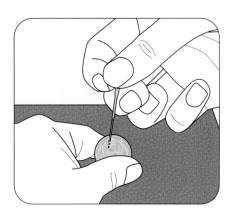

4 As the part you are felting begins to firm, roll the ball a little to reveal a fuzzier section and felt again until firm. As you near the end of the process you will not need to poke the needle all the way through. Firm up any surface fuzzy spots by poking with the needle.

5 While it isn't always necessary, you can smooth excess fuzziness. Put a drop of detergent in a cup or glass and add hot water. Wet the felted ball in the soapy water, and roll between your fingers to smooth the fibres and maintain the ball shape. Rinse briefly in hot water and allow to dry completely.

Felting needles

Felting needles are very sharp with barbs all down the sides so watch your fingers as you work – it's very easy to stab yourself accidentally. The needles come in different sizes; for beadmaking you will need larger needles for moulding and shaping. The smaller needles are for adding felted detailing.

Felt beads are easy to decorate with fabric dye pens.

Decorating felt beads

Fleece to make felt beads can be bought in a wide range of colours, but you can also add surface decoration to your felt beads.

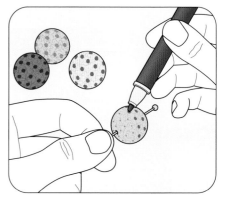

1 Press a pin into opposite sides of the bead so you can hold it while you decorate it, without obstructing the design. Using fabric dye pens, slowly revolve the bead against the pen to make a stripe.

2 You can also use the fabric dye pens to draw spots – it's best to mark the position of spots with a faint dot first to check the design. When you are happy with the positioning, go over the dots with the dye pens to make them into bigger spots.

Stitching into felt

Stitch securely right into the felt and make sure the initial and final knots in the thread are tight so the tiny beads you are adding to the surface will not come adrift later.

Positioning random beads at different angles to catch the light makes a livelier design.

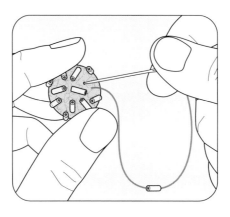

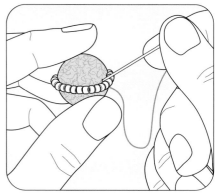

3 Felt is very easy to stitch into so you can use transparent nylon thread and a beading needle to attach bugle beads in a random design over the surface of the bead.

4 Alternatively you could add a row of tiny seed beads around the middle of the felt bead. Thread the seed beads onto transparent nylon thread and wrap the beaded thread around the felt bead, attaching it to the felt with a few small stitches at intervals.

paper beads

Using recycled paper is one of the cheapest ways to make beads – and the techniques are also very easy. Paper is also lightweight so quite large beads can be made.

Papier mâché

You can make papier mâché from old newsprint or computer printout paper as described below, or you can buy bags of dry paper pulp ready to mould. If you are using the pre-prepared pulp, omit steps 1–4, follow the manufacturer's instructions to make up the pulp and begin making your beads at step 5.

1 Tear the newsprint into small pieces and place in a heatproof bowl. Cover with boiling water and leave to soak for at least three hours.

2 Using an electric hand blender or whisk, blend the paper into a smooth pulp – be careful not to overwork your blender, add more water if necessary.

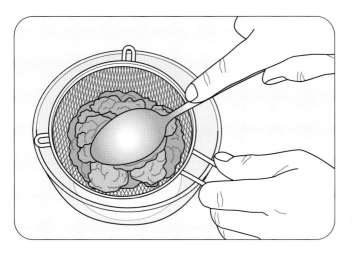

3 Place the blended pulp into a metal strainer and squeeze out the excess water by pressing a spoon firmly all over the surface.

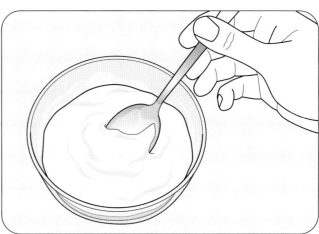

4 Mix the paper pulp with water-soluble paste to form a clay-like consistency. You could also add a little decorator's filler at this stage.

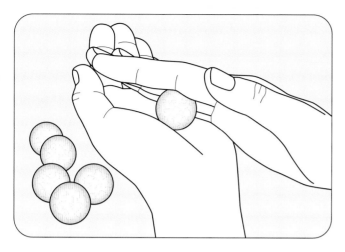

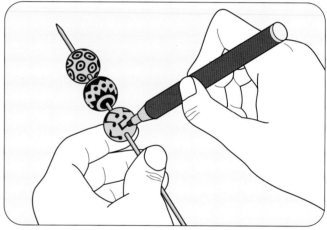

5 Roll a piece of the mixture between your palms to make a bead of the desired size. Pierce with a darning needle from both sides, then thread the bead onto a wooden skewer and allow it to dry completely.

6 The beads may take several days to dry and the surface may become pitted. Use very fine grit sandpaper to smooth the bead and remove any imperfections.

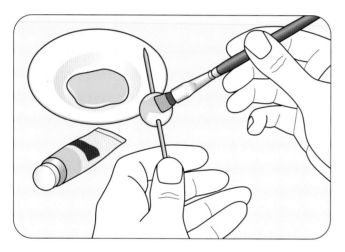

7 Using a soft paintbrush and working with the bead still on the wooden skewer, apply a base colour all over the bead using artist's acrylic paint. Allow to dry.

8 Decorate the beads by painting a design on them using acrylic paint, or by drawing motifs with permanent marker pens. Spray the finished beads with matte or gloss varnish.

Paste for papier mâché

Papier mâché can be made with wallpaper paste, mixed according to the manufacturer's instructions, but this often includes a fungicide so it is not suitable if you are working with young children who may accidentally swallow small amounts of the glue.

Watered down white PVA is also suitable, but this can become an expensive option if you are making lots of beads.

The traditional adhesive for papier mâché is flour and water paste: mix plain flour into water at a ratio of 1:4 to make a thick cream. Dilute with about five times as much boiling water, stirring into the paste so it becomes translucent and thickens. Allow to cool and then dilute further as required. One tablespoon of salt per six cups of paste will stop it hardening too quickly. The paste will keep in the refrigerator for several days and can also be used for paper flowers.

Paper flowers

Tiny paper roses made from tissue paper can be unusual and colourful beads. They will be fairly delicate, but it's easy to make a few more.

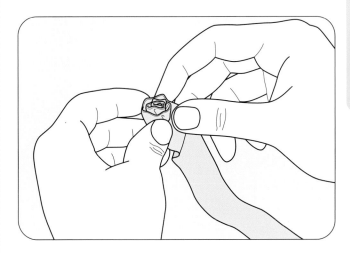

1 Spread paste (see tip box, left) over a strip of tissue paper and fold it in half lengthways. Wind the strip into a spiral, squeezing the base as you go to create a flower effect.

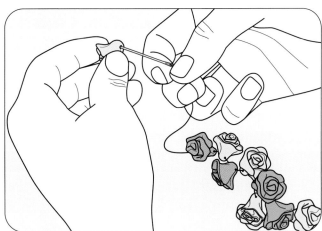

2 Once the flowers are dry, use a sharp darning needle to pierce a hole through the base of each flower. Thread the flowers onto elastic or stranded embroidery thread.

Delicate tissue roses can be hardened with a glossy varnish.

Rolled paper beads

Almost any type of paper can be used to make these beads, which are lightweight but surprisingly strong.

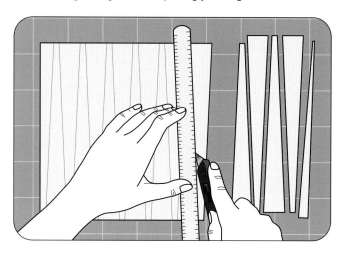

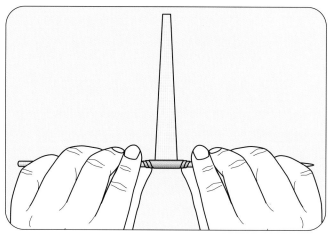

1 Mark out tapered strips on the back of the patterned paper – as a rough guide, to make a bead 2.5cm (1in) long the strips should be about 2.5cm (1in) wide at the wide end, 6mm (¼in) wide at the narrow end and 21.5cm (8½in) long. Cut the strips out.

2 Smear a little petroleum jelly on a knitting needle as a release agent. Starting at the wide end of the strip, begin rolling it tightly round the needle. Make sure it is rolling centrally and evenly. Put a dab of glue on the end and press down for a few seconds to hold the bead in place. Set aside to dry.

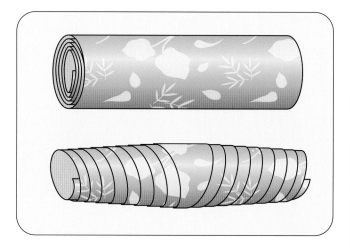

3 Using tapered strips of paper will create shaped beads that are fatter in the middle than at the ends; the longer the strip, the fatter the bead will be. For tubular beads, cut the strips to an even width along the length of the strip.

Colouring beads

If you make your paper beads from gift wrapping paper or a similar printed design paper you probably won't need to colour them and it's a quick option for a fast result. Alternatively you can make them from plain paper or newspaper and paint the finished bead with acrylic paint.

Rolled paper beads are surprisingly firm and robust – the layers give them stability – so they will be fairly longlasting if used in jewellery. However, remember that they will not be washable.

using natural materials and found items

There are many items that can be found in nature that make wonderful beads – and if you use spices, they will also be perfumed. Use seeds and shells in their natural colour, or you can paint them if you prefer.

Seeds

Many seeds are an ideal bead shape and can easily be pierced and threaded.

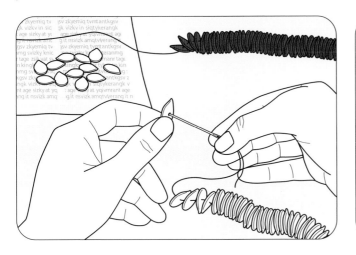

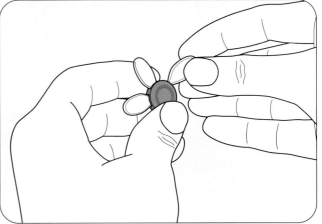

1 Wash the seeds and remove any pith, then lay them out on newspaper and leave them to dry out thoroughly. Pierce the dried seeds with a sharp darning needle and then string them onto beading thread.

2 To make a seed flower, roll a small ball of self-hardening clay and then squash it flat to form the centre of the flower. Press the pointed end of five seeds into the edge of the clay disk to form the petals of a flower.

3 Remove the seeds and allow the clay to dry and harden. Glue the seed petals into place and allow the glue to dry. Paint with clear varnish or nail polish to protect the surface. Pierce the tip of one seed to hang the flower bead.

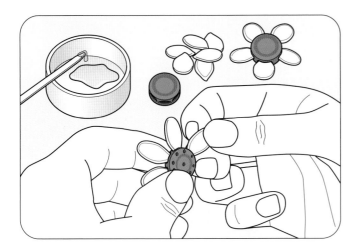

Slate

Slate is quite soft and pieces on the beach have often been worn into lovely natural shapes.

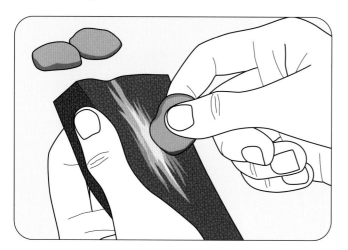

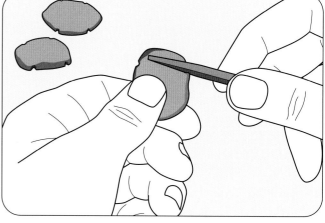

1 Use fairly small pieces of slate because larger ones may be too heavy. If necessary, sand the edges of the slate on a sanding sponge to remove any odd rough edges or to adjust the shape slightly.

2 On each side of the pieces of slate file a pair of small notches, one pair near the top and one near the bottom, using a needle file. If you prefer you can drill holes in the slate instead, following the instructions for shells on page 76.

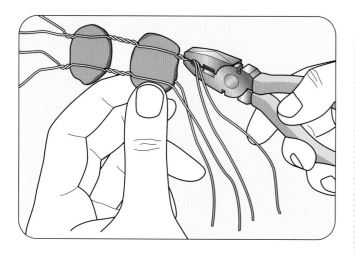

3 To join notched slates, use two pairs of wires, one pair for the top notches and one for the bottom. Slide the slate between a pair of wires and twist the wires together on each side using pliers, so the wire tightens into the notches and holds the slate securely.

Slate necklace

When making the slates into a necklace, add extra colour or sparkle by threading a glass bead onto the wires between slates.

It also adds extra interest if you run one of the wires across the surface of the slate from top to bottom at irregular intervals.

Seaworn slate combined with plastic-coated wire and frosted glass beads.

Shells

Shells come in beautiful shapes and sometimes in pretty pastel colours. They can be quite delicate, so choose sturdier types to make into beads.

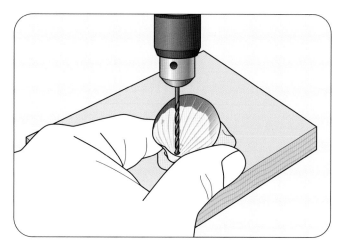

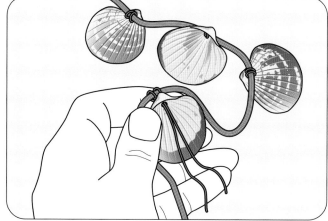

1 Wash and dry the shell. To drill a threading hole, position the part of the shell that is to be drilled against a piece of wood and support it with a piece of modelling clay. Drill steadily but without applying too much pressure to avoid breaking the shell.

2 You could use a jump ring to attach the shell, but a softer alternative method is to thread a short length of embroidery thread through the hole and use this to tie or stitch on the shell. Here the shell is being attached to a decorative cord.

Spices

Spices often come in exotic shapes and rich colours, so they add texture and colour to jewellery as well as scent.

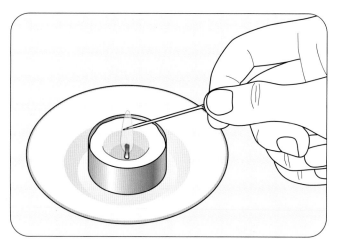

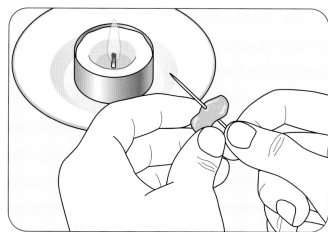

1 When making holes in small or soft items such as incense, it may be easier to pierce them with a hot needle. Heat the tip of the needle in a candle flame – but be careful not to burn your fingers.

2 Wipe any soot off the needle with a cloth, then pierce or melt a hole through the incense.

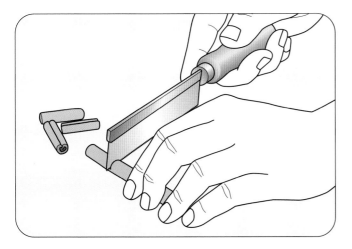

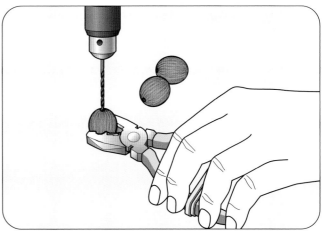

3 Long shapes such as cinnamon sticks can be cut into shorter lengths using a small saw. Select cinnamon sticks that are compact and not too flaky and mark them into regular lengths using a ruler. Saw from the bridge on the back to minimize the risk of flaking.

4 To drill into small round spices such as nutmeg, secure them in the jaws of a pair of pliers. Wrap a strong rubber band around the handle of the pliers to keep them secure. Press a dent in the top with the drill bit, and then drill slowly through.

5 Brittle shapes, such as star anise, may be difficult to drill. Decide which way round you want the star to hang, place the top point against a piece of wood and drill through it slowly and carefully.

6 Some spices, such as cloves, will be easier to thread if you soak them in water overnight so they become soft and pliable. Use a sewing needle and a doubled length of thread to string as required.

bead jewellery

You can make beautiful and unique pieces of jewellery with purchased beads, beads you have made or by recycling beads from old or broken pieces of jewellery. You may need other components, known as findings, to complete your pieces but these are widely available from bead stores and jewellery-making suppliers.

basic jewellery-making techniques

The techniques in this section are mostly general ones that will be used over and over again in many forms of jewellery making. You will find the more specialized techniques covered in detail from page 92 onward.

Opening and closing a jump ring

Jump rings are not solid rings; they can be opened along a join to attach the individual parts of a piece of jewellery together. It's not a good idea to pull the ends apart to open a jump ring because this distorts the ring and it may be impossible to close it again into a perfect circle – instead, use the technique shown here.

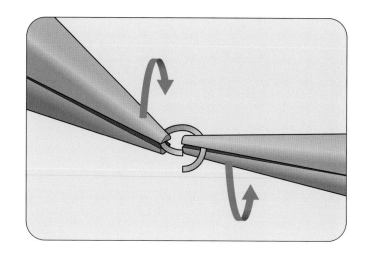

1 To open the jump ring, hold it on either side of the join with a pair of pliers. Push back with one pair of pliers and pull forward with the other pair to open up a gap in the ring.

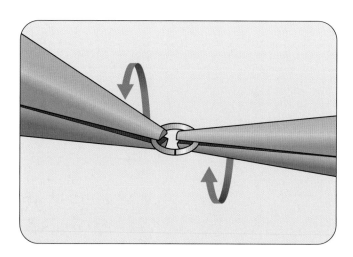

2 To close the jump ring again, repeat the same motion in reverse to bring the two ends of the ring back in line with one another.

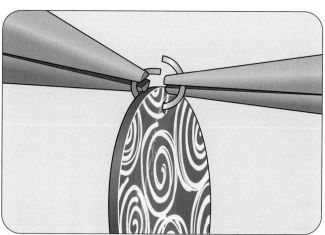

3 Jump rings can be added to pendant beads so that they can hang from a chain or cord, or used to add end clasps to a necklace or bracelet.

Attaching a pendant holder

These come in two basic forms; a triangular-shape jump ring or as a decorative clasp. They are used to hold a pendant bead at the top – so it can be added to a necklace or bracelet – instead of using a plain jump ring. Alternatively you can make your own wrapped pendant holder with wire – see page 83.

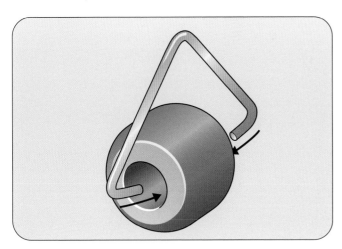

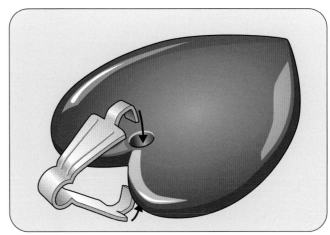

1 A triangular pendant holder usually comes with the arms already opened apart. Slip the bead onto one side and then close the pendant holder with a pair of pliers.

2 A decorative pendant holder has claws to grip the bead, which can be opened outward. Slip the bead onto one claw and then squeeze the pendant holder closed with the pliers.

Choosing pliers

For simple techniques like this you can use needle-nosed pliers (also known as snipe-nosed or chain-nosed pliers), flat-nosed or half-round-nosed pliers – or even general purpose pliers.

When working with softer polished metals, be careful not to scratch the shiny surface with the pliers by gripping too tightly. It is possible to buy pliers with nylon jaws that will not mark metal if you plan to do a lot of jewellery making.

Wrapped pendant bead

Pendant beads have holes drilled through the top, either from front to back or from side to side, instead of holes drilled from top to bottom. They can be attached using a simple jump ring or pendant holder (see page 81), but making a wrapped loop gives a more professional-looking finish.

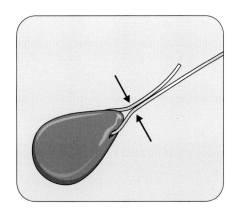

1 Cut a piece of wire about 8cm (3in) long. Slide the pendant bead about two-thirds of the way down the length of wire. Pinch the wire together just above the apex of the bead.

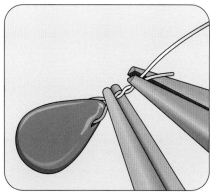

2 Hold the apex of the wire with the round-nosed pliers and use a second pair of pliers to twist the wire together two or three times. Using wire cutters, cut the short end of the wire right above the twist.

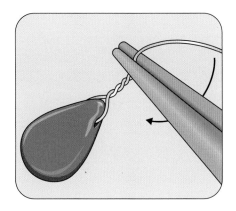

3 Directly above the twist grip the long end of wire with the round-nosed pliers and bend it towards you. With the finger and thumb of your other hand, bend the tail of wire back over the top jaw of the pliers to form a loop.

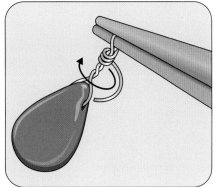

4 Once the long end of the wire meets the short end underneath the pliers, move the loop from the top jaw to the bottom jaw, about one-third of the way from the tip. Holding the loop with the pliers, wrap the tail of wire around the twisted section. Cut off the excess wire.

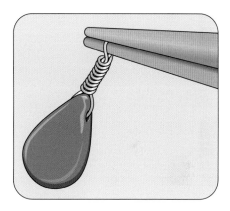

5 Use the round-nosed pliers to push the end of the wire against the coil. The wrapped pendant can now be attached using a jump ring, or threaded on cord or chain.

Organza ribbon and silver thread combined with pretty crystal beads.

Attaching findings to thread

To attach findings to bead thread or wire you will either have to use a crimp bead or a calotte end. A crimp bead is a simple tube of metal that can be squashed to grip the thread, while a calotte end has two tiny half-spheres joined at the base like an oyster shell with a hole at the base to take the beading thread.

Crimp bead

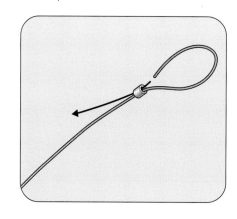

1 Cut the desired length of beading wire. Hold the wire in one hand about 4cm (1½in) from the end and slide on a crimp bead. Push the short end of the stringing wire back through the bead, creating a loop.

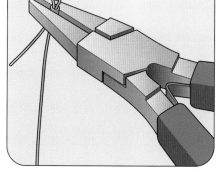

2 Adjust the size of the loop by pulling the crimp bead towards it, making it smaller, but large enough to let a jump ring move freely. Squeeze the crimp bead gently with flat-nosed pliers so it grips the wire.

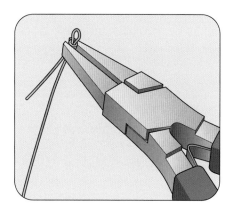

3 If you just squeeze in one place the crimped bead will be flattened, so move the pliers round slightly and squeeze again firmly. You can gently rock the crimped bead between the jaws of the very tip of the pliers to make it rounder if you wish.

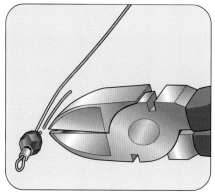

4 Slide the first bead onto the strand of stringing wire and over the tail of the wire from the crimped loop, if the bead hole is big enough. Trim the excess wire and then string on all the beads for the project.

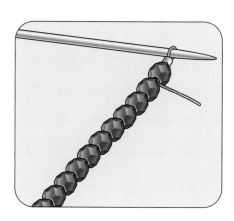

5 After the last bead slip on another crimp bead. Pull the tail end of the wire through the hole of the crimp bead and through the bead next to it, creating a loop as in step 1. Holding the loop firmly, pull the end of the wire to take up the slack so the crimp bead rests snugly next to the last bead. Squeeze the crimp bead as in steps 2 and 3. Use a jump ring (see page 80) to attach the two parts of the clasp to the end loops.

Calotte end

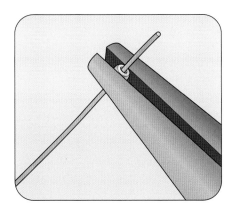

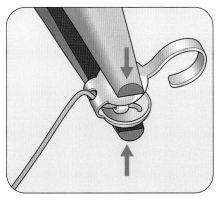

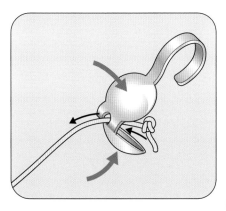

1 Thread a crimp bead onto the end of the thread or wire and squeeze in place with a pair of half-round or flat-nosed pliers. Make sure the crimp bead grips firmly and will not move.

2 Thread on the calotte end so the rounded sections cup the crimp bead. Very gently, squeeze the calotte closed with the pliers.

3 On nylon beading thread, instead of using a crimp bead, you can tie a couple of tight knots – one over the other – in the end of the thread. Thread on the calotte and pull up to the knots so they are inside the rounded section. Trim the thread end so it is also concealed inside. Close the calotte gently onto the knots using the pliers.

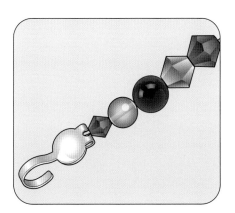

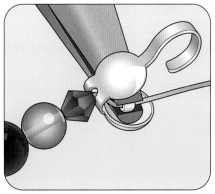

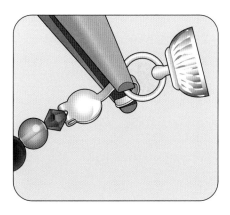

4 Thread on the beads as normal, with the first bead sitting against the base of the calotte.

5 Thread a second calotte onto the end of the necklace and add a crimp bead to hold it in place as described in step 1.

6 Attach the halves of the clasp to each end by threading it onto the hook on the calotte. Gently squeeze the hook closed into a ring.

Using cord ends

These can be used to attach a clasp to the ends of leather or fabric cord or ribbon and come in three basic types.

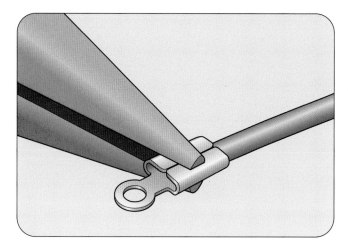

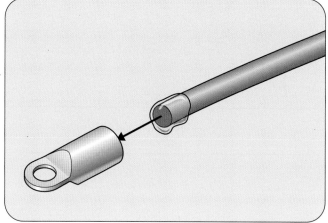

1 If using the type with the ring at the end of a flat metal piece, place a dab of glue on the end of the cord or ribbon and position it over the flat section. Fold over each side of the flat metal piece, one after the other, and close tightly onto the cord using flat-nosed pliers.

2 The type of cord end with a solid cylinder attached to the ring comes in different sizes so choose the one that fits your cord or ribbon best. Place a dab of glue on the end of the cord or ribbon and slide it into the cylinder. Leave to dry thoroughly before proceeding.

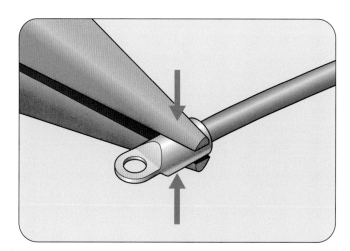

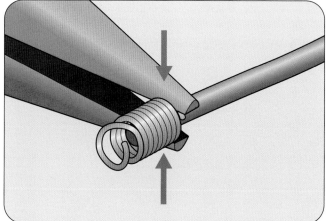

3 The cylinder should fit as snugly as possible, but squeeze it gently with the pliers so it grips tightly for extra security, moving the pliers around the cylinder so it is compressed equally on all sides.

4 With the type of cord end that has a twisted wire cylinder, slide the cord or ribbon inside and then squeeze the last coil only with the pliers until it grips securely. You can make your own version of this type using coloured wire.

Anchoring beads

For a string of beads without a finding at one end, the final bead needs to act as an anchor to hold the rest in place.

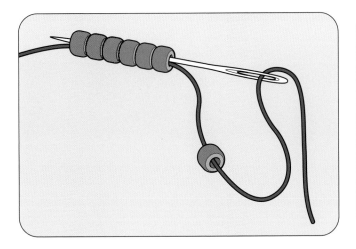

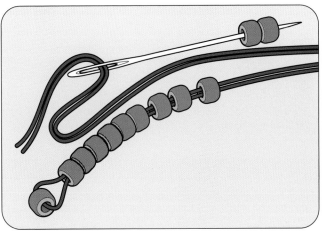

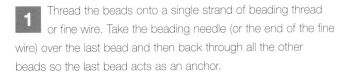

1 Thread the beads onto a single strand of beading thread or fine wire. Take the beading needle (or the end of the fine wire) over the last bead and then back through all the other beads so the last bead acts as an anchor.

2 Alternatively, thread a single bead onto the beading thread or fine wire. Bring the two ends of the thread or wire together so the single bead sits in a loop at the bottom and then thread all the remaining beads onto both strands.

Using a head pin

One or more beads threaded onto a head pin can be hung from a chain or from an earring wire to create instant simple jewellery. You can use a simple head pin or one of the types with a decorative end for extra interest.

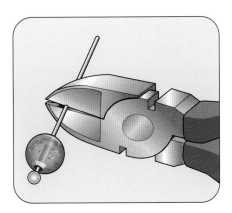

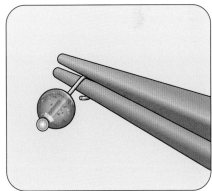

1 Thread a bead or selection of beads onto a head pin – if some of the beads have a large hole, start with a small bead against the head of the head pin so it won't slip through. Cut off the excess head pin wire, leaving about 6mm (¼in) above the last bead.

2 Using round-nosed pliers, bend the wire over into a loop. When you have made a complete loop, push it back the other way a little so it is centred over the bead.

Turquoise chips and silver beads threaded onto silver cord.

Making jump rings

Jump rings are inexpensive and available in a range of
different metals and sizes, but you can also easily make
your own if you want a different shape or an unusual size.

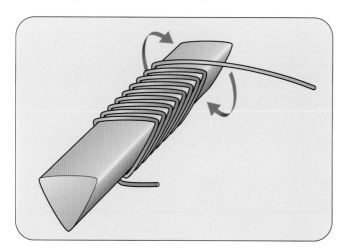

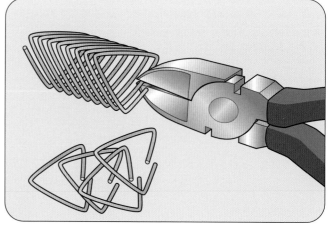

1 Choose a rod that is the same size and shape as the jump
ring should be – jump rings do not have to be round, they
could be square, rectangular or triangular. Wrap wire tightly
around the rod several times.

2 Slide the wrapped wire off the rod. Use wire cutters to snip
sections off to make individual jump rings. You can also
use this technique to make different shape pendant holders.

Colouring findings

Most findings are only available in a fairly limited range of colours and finishes, but you can change them into something unique to suit what you want to make.

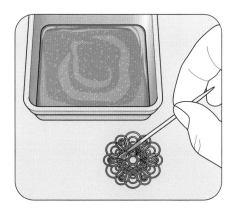

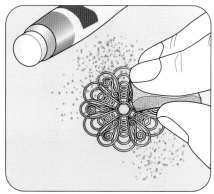

1 Many metal findings can be coated with coloured resin, which comes in a wide range of shades. You can also create your own special effects by adding glitter or mica flakes to the resin.

2 Metallic waxes can be used to change the colour of findings from gold to silver, and vice versa, or to add a different colour or an antique effect.

3 Brushing the surface of a metal finding with a brass brush creates a more subtle soft matte surface instead of a bright shiny one. Brush in one direction for an even finish. Finish off by polishing with a soft cloth.

4 Liver of sulphur will create a deep gunmetal colour on copper alloys and silver. Drop a couple of nuggets of liver of sulphur into very warm water and allow to dissolve. Dip the metal piece in the solution until the desired finish has developed. Note that the smell will be awful so use in a well-ventilated area or outside in the fresh air.

5 For shades of blue on copper and brass, mix an ammonia solution of 2 parts water, 1 part ammonia and 1 tablespoon of salt in a sealable plastic container. Fold a piece of metal mesh into a rack or scrumple up a piece of cloth and place this in the base of the container so the finding will not touch the solution directly. Place the finding carefully onto the rack or onto the cloth and sprinkle with a little salt. Seal the container and leave it for several hours – the longer the time, the more intense the blue.

Recycling old jewellery

Jewellery boxes and inherited pieces can offer a treasure trove of beautiful and unique beads that can be recycled and revamped to create modern earrings, chokers and pendants. Save old and broken jewellery; it can be taken apart and the beads given a new lease of life.

Attach odd beads on head pins to make pendants, or if you have pairs of odd beads use them to make a pair of matching earrings. If there are enough beads left over you could recycle them into a matching bracelet – consider threading them on elastic, see page 110. Hang a single beautiful bead on a chain or from a velvet ribbon choker and update an old beaded pendant by hanging it on a brightly coloured leather cord for a contemporary look. Old hat pins can be made into contemporary stick pins by threading on a few attractive beads and securing the last one with a dab of glue.

Knots

The reef or square knot and the surgeon's knot can be used if there are two ends to work with. To make a knot with only one end, use the overhand or half-hitch knot.

Reef knot

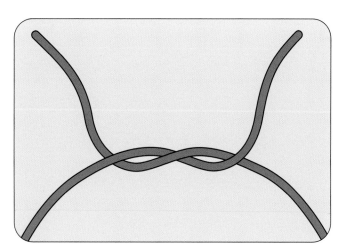

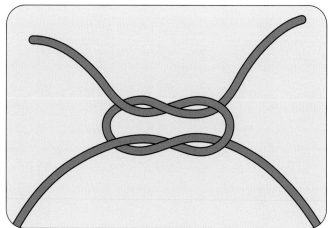

1 Cross the left-hand thread over the right-hand thread and wrap right around.

2 Cross the right-hand thread over the left-hand thread. Pull up through the hole and tighten the knot.

Surgeon's knot

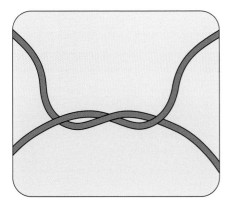

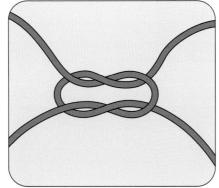

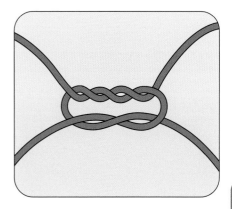

1 Cross the left-hand thread end over the right-hand thread end and wrap right around.

2 Cross the right-hand thread over the left-hand thread and pull up through the hole.

3 Wrap underneath, and pull up through the hole again.

Controlling beads

Round beads have a tendency to roll so it can be difficult to keep them in place while you work. One solution is to lay out the design on an old towel – use white or a flesh tone, because a strong colour will affect the appearance of the beads, which may throw off your design.

If you plan to do a lot of stringing, a beading board is a good investment – it has parallel grooves with numbering so it is easy to lay out a multi-strand design and see how it will look before you begin stringing. It also has several useful indented sections to keep loose beads in before they are positioned in the design.

Overhand knot

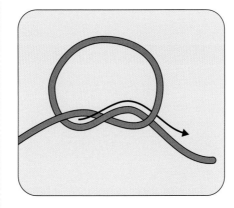

Make a loop with the thread, curve the thread around and pass back through the loop. Pull tight.

Half-hitch knot

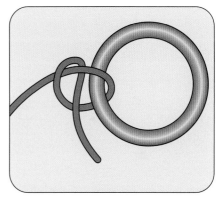

Form a loop around the wire or ring. Pass the end around the thread and through the loop. Pull tight.

traditional bead stringing

Bead stringing using a needle and thread is a technique that has been utilized for hundreds of years and it gives a traditional quality finish – especially when threading real pearls or semi-precious gemstone beads.

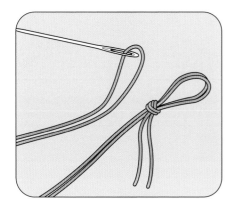

1 Thread a beading needle with the required amount of thread, doubling up the thread and closing with a slip knot at the end. Stretch the thread overnight (see pre-stretching details in the tip box, above right).

Pre-stretching

Over time beading thread will stretch, creating unattractive spaces between the beads and the clasp. You can prevent this to an extent by stretching the thread overnight – suspend an object weighing 0.5kg (1lb) from the length of thread prior to stringing with beads.

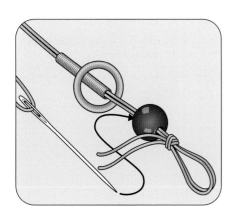

2 String on one bead and then a jump ring, followed by a section of French wire. Hold the French wire gently as you slide it on, because it may catch the fibres of the thread and snag.

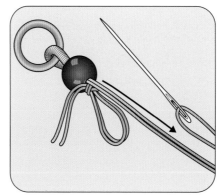

3 Pass the threaded needle back down through the hole of the bead next to the French wire on the adjacent side of the jump ring. Bring the needle out of the bottom hole of the bead next to the slip knot, and pull the thread through gently to form a French wire loop at the top around the edge of the jump ring.

French wire

French wire, also known as bullion or gimp, is very fine wire that is tightly coiled. A short length is threaded onto the end of the beading thread or wire and then bent over into a loop and the finding is then attached to the loop. The French wire protects the main beading thread or wire from abrasion on the finding and creates a professional-looking finish.

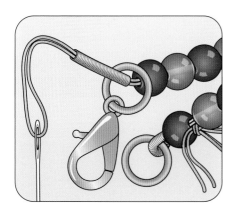

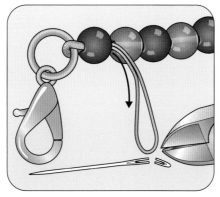

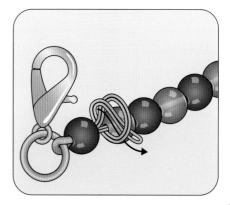

4 String on the rest of your beads, following the pattern you have designed if they are different colours, then slide on another piece of French wire followed by the jump ring on the clasp.

5 Pass the beading needle back through the last bead and pull the thread through gently to pull the French wire into a loop at the top with the jump ring held in the loop. Cut the eye of the needle with wire cutters and remove the needle from the thread.

6 Make sure the jump ring on its French wire loop is sitting snugly next to the last bead. Tie a half-hitch knot (see page 91) by crossing the short end of the thread under and then over the thread of the long strand. Next, tie an overhand knot (see page 91).

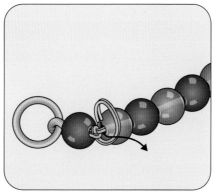

7 At the other end of the necklace, slide the beads, except for the last two beads, down towards the clasp added in step 6. Undo the slip knot. With the thumb and forefinger of one hand, hold onto the French wire loop gently. With the thumb and forefinger of the other hand, pull the tail of the thread, tightening the slack between beads around the point of an awl.

8 Use your fingernail right next to the bead to tighten the thread firmly. The jump ring on its French wire loop should remain snugly next to the last bead and there should be no other gaps between beads. Tie a half-hitch knot with the short end of thread, and put the tip of your awl in the centre of the loop, right next to the bead. Tighten the loop by taking up slack as you pull the thread until it knots firmly around the awl. Next, tie an overhand knot.

9 Use your fingernail as leverage to hold the knot tight against the bead as you release the awl. Put a dab of glue on the thread with the tip of a straight pin, let it dry for a few minutes, and trim with scissors or wire cutters.

knotted beads

Precious beads, such as pearls, often have the stringing thread knotted between each bead. This not only prevents the beads from rubbing against each other but also means that if the thread breaks only one or two beads can fall off.

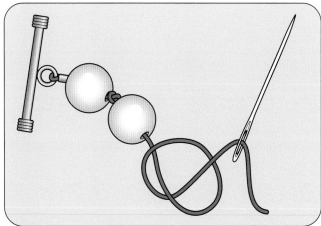

1 Pre-stretch the thread as explained in the tip on page 92. Add a finding or clasp to the end using your chosen method. Thread on the first bead, and then tie the thread into a loose overhand knot (see page 91).

2 Place the tip of the needle, or an awl, in the knot and hold it next to the bead. Gently pull the thread to tighten the knot around the needle, and then pull the needle out of the knot ready to thread the next bead.

A knotted pearl necklace.

Knotting

Knotting between beads can also be used to make inexpensive beads look as if they are more expensive, and to make a longer necklace or bracelet if you have too few beads.

Make sure the beads you use do not have too large a hole or the knot will just slip inside.

You will need to use traditional bead stringing thread for knotting – nylon thread or wire will not knot neatly and evenly.

daisy beading

This sequence of beading creates a row of little flowers – it will look most effective if the petals are in a different colour to the centre bead. A variation has the daisies separated by two or three beads – which could be in a third colour – so the flowers are spaced out a little more.

bead jewellery

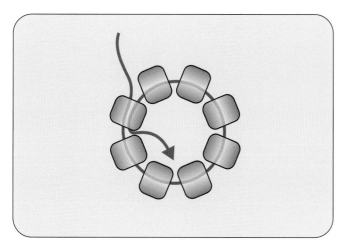

1 The first ring of beads will be the petals of the daisy chain. Thread the needle with a long length of thread – around 150cm (60in) maximum. Pick up eight beads in the petal colour and then pass the needle back through the first bead and pull tight to bring the beads round into a circle.

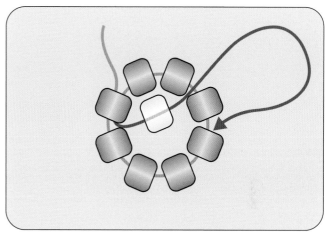

2 Pick up a different colour bead for the centre of the flower. Count back three beads behind the bead that the thread comes out of and pass the needle down through the fourth bead.

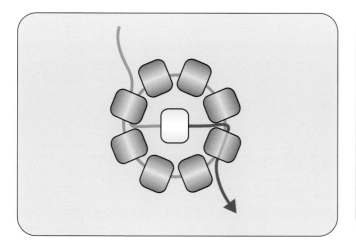

3 Pull on the thread so that the contrast colour bead is centred inside the ring of eight beads. The first flower is now complete.

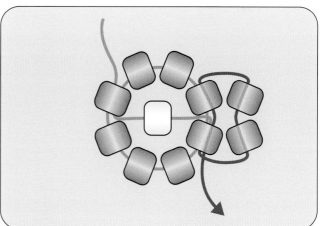

4 Pick up another two petal colour seed beads. Pass the needle back through the bead above the one where the thread came out in the first flower, and through the bead below, so the two new beads just added sit neatly next to the first flower.

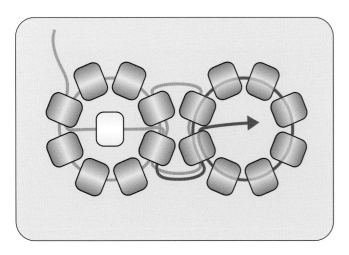 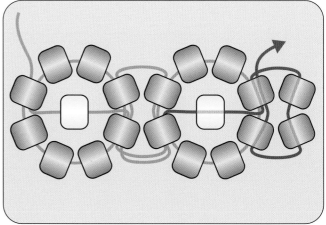

5 Go back up through the two new beads and then pick up another six beads in the petal colour. Take the needle back up through the first bead in the second flower. Pull tightly so the eight new beads form a new flower.

6 Pick up a different colour bead for the centre of the flower. Count back three beads from the bead that the thread comes out of and pass the needle up through the fourth bead. Repeat these steps until the daisy chain is the length you need.

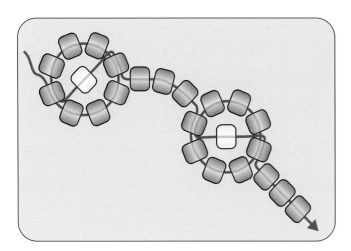 

7 A slightly different method of daisy beading has the flowers connecting with only one bead – which means you can also add a few different colour beads between each flower to space them out if you choose.

A sparkling necklace with daisy beading.

multi-strands

Using several strands together is an effective way to make more of smaller beads. The strands can be identical beads, or each strand can be different. For a choker or bracelet the different strands are usually the same length, but on a longer necklace they are usually graded lengths so each strand hangs at a different level.

Using a multi-strand clasp

A multi-strand clasp has several rings, each of which can hold one or more strands of beads. There are also findings with several rings on one side and one on the other, which can be used to convert a single clasp to a multi-strand type.

Twisting strands

For a different look, attach the multi-strands at one end and then twist or braid them together for a rope effect before attaching them at the other end.

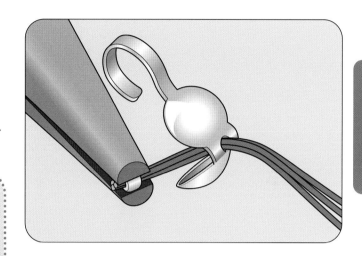

1 Cut three lengths of nylon beading wire each 40cm (16in) long, another three each 46cm (18in) long and another three each 50cm (20in) long. Attach each set of three wires of the same length together using a crimp and calotte end as described on page 85.

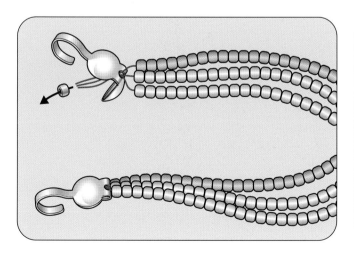

2 Thread the beads onto each wire in your chosen design. Join the three strands together at the other end using a crimp and calotte end as before.

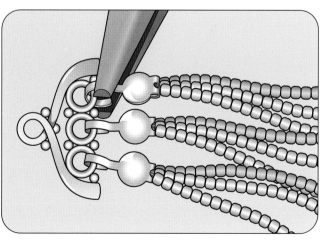

3 Close the calotte end hook on each set of strands over one ring of the multi-strand finding or clasp. Repeat at the other end of the necklace.

Using spacer bars

Spacer bars hold several strands parallel to each other. They can be used to create a wider bracelet or necklace from several narrow strands, or to control several strands around the back of the neck, which are then allowed to fall naturally at the front.

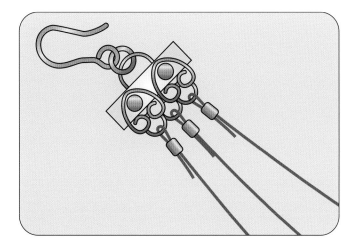

1 Cut one strand of beading wire for each ring on the multi-strand clasp and attach to the rings using a crimp bead, as described on page 84.

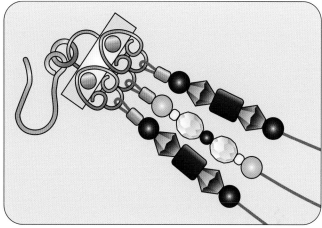

2 Begin to thread beads onto each wire, either in a specific design or randomly. Each strand should be beaded for the same length.

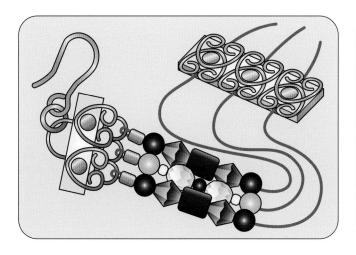

3 The clasp and the spacer bar should have the same number of rings/holes. Thread one strand of the beading wire through each hole in the spacer bar.

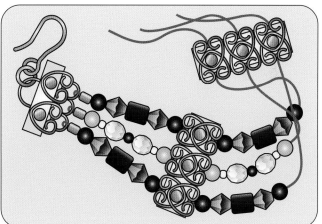

4 Carry on threading beads after the spacer bar as before. Add spacer bars at regular intervals and the other half of the multi-clasp at the end.

Beads and crystals combined in a multi-strand choker.

Using a bead spinner

If you need to string large quantities of small beads in random order onto thread or fine wire, a bead spinner will save a great deal of time.

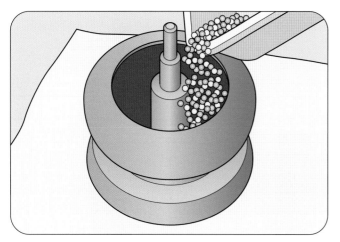

1 Place the bead spinner on a small towel to catch any beads that may spin out. Fill the bowl half to three-quarters full with seed beads.

2 Insert the tip of a curved beading needle or the end of the wire just below the surface of the beads, at a slight angle. Spin the bead bowl, so the needle or wire end lightly skims the surface of the spinning beads, picking up beads.

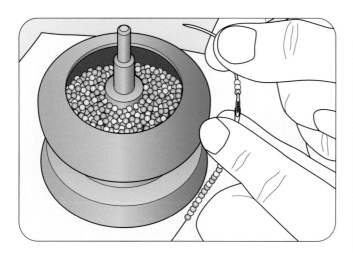

3 When around 5cm (2in) of beads have been picked up, stop and push them down the thread. Repeat steps 2 and 3 until you have strung all the beads you need.

Spinning beads

Do not spin the bowl too fast – a smooth, steady speed is best.

Don't let the end of the needle or wire scrape along the sides of the bowl – you need to find exactly the right angle so the beads just flow onto the needle.

spaced beads on nylon wire

Beads spaced out and held in place along transparent nylon wire will appear to be floating, but this unusual effect is very easy to achieve.

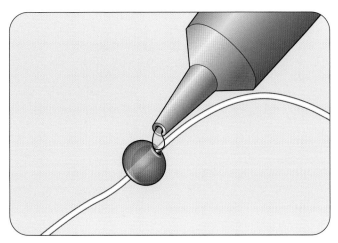

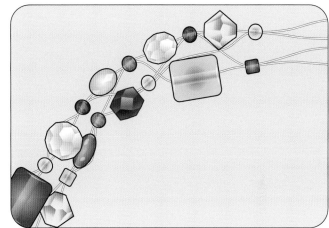

1 When using very tiny seed beads super glue can be used to hold them in place. Thread the beads onto a nylon line, securing every third or fourth bead by putting a tiny dab of superglue on the line and sliding the bead over it. Hold in place for a minute or so until the glue sets.

2 You will need at least four strands of nylon line and a mixture of large beads and seed beads. Join the strands together at the end onto a jump ring or clasp (see page 84). Thread on the beads at random, with each large bead on only one strand of wire but the seed beads on two strands. Thread the seed beads on a different two wires each time for a braided effect with the large beads floating between them.

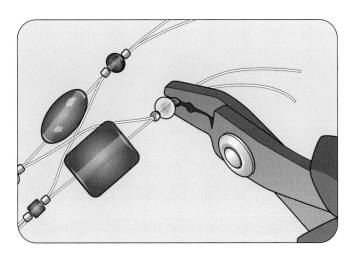

3 You can also use crimp beads to hold seed beads or even quite large beads in place. Thread on each bead with a crimp bead before and after it, but do not crimp at this stage. Arrange the beads and then close the crimp beads using flat-nosed pliers to hold them in position.

making beaded links

Single or multiple beads can be threaded onto short lengths of wire, creating a loop at each end, so they can be used as links. Making wire-wrapped beaded link is much the same technique but is a more decorative version.

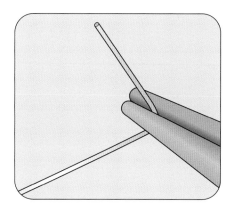

1 Cut a piece of wire about 5cm (2in) long. Hold the wire with round-nosed pliers about a third of the way down and bend at a right angle.

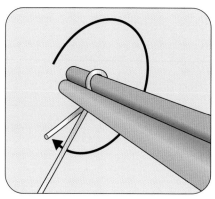

2 With a finger and thumb bend the short tail of wire back over the top of the pliers. Once the short end meets the long end underneath the pliers, remove the loop from the top jaw and place it on the bottom jaw.

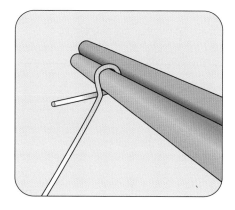

3 Continue to bend the wire as before, crossing the short tail over the long tail of wire, making a 30-degree angle with the short tail.

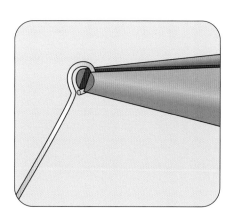

4 Using wire cutters, trim the short tail of wire at the base of the rounded loop. Use needle-nosed pliers to adjust the loop so it is centred on the wire.

Eye pins

To save time you can thread the beads onto an eye pin and omit steps 1–4. Make the loop at the other end the same size as the 'eye' of the eye pin.

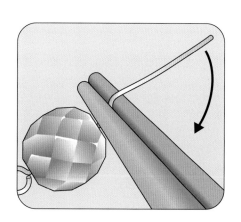

5 Slide on a bead. Holding the loop flat between thumb and forefinger, bend the tail of wire towards you, as before. With the finger and thumb of the other hand, bend the short tail of wire back over the top jaw of the pliers.

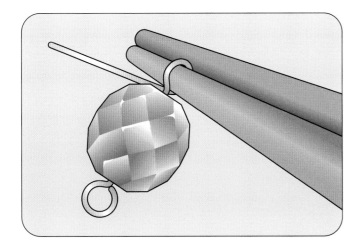

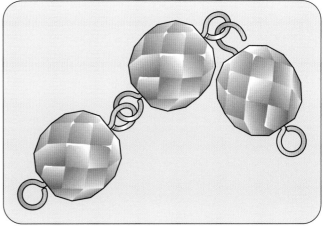

6 Once the short end meets the long end underneath the pliers, switch the loop from the top jaw to the bottom jaw, again one-third of the way from the tip. Continue to bend the wire as before to make a 30-degree angle with the short tail. Using wire cutters, trim the short tail of wire at the base of the loop. Use needle-nosed pliers to adjust the loop.

7 Beaded links can be attached to one another to make a simple necklace, or the beaded links can be used to join different parts of a piece of jewellery together instead of using a simple jump ring.

Assorted beads and crystals hung from a chain.

Chain and beads can also be used to create flamboyant dangly earrings.

Wrapped bead links

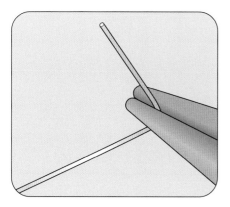

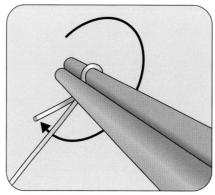

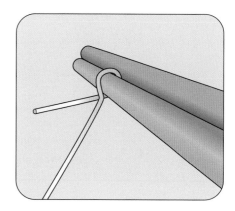

1 For a wire-wrapped loop, start with a longer tail of wire, such as 2.5cm (1in). Make a right angle in the wire by bending the top third of the wire towards you over the round-nosed pliers.

2 Using a finger and thumb, bend the short tail of wire back over the top of the pliers to form a loop. Once the short end meets the long end underneath the pliers, move the loop from the top jaw to the bottom jaw.

3 Continue to bend the wire as before, crossing the short tail over the long tail of wire, making a 30-degree angle with the short tail and turning it away from you.

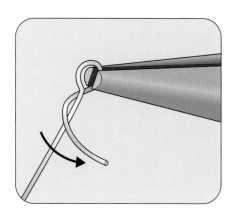

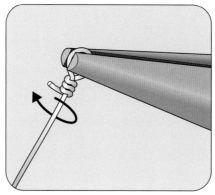

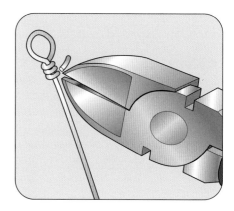

4 Instead of cutting the wire at the base of the loop, grasp the top of the loop with the chain-nosed pliers and with your other hand begin to twist the short tail towards you.

5 Keep twisting the short tail of wire around the long end at the base of the loop until it is wrapped around two or three times.

6 Using wire cutters, cut the excess wire off the short end under the wrapped coil.

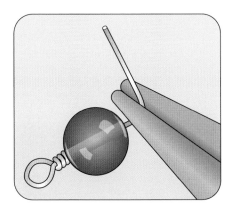

7 Slide on the bead or beads and repeat steps 2–5, making the initial right angle about 2mm (¹⁄₈in) above the top of the bead.

bead jewellery

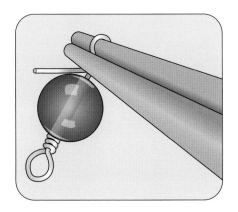

8 Continue to bend the wire as you did before, crossing the short tail over the long tail of wire, making a 30-degree angle with the short tail and turning it away from you.

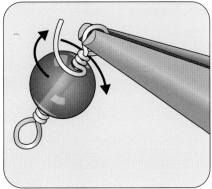

9 Wrap the short end of the wire two or three times around, as shown in steps 4–5.

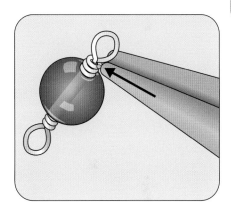

10 Using wire cutters, trim the short tail of wire near the coil. Use the tip of the round-nosed pliers to push the end of the wire against the coil.

using chain

Chains are available with quite large decorative links, which can be taken apart and combined with suitable beads for unusual and expensive-looking jewellery.

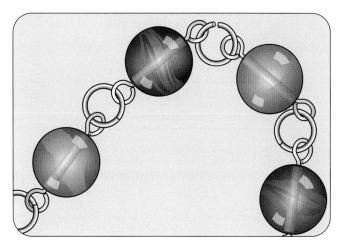

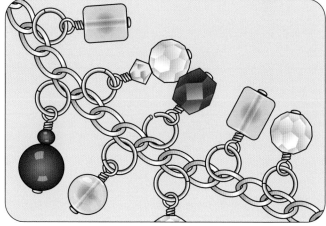

1 Beaded links (see page 102) can be joined with a large jump ring between each to give a beaded chain effect. Alternatively, short lengths of the chain can be joined with a beaded link into longer lengths – this is a good way of using up odd lengths of chain.

2 Hang an assortment of small beads from the links of a length of chain using jump rings. This is great to decorate a plain chain, or short lengths of beaded chain can be turned into earrings or a bracelet.

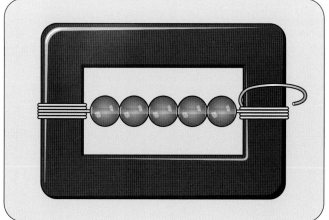

3 A single large round link can have a suitable size bead hanging inside it. Thread the bead onto a head pin (see page 87), add the loop at the top to a jump ring and hang this from the top of the link. You can thread a thin chain through the jump ring to make the unit into a pendant for a necklace – or make two units to hang on a pair of earring wires.

4 Tiny beads can also be suspended across the centre of a very large link. Cut a length of wire a little longer than the length of the link and wrap one end around the link at one end. Thread on several tiny beads, and then wrap the wire around the link at the other end.

wiring beads with fine wire

With this technique the beads can stand out from the main strand of jewellery and the wire can be manipulated to create different shapes.

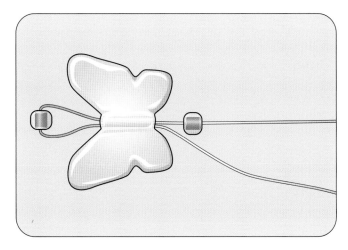

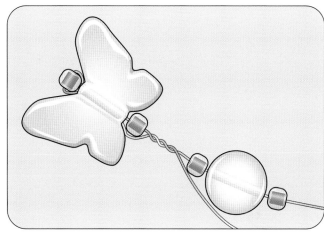

1 Thread a rocaille bead onto very fine wire and fold the ends together so the bead sits in the loop. Insert both ends of the wire through the hole of a bigger bead – here a butterfly shape – then thread another rocaille bead onto only one strand of the wire.

2 Twist the wires together twice after the second rocaille bead to anchor the beads in place. To add more beads, thread a rocaille bead onto one strand of the wire about 6mm (¼in) from the twisted wire. Thread on another larger bead – here a plain disk – and then another rocaille bead.

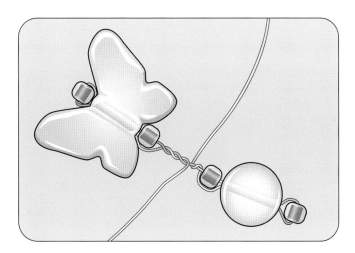

3 Insert the wire back through the second large bead and twist the two wires together at a central point between the two groups of beads. Carry on making groups of beads, and wire the groups together to make jewellery.

Glass flowers, leaves and butterflies on fine silver wire.

crocheted wire necklace

Very fine wire (0.2mm/US 32 gauge) can be crocheted and if you add beads as you work you can make delicate beaded jewellery. The technique shown here uses simple chain stitch, but see chapter 6 (page 198) for more beaded crochet and knitting stitches.

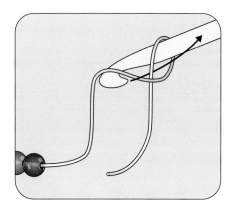

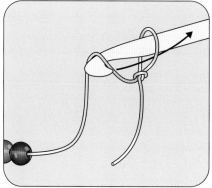

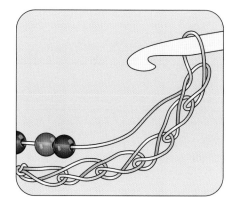

1 Thread seven to nine rocaille beads onto the wire followed by one larger bead. Make a slip knot on the hook at one end of the wire in exactly the same way as you would for normal crochet (see page 203). This is the first stitch.

2 Holding the hook in your right hand and the extending wire in your left, take the wire over the hook, catching and pulling a loop through the first stitch.

3 Carry on repeating step 2 in the same way until you have made six chain stitches.

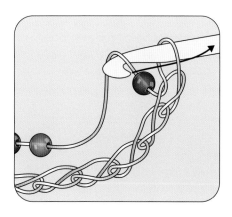

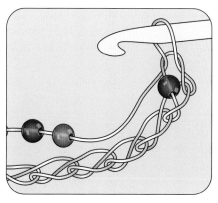

4 Slide the first bead along the wire so it sits next to the hook and then catch the wire behind it with the hook.

5 Draw a loop of wire through the stitch. Work another chain stitch and then add another bead in the same way. Continue the sequence adding a bead every other stitch.

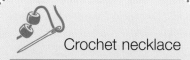

Crochet necklace

Make a length of beaded chain stitch crochet about 4.5m (5yd) long and fold it into lengths of about 42cm (16½in) long. Wrap the folded ends tightly with wire to secure, then add a clasp using jump rings.

Green glass beads crocheted with fine gold wire.

elasticated jewellery

Elastic cord is great for creating simple beaded bracelets that extend to fit a range of sizes. Thread on the beads and tie off the ends in one of two ways.

Concealed ends

This elasticated bracelet has a simple repeating bead pattern and the ends of the elastic are concealed.

Using elastic

Don't pull the elastic too tight when you are threading and knotting or you will use up all the stretch. The beads should sit closely and neatly together but not be too crowded.

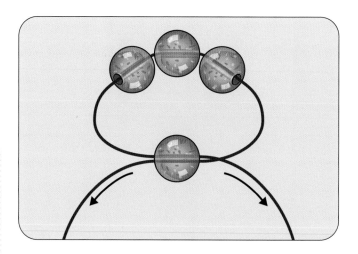

1 Cut a length of elastic cording – for an average-size wrist you will need around 60cm (24in). Thread on three beads and pull them to the centre of the cord. Add a fourth bead, taking each strand of the elastic through it from opposite directions.

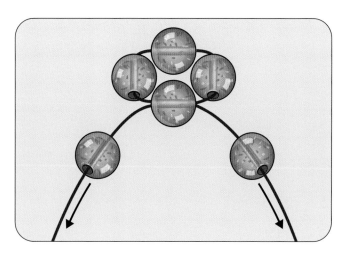

2 Tighten the beads together and then add another bead onto each strand. Add a third bead to this group, again taking each strand of the elastic through it from opposite directions. Keep going until there is only 5cm (2in) of free cord on each end for tying.

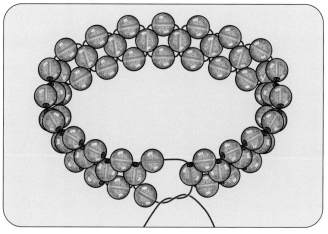

3 Add one more bead to each strand and then tie the ends of the elastic cording together in a tight reef knot (see page 90). Cut the cord ends down if necessary, then add a dab of glue to each and thread the end back inside the nearest bead so they are concealed.

Chinese knot

This simple decorative knot leaves the ends of the cord free, so add a bead to each to finish them off.

Elastic cord

Elasticated cord is available in a small range of colours so you can choose one to match or tone with your beads. It comes in several thicknesses – the most popular for jewellery making is 2mm (⅛in) but you can also find much thinner types for threading seed beads.

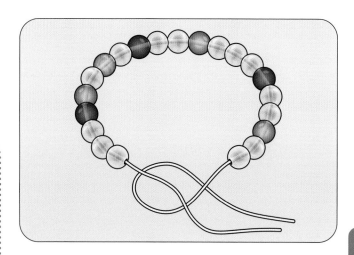

1 Cut a length of elastic cording – for an average-size wrist you will need around 30cm (12in). Thread on the beads randomly or in your chosen colour sequence. Start making the knot by crossing the strand from the left-hand side over the one from the right-hand side and then taking the right-hand end underneath both strands.

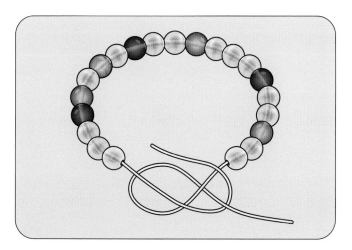

2 Take the strand coming from the left-hand side of the bracelet under the other strand and then curve it around over the top of the same strand just below the beads.

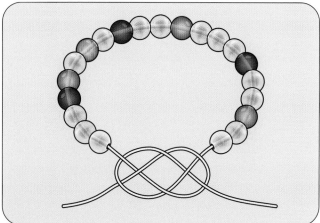

3 Carry on taking the strand from the left-hand side under, over and under the other strand as shown to make the knot. Gently tighten the knot towards the beads, keeping it flat so it doesn't distort. Trim the ends to a suitable length and glue a bead onto each to finish.

using ribbon

Beads can be threaded onto ribbon for a light and pretty effect, or ribbon can be combined with beads for jewellery in other ways.

Beaded ribbon

Ribbon comes in many materials, widths and colours so there is a very wide choice.

Threaded ribbon

Narrow ribbon can be threaded with beads in the same way as wire or cord, but the beads can be spaced out to show the ribbon between.

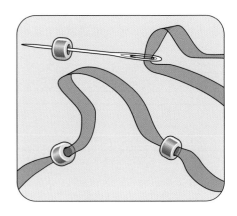

Securing the beads

Light beads will stay in place on the ribbon and can be moved around for a different look. Heavier beads may need to be secured in place with a dab of glue.

Thread narrow organza ribbon into a large-eyed needle. Choose beads with a fairly large hole and thread them onto the ribbon, spacing them out along the length and securing with a dab of glue if necessary. Make up several lengths and stitch together at one end. Add a cord end and clasp (see page 86).

Stitched ribbon

Organza ribbon stitched with metallic thread and crystal seed beads makes a delicate and pretty piece of jewellery.

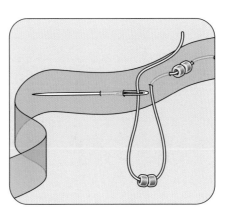

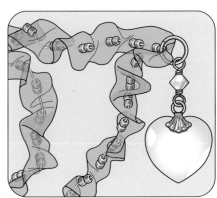

1 Thread an embroidery needle with silver thread and tie a knot at one end. Cut a length of narrow organza ribbon. Work a running stitch along the centre of the ribbon, with stitches about 6mm (¼in) long, threading two rocaille beads onto one side of the ribbon on each stitch.

2 Gather the ribbon gently, making a double stitch every 2.5cm (1in) to secure the gathers in place until there is around 50cm (20in) of gathered ribbon. Add a pendant with a jump ring and a cord end and clasp (see page 86).

Pleated ribbon

Pleated metallic ribbon is simple and inexpensive but can look very effective. The mother-of-pearl chips and gold rocaille beads used here create an attractive studded effect.

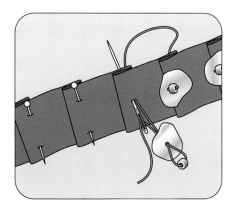

1 Starting around 3cm (1¼in) from one end, press the ribbon into knife pleats about 6mm (¼in) deep and 1.5cm (⅝in) apart. Pin the pleats in place. Thread an embroidery needle with matching thread and knot the end. Bring the thread through the centre of the pleat and thread on a mother-of-pearl chip and a gold rocaille bead. Take the thread over the rocaille bead and back down through the chip to the reverse of the ribbon. Take a small double stitch on the back to secure, and then repeat the stitching sequence on the next pleat.

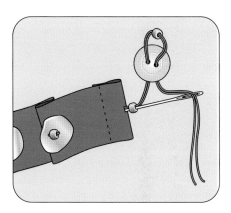

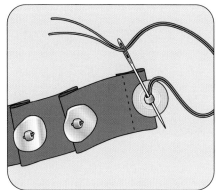

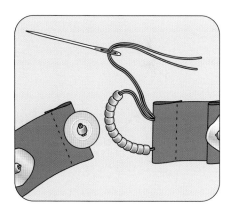

2 When all the pleats are stitched, turn under the ends of the ribbon and hem in place. To add a button fastener, thread the embroidery needle with a double length of thread and secure the end on the reverse of the ribbon. Bring the needle up to the right side of the ribbon at the centre just inside one end. Thread on a rocaille bead, then come through the hole in the button and thread on another rocaille bead. Come back down through the second hole in the button and through the first rocaille bead into the fabric.

3 Secure the button in place with a few stitches, each time coming up through the bottom rocaille bead, through a hole in the button and the top rocaille bead, then back down through the second hole in the button and through the bottom rocaille bead into the fabric. When the button is secure, take a couple of small stitches on the reverse to secure the end of the thread and trim the excess off.

4 To make a matching bead loop, fasten a double length of thread to the other end of the ribbon 6mm (¼in) above the lower edge. Thread on enough rocaille beads to go around the button. Take a stitch 6mm (¼in) below the upper edge and pull gently to tighten the beads on the loop. Fasten the thread off.

using a perforated disk

Beads can be stitched or wired through the holes of a perforated disk, and then the bead fixings are concealed by adding a backing disk.

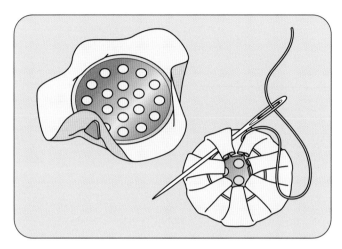

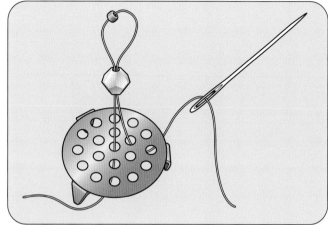

1 The disk can be covered with fabric to match the beads before you begin, which will hide any gaps between beads. Draw around the perforated disk onto the fabric adding a 6mm (¼in) margin all around. Cut out the fabric circle and then lay the disk down in the centre. The disk may have claws around the edge (sometimes they are on the disk back instead) – if so, pierce a hole at the claw position and slip the fabric over the claws. Gather around the fabric with a running stitch and fasten off the thread securely.

2 Alternatively, you can leave the disk uncovered, in which case the metal may show through the beads in places. Thread a length of nylon beading wire through the centre hole in the perforated disk, leaving a 5cm (2in) tail at the back to tie off later. On the front, thread on a crystal and a delica. Go back through the crystal and pass the thread back down through a different hole in the disk. Make sure you hold the thread securely as you work to stop the end slipping through the hole.

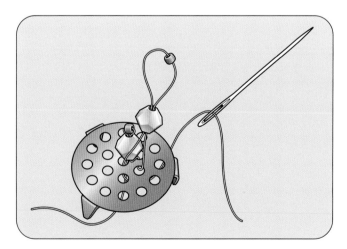

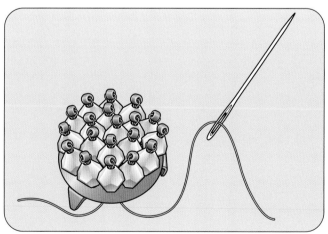

3 Bring the nylon up through the next hole and repeat the threading pattern with the beads, this time taking the thread back down through the centre hole. Pull firmly to sit the crystal against the finding.

4 Repeat the threading pattern until the disk is closely clustered all over with beads.

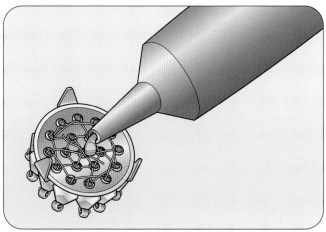

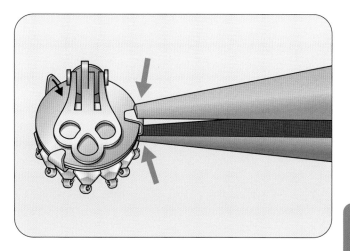

5 On the reverse, tie off the ends of the nylon with a reef knot (see page 90) and put a dab of glue on the knot to hold it secure. Trim off any excess nylon thread.

6 Attach the backing disk – this one incorporates an earring finding – to the back to conceal the fixings and gently squeeze the claws closed with pliers.

Beads

If you stitch drop beads onto the perforated disk, the holes will be at one end and will be concealed under the bead. In this case there will be no need to use a tiny crystal to conceal the upper hole as detailed in the steps.

Drop beads stitched onto a perforated disk ring.

combining sizes and shapes

Using several different size beads or different types of beads in one piece of jewellery can make the design look livelier. This can be done on one strand or using several strands.

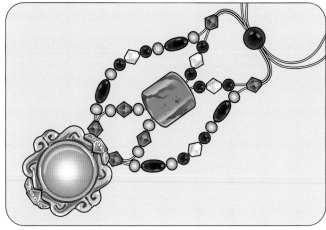

1 With one strand, add a calotte end to the beading thread as described on page 85. Lay out the beads in order and adjust until you are happy with the design. Begin threading the beads. When combining a very large bead with much smaller beads, grade the size down by adding a medium-size bead on each side of the large bead. This will also stop the small beads from sliding into the hole of the large bead.

2 This way of using multiple strands with different-size beads begins by joining four strands (here onto a pendant finding). Thread a small bead onto the two outer strands together then separate all the strands and thread a few small beads on each. Take the two centre stands through the large bead but carry on adding small beads on the two outer strands. On the other side of the large bead add a few more beads to the centre strand then take all strands through one bead. Repeat the beading pattern as required.

Advance planning

When working out more complicated designs it is always worth either drawing the design at full size or laying out the beads on a beading board so you can judge the effect and make any necessary adjustments before you begin threading.

alternative ideas

Beaded strands do not have to be used to make a simple circle with a clasp joining the two ends – other ways of using them can be more interesting in the right piece of jewellery. Also consider combining other decorative items, such as buttons, into jewellery.

Binding shapes

Tiny multi-colour rocaille beads really need to be used en masse to make the most of their coordinating colours.

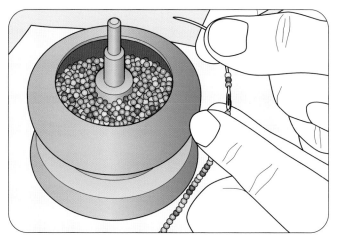

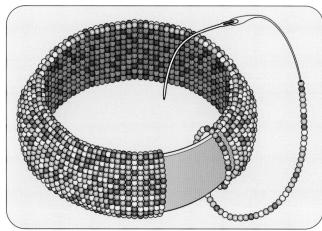

1 Thread a long length of beading thread into a beading needle, pull through to double it and knot the ends together. Thread with around 3,000 rocaille beads – a bead spinner (see page 100) will make this process much faster.

2 Take the needle through the centre of a plastic bangle and then between the two threads at the end, just above the knot. Glue the knot to the bangle. Wrap the beaded thread closely around the bangle to completely cover it. If the thread runs out, cut off the needle and glue the thread ends to the bangle. Start a new length as before close to the last bead. When the bangle is covered, part the first couple of rows and bind the thread around the bangle. Cut off the needle and glue the thread ends in place.

A bangle bound with subtly-toned rocaille beads.

Lariats

A lariat necklace is a single long strand of beads with no clasp that can be worn in a variety of ways.

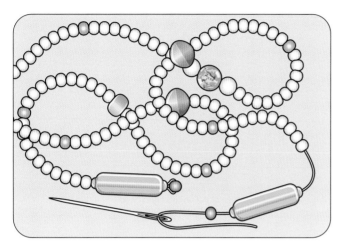

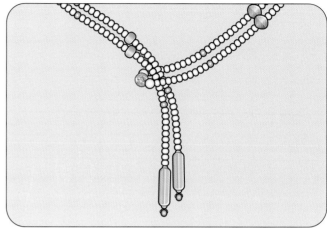

1 To secure the end, leaving a trailing end of 10cm (4in), begin threading the beads onto the beading nylon, beginning with a small bead as an anchor bead (see page 87). When a good length is beaded, insert the trailing end back up through the beads starting at the second one along. Continue beading until the lariat is around 145cm (57in) then make an anchor bead at the other end.

2 To wear the lariat, fold it in half and pull the ends through the loop or knot the ends loosely at the front.

3 A loop necklace is another version of the lariat, with a loop of beads created at one end of the strand that the other end is threaded through. Make the lariat as described in step 1 until it is around 75cm (30in) long and ending with a medium-size bead. To make the loop, thread on smaller beads in sequence for 7.5cm (3in) and then thread the beading wire back through the medium-size bead and the next few beads behind it, creating a loop. Add a dab of glue to the beading nylon just before the medium bead and pull it into the bead. Cut off excess thread.

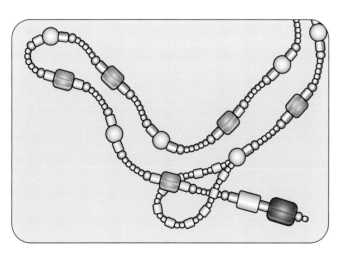

Tiny seed beads and stars used to create a delicate multi-strand lariat.

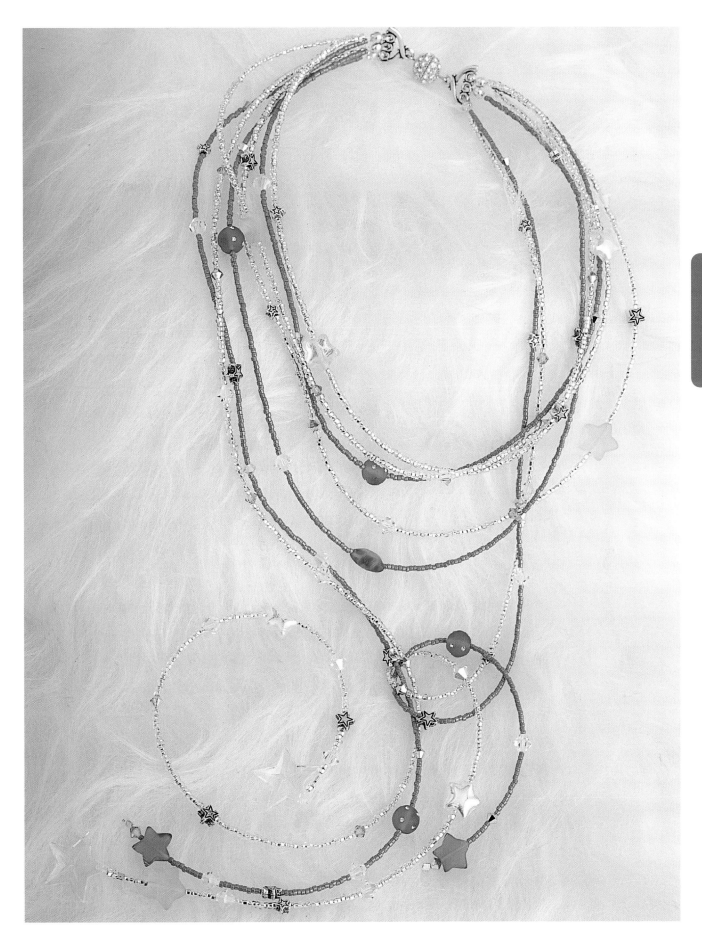

Incorporating buttons

For a contemporary look, try mixing buttons with beads, using them like large flat beads. Buttons can be stitched in place, or can be secured with pendant holders.

The claws on a decorative pendant can be used to clip onto one hole in the button as described on page 81. Look out for unusual shape or interesting colour buttons to use as 'beads'.

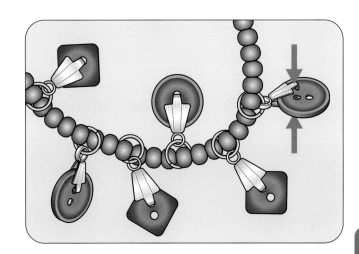

Using cord

It's not always necessary to use specialist stringing materials with beads; coloured embroidery thread or fine cord can make a delicate and unusual piece.

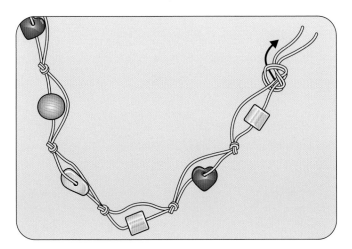

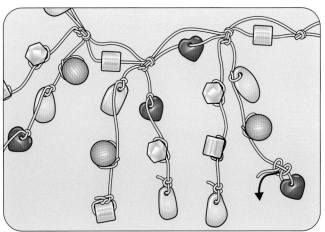

1 Cut two 80cm (32in) lengths of green embroidery thread and knot together at one end. Thread one strand into a needle and thread on about 30 assorted beads. Slide the first bead to the knot and then knot both strands together with an overhand knot (see page 91) 1.5cm (⅝in) from the bead. Repeat to capture each bead between knots. Add a calotte end to each end as described on page 85 and then add the clasp.

2 For the fringe, cut three 30cm (12in) lengths of thread. Lay the necklace out flat and thread one of the short lengths through a knot so the two ends hang down. Tie the ends together over the knot to secure and tighten the necklace knot again. Tie on beads at intervals down the hanging strands, with a bead at the end tied with a double overhand knot. Repeat to add further beaded fringes.

Interesting buttons can be incorporated with beads to great effect.

wirework
with beads

Wire and beads are an ideal combination and they can be used to make a wide range of things. This section includes wire-wrapped jewellery and French beading, as well as larger items for the home made from wire and beads.

basic wire-working techniques

Many of the wire and beading techniques in this section incorporate curved wire in various shapes, including scrolls, spirals and hearts.

Decorative ends

Wire scrolls and double-ended scrolls are a great way to create decorative ends on a length of wire.

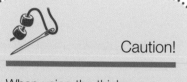

Caution!

When using the thicker gauges of wire, use gloves to protect your hands from sharp ends. It's also a good idea to wear goggles to protect your eyes when cutting wire in case a small piece flies up.

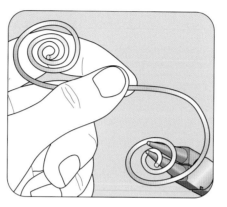

1 For a scroll, use round-nosed pliers to form a small circle at both ends of a length of wire. Holding one of the circles with the pliers, wind the length of wire around to form an evenly spaced spiral. Do the same at the other end, coiling the spiral in the opposite direction.

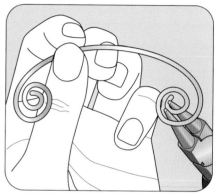

2 A double-ended spiral is similar to the scroll, but the ends curve in the same direction. If the spirals need to be a precise size and shape, draw a template first to check the wire against. Use round-nosed pliers to form a small circle at both ends of a length of wire. Holding one of the circles with the pliers, wind the length of wire around to form an evenly spaced spiral. Do the same at the other end, coiling the spiral in the same direction.

Wire heart

This is based on a double-ended spiral, leaving enough wire between the two ends to form the body of the heart.

Make a small double-ended spiral as explained above. Place a finger in the centre of the straight length of wire and push the coiled ends together with your thumbs. For a more pointed tip to the base, bend the wire around round-nosed pliers instead of using your finger.

Wire spiral

This can be made as a single open spiral similar to one end of the double-ended spiral on page 124, or as a much more tightly coiled version.

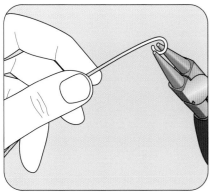

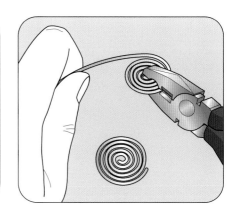

1 Hold the end of the wire with a pair of round-nosed pliers and twist the length of the wire around the tip of the pliers to form a small loop.

2 For an open spiral, hold the central loop with the pliers and continue to twist the wire into a spiral. Brace the length of the wire between your thumb and forefinger to control it and keep the spiral smooth and even.

3 For a closed spiral, hold the central loop flat between a pair of parallel pliers – ordinary household pliers will do as an alternative – and wind the wire into a spiral. Reposition the wire between the jaws of the pliers as necessary to keep the spiral flat.

Joining wires

When you are making up a large item in wire, it may be necessary to join two or more lengths of wire.

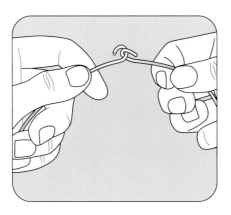

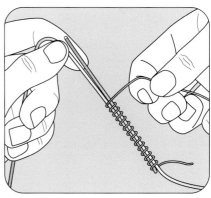

1 Hooking ends is the simplest technique to join two ends together. Use a pair of round-nosed pliers to form a small loop at the end of each wire. Link the loops together and squeeze them closed with the pliers.

2 This technique is used to join two wires along their length. Place the wires side by side, then bind them together by wrapping a length of finer wire tightly around both strands.

Flattened coil

This easy technique will create a line of flat wire loops.

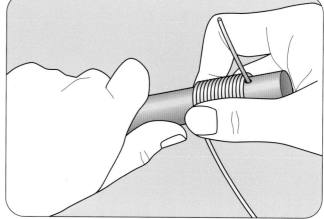

1 Drill a hole through the end of a length of dowel, then rub a piece of candle over the dowel so that the wire will slide off it more easily after coiling. Thread the end of the wire through the hole in the dowel to keep it in place while coiling.

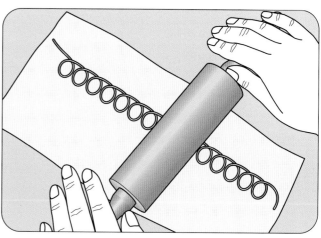

2 Using your thumb to brace the wire against the dowel, twist the dowel around until you achieve a tight, even coil of wire. Gradually slide your thumb along the dowel as the coil lengthens. To remove the finished coil, cut off the end of the wire that is threaded through the hole in the dowel and then twist the coil along the dowel and off the end.

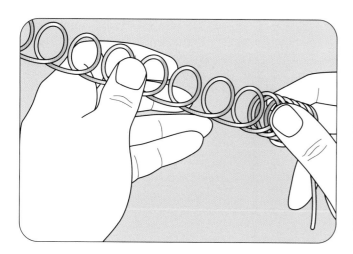

3 Extend the coil out sideways by gripping it firmly between both thumbs and pulling it out to the side so that the loops lie side by side.

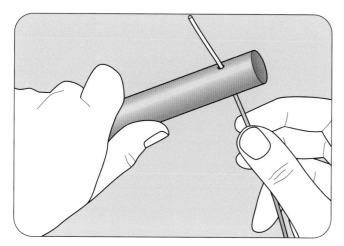

4 Place the extended coil of wire on a cloth to protect your worktop, because the wire may emboss its pattern into the surface. Flatten the coil with a rolling pin.

Wiggly wire

Making the jig may seem a bit time consuming for this technique, but it's worth it to achieve even wiggles in the wire.

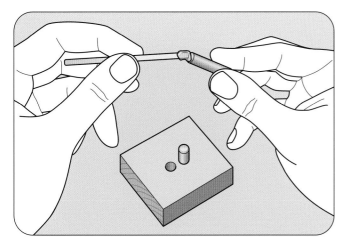

1 Decide on the depth of curves you require, then mark two points on a piece of wood this distance apart. Make two small pegs from dowel and drill two holes in the piece of wood at the marked points large enough to accommodate the pegs. Glue the pegs in position.

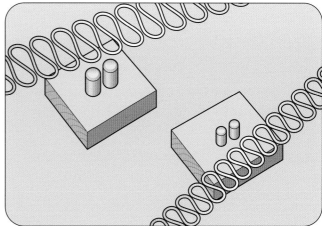

2 The finished wooden structure is called a jig. For small loops, use pegs made from thin dowel; for larger loops use thicker dowel. Try using different thicknesses of wire for different effects.

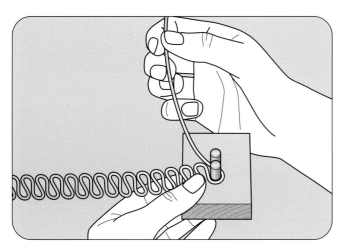

3 Hold the jig firmly in one hand, with the two pegs perpendicular to your body. Using your thumb to hold the end of the wire firmly against the block of wood, bring the remaining length of wire down toward the bottom peg at a right angle and bend it around the base of the peg. Then bend the wire up between the two pegs and around the top peg. Lift the curled wire off the pegs and move it to the side so that you can repeat the process to create two more curls. Continue until you have achieved the required length of wiggly wire.

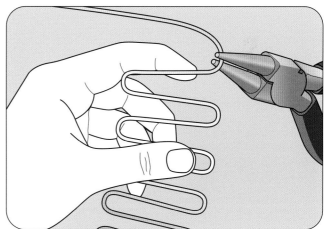

4 Instead of using a jig you can make wiggly wire freehand, using round-nosed pliers to bend the wire. To make sure that the depth of the curls is consistent throughout, mark the required depth at regular intervals along the straight wire before bending it. Use your fingers to gauge the width of the loops.

wire-wrapping

Wire can not only be used to thread beads but also for wrapping to add texture and to create more complex and interesting shapes.

Wire-wrapping a bead

Most medium to large beads can be wire-wrapped – the larger the bead, the easier it is to wrap. The wrapping can be simple swirls of wire or quite complicated designs with scrolls and coils.

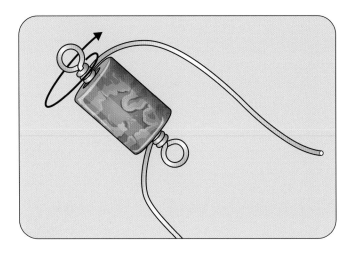

1 Take a fairly large bead and thread it onto around 10cm (4in) of wire. Bend the wire into a loop on both sides of the bead leaving long ends.

Wire wrapping and pearls combined to make an elegant necklace.

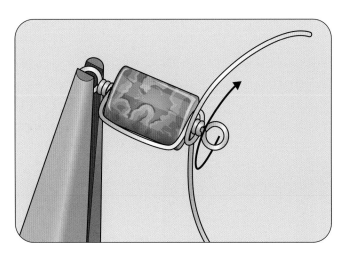

2 Holding one of the end loops in the pliers, begin twisting the other long end randomly around the bead in a decorative design.

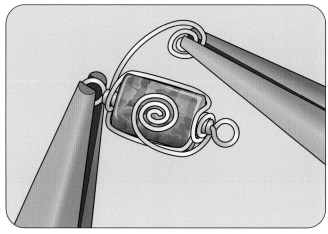

3 Repeat with the other long end. Curl both the wire ends into small spirals sitting flat against the bead.

Wire-wrapped dangles

Combining threading and wire wrapping is a great way to make more eye-catching elements using smaller beads. The resulting dangles can be used in jewellery or used to decorate other items.

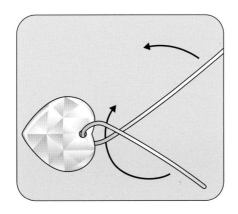

1 Make a sharp bend in the wire with the flat-nosed pliers, leaving one 2cm (¾in) end. Thread a crystal heart on the long end and, very gently, make another bend with the pliers to create a U-shape. With your fingers, bend the long end forward to cross the other wire. If you are too heavy handed you will crack the crystal, so be careful.

2 Hold the triangle of wire with one pair of pliers, and with another wrap the shorter end around the longer twice. Trim close to the stem.

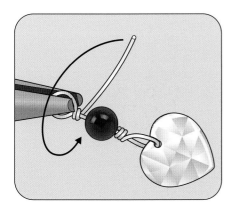

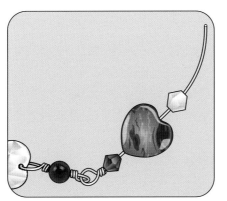

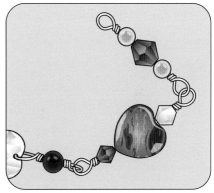

3 Thread on a 5mm pearl; make a top loop; and make a wrapped loop (see page 83).

4 With another piece of wire, make a loop; thread through the previous loop; wrap; and add a 4mm crystal, a bead heart and a 5mm crystal.

5 Make a loop and wrap at the top of this second component. Add the top component in the same way but using a 4mm pearl, an 8mm crystal and a 4mm pearl. Finish with a top loop, and wrap.

Wire-wrapped bead clusters

To make small beads look more dramatic, thread them onto wire and twist them into clusters, then wrap the clusters with delicate silver wire. The clusters are large but not heavy, so will combine well with more delicate materials such as wispy feathers.

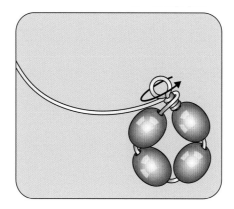

1 Make a wrapped loop at the end of a 20cm (8in) piece of wire, thread on four pearls and curve around to create a loop. Wrap the wire end twice around the wrapped loop.

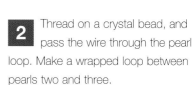

2 Thread on a crystal bead, and pass the wire through the pearl loop. Make a wrapped loop between pearls two and three.

3 Group seven strands of feather in one hand, and trim the top edges to neaten. Put a dab of glue inside a cord end, and push the feathers into it. Crush the cord end tightly around the feathers with flat-nosed pliers. Open and attach a jump ring to the top of the cord end.

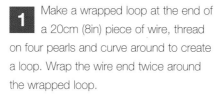
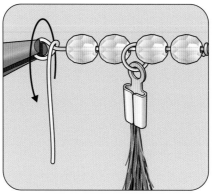

4 Make a wrapped loop with a short piece of wire. Thread on two crystal beads, the feather component, two more crystal beads, and make another wrapped loop. Slightly curve this piece.

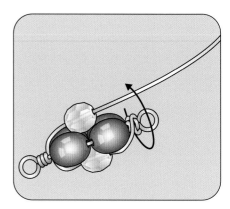

5 Turn over the pearl circle, and thread on another crystal bead to the back. Wrap around the loop once more. Thread on four more pearls; make a circle and wrap at the top; then repeat steps 2 and 5. Attach the long feather piece to each side of the pearl flowers with 4mm jump rings and attach a fishhook earring finding at the top.

building bead shapes

Since wire is a rigid threading material, it can be combined with beads to make quite large and intricate semi-rigid shapes, such as this circle of beaded spokes around a central scarab bead.

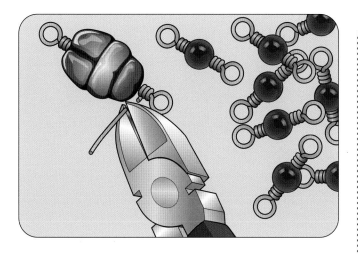

1 Make a small wrapped loop on a 5cm (2in) length of wire. Thread on the scarab bead, and wrap and trim the other end. Repeat for 10 black jet beads to make the wire bead spoke components.

Jet beads

Jet is a semi-precious stone although it is not a real gem since it is not completely of mineral origin – it was formed under pressure from decayed wood over millions of years. It is very easy to cut and polish to create sparkling faceted beads and was very popular in Victorian times, particularly for mourning jewellery. Black glass is often used to imitate jet, but real jet is warm to the touch because it does not conduct heat well.

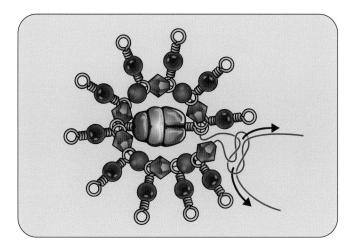

2 Take a 12.5cm (5in) length of nylon wire and thread on one end of the scarab, a black jet spoke, a 6mm crystal, jet spoke, 6mm matte bead, jet spoke, 6mm crystal, jet spoke, 6mm matte bead, jet spoke, 6mm crystal, jet spoke, other end of the scarab, 6mm crystal and so on, repeating the pattern symmetrically. Tie the nylon wire in a surgeon's knot (see page 91) and put a dot of glue on the knot. Trim the ends.

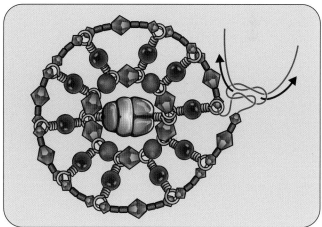

3 Cut an 18cm (7in) length of nylon wire and, starting at the top of the scarab, thread on the other end of an jet spoke, then a 4mm crystal, a small bugle bead, a 6mm crystal, bugle bead, 4mm crystal, jet spoke, 4mm crystal, two bugle beads, 4mm crystal, jet spoke, 4mm crystal, two bugle beads, 6mm crystal, two bugle beads, 4mm crystal, jet spoke; repeat symmetrically all around the inner circle. Tie the nylon wire in a surgeon's knot and put a dot of glue on the knot. Trim the ends.

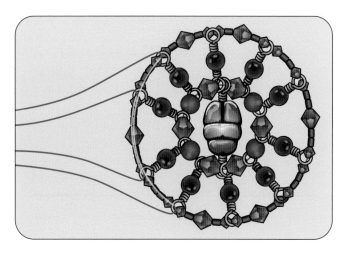

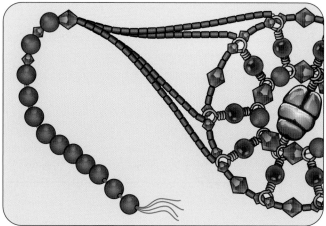

4 Cut two 50cm (20in) lengths of nylon wire, and thread one into the outer circumference of beads at the second spoke, around through each bead in the outer circumference to the fifth spoke and out again on the same side. Repeat with the second thread using the third and fourth spokes.

5 Thread 5cm (2in) of bugle beads onto the outer two side threads and about 4.5cm (1¾in) onto each inner thread. Adjust the number of beads until all four threads lie flat when joined to enter a 6mm crystal. Thread all four strands through a matte bead, 4mm crystal, a matte bead, 4mm crystal and 10 matte beads.

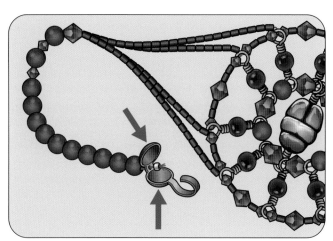

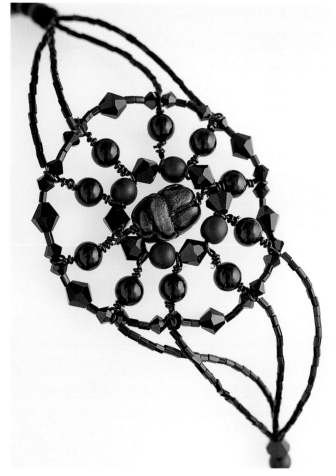

6 Thread on a necklace end and a crimp, and crush the crimp with flat-nosed pliers. Trim the wires and close the necklace end. Attach one end of a clasp with round-nosed pliers. Repeat from step 4 on the other side.

Jet beads make a very dramatic piece.

memory wire

This is a great type of wire that 'remembers' its coiled shape, so even if you pull it out straight it will coil itself up again. When used for bracelets or necklaces it will not need a clasp since it just coils around the arm or neck.

Basic memory wire necklace

Memory wire is great for a very simple necklace; for a more decorative version, add a selection of wire-wrapped dangles between the beads at the front.

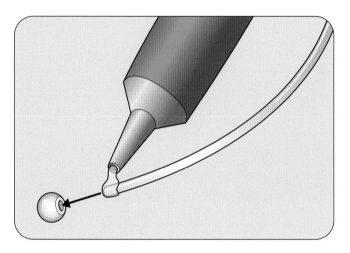

1 Cut a length of memory wire 1¾ coils long. Glue the first end cap onto one end of the memory wire with epoxy glue; leave it to set until completely solid.

2 Thread on imitation pearls along the length of the wire. Snip off any extra wire, but leave 6mm (¼in) to glue the other end cap in place.

Working with memory wire

Do not cut memory wire with ordinary wire cutters – it is made of steel and will quickly spoil them. Use special memory wire cutters.

Memory wire may not need a clasp but the ends will need to be finished, both for neatness and to prevent them scratching. Special memory wire end caps are available – they look like a small bead with a hole only part way through and come in several sizes and finishes. For a secure finish when gluing on end caps, sand the ends of the wire slightly before applying glue so it has a rough surface to grip onto.

Set screw findings for memory wire also have a hole partway through into which the wire end is inserted, with a tiny set screw on one side that must be tightened onto the wire using a miniature screwdriver.

Memory wire with spacers

This type of wire doesn't have to be used in continuous coils – it can also be used in separate strands like ordinary wire with the strands held in place with spacers.

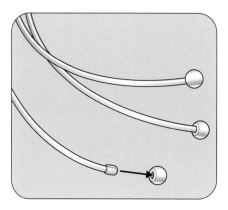

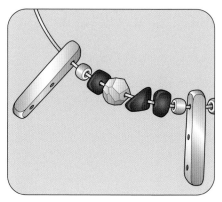

1 Add a little epoxy glue onto the tip of a cocktail stick and use to glue a memory-wire end to one end of three lengths of wire. Don't worry if you get a tiny bulb of glue at the foot of the bead; it will dry clear. Leave to dry according to the manufacturer's instructions.

2 When the glue is completely set, thread on a gold bead, a spacer, and a gold bead. Then thread on two tumble chips, a pyrite piece, a chip, another gold bead, and a second spacer.

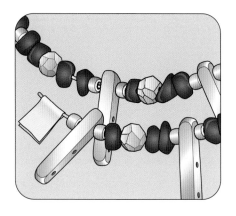

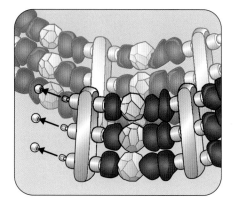

3 Thread on about 6.5cm (2½in) of assorted chips and beads, placing a gold bead either side of the faceted stones. Thread on a gold bead, a spacer and a gold bead. Wrap a bit of tape on the end of the wire to hold the beads in place until the final cap can be glued on.

4 Repeat steps 2 and 3 for the second and third wires, threading them through the middle and bottom holes in the spacers. Make sure the length of stones between each spacer is exactly the same as the first – you may have to add or subtract beads if they are all irregular shapes and sizes.

5 Snip off any excess memory wire with the appropriate cutters, leaving 3mm (⅛in) to glue into a memory-wire end. Be careful: you don't want all the beads to fall off. Glue the remaining three ends to the ends of each wire using the epoxy glue and a cocktail stick. Leave to dry thoroughly.

Memory wire hoops

Since memory wire remembers its circular shape, it's a great material with which to created beaded hoops. It will be very stiff when trying to bend the end loops, but try and make a complete tiny round loop with no gap.

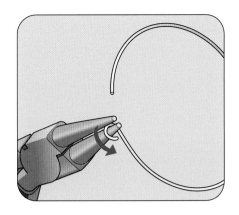

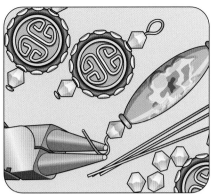

1 Grip the very end of one piece of memory wire with a pair of round-nosed pliers, and curve it outward into a loop. Place it to one side.

2 Thread a series of decorative beads onto each of three head pins and make a neat top loop so you have a pair of dangles and a centre dangle.

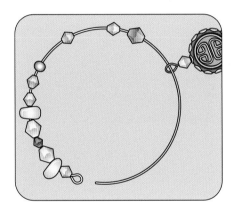

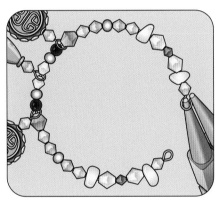

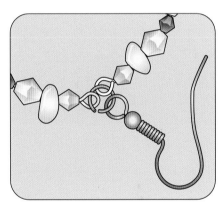

3 Thread a series of small beads onto the memory wire loop, then add one of the pair of dangles made in step 2.

4 Thread a few more beads, then the centre dangle. Repeat the bead threading symmetrically on the other side. Leave 1cm (½in) of wire showing. Snip off any excess, and then make another loop with the round-nosed pliers.

5 Open a jump ring and thread through the loops from each side of the memory wire. To turn into earrings, thread on a fishhook earring finding, and twist the jump ring to close. Make a second hoop in the same way for the other ear.

wirework with beads

french beading

This is a very old way of using wire and beads – it dates back more than 500 years – traditionally to create beaded flowers, although it is possible to make other shapes with the same techniques. Usually seed or rocaille beads are used, or occasionally small crystal beads. The flowers were often used in bouquets or memorial wreaths, and later as hairpins or as decoration on gowns.

Single loop

The simplest flower can be made using just the single loop technique. Once you have mastered this, you will be able to make star flowers and gypsophila.

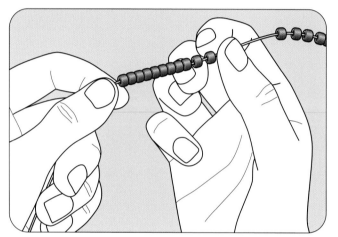

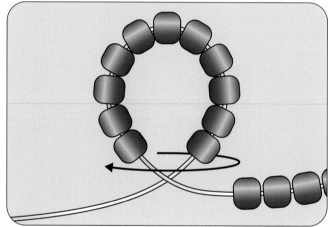

1 Twist the end of a length of fine wire into a knot and thread on more than enough beads for the petals – in this case at least 55 beads. Place the finger and thumb of your left hand onto the wire, around 10cm (4in) from the knot (this length will become the stem, so when following a pattern the distance from the knot is the length of the stem). Using your right hand, push eleven beads along the wire to the finger and thumb of your left hand.

2 Bend the wire with the eleven beads to form a loop of beads. Holding the loop at the base, twist the wire two or three times in a clockwise direction to hold the loop securely in place. This is the first petal.

Making a stem

If you are making a bare wire stem, you will need to twist the wires together all the way to the bottom of the flower. To get the best finish, hold the flower in your left hand, separate the wires into two pairs, creating an angle of about 70 degrees. Use your right-hand finger and thumb to maintain this position with the wires and use your left hand to twist the flower around. The wires should twist around each other evenly to create a neatly twisted stem. You will need to use this technique when you are making gypsophila.

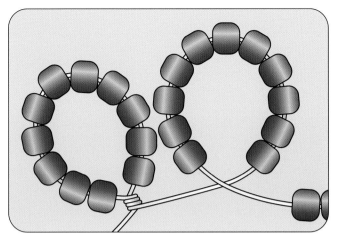

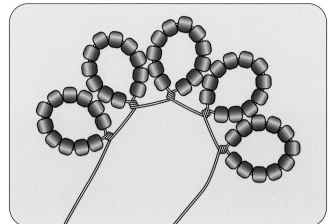

3 Shape the loop so it resembles a petal. Hold the petal in your left hand and use your right hand to pass another eleven beads along the wire until they are about 6mm (¼in) from the base of the first petal – you need to leave this space so you have room to create the loop and twist the wire. Repeat step 2 to form a second petal.

4 Repeat another three times so that you have a row of five petals. Cut the wire 10cm (4in) – or the specific stem length – from the end of your final petal. If there are any remaining beads on the wire leading from the spool, knot the end again to prevent them falling off.

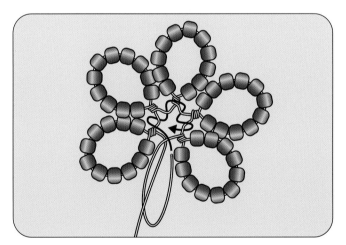

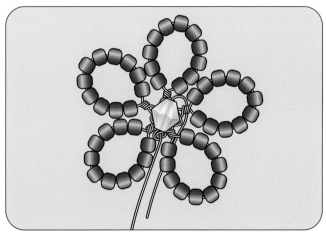

5 To form a flower, wrap the end of wire you have just cut off over the top of the twisted wire at the base of the first petal and down between the first and second petals to form a circle. Take the wire under the twist at the base of the second petal and up between the second and third petals, then over the top of the twist at the base of the third petal and down between the third and fourth petals, then up between the fourth and fifth petals and finally down over the fifth petal.

6 Add a centre bead by threading a single bead onto the wire end and then passing the end over the top of the flower so the bead sits in the centre. Pass the wire down between two petals roughly opposite the point from which you started. Your two ends of wire should now be sitting roughly opposite each other underneath the flower, ready to be twisted together to make the stem. In some patterns you may be required to add a separate centre, in which case, omit this step. Cut the knot off your first piece of wire and twist the stem wires together. Follow the instructions in the tip box (opposite) for finishing off the stem.

Double loop

Once you have mastered the technique for making a single loop, you can make a similar flower using a double loop. Again you need to thread on all the beads you need to complete the flower at the start.

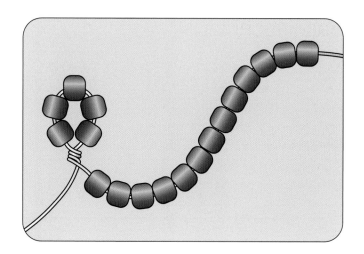

1 Make a single loop with five beads in the loop and leaving a 12.5cm (5in) length of wire for the stem. Instead of making a second single loop, push about 13 beads from the spool of wire right up to your existing single loop.

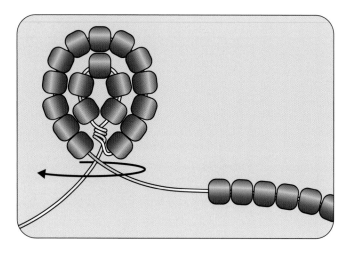

2 Wrap these beads around the outside of the single loop and adjust the number of beads so that they sit snugly round the single loop. Hold the petal with your left hand, holding the wire just below the petal with the thumb and forefinger of your right hand. Twist the petal just as you did for the single loop. Both rows of beads should now be secured in place.

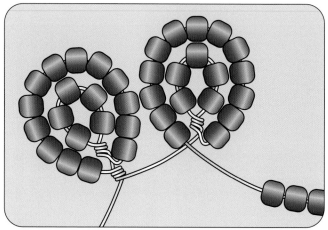

3 Repeat steps 1 and 2 to make another petal using the double loop method. You will need to leave slightly more than 6mm (¼in) gap between the end of the first petal and the start of your next loop, so that there is enough wire to allow for the two sets of twists.

Basic technique

Despite its name, this technique is a little more advanced than the loop techniques. It is used to make individual petals and leaves rather than whole flowers and can be used to create petals with round or pointed ends or to create cone-shaped centres.

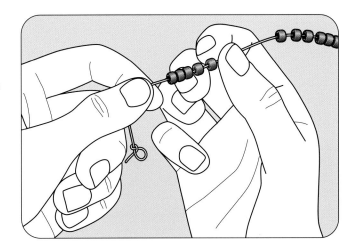

1 Begin by threading at least enough beads onto the spool of wire for a single petal, then knot the end of the wire. Unravel a long length of wire, keeping the beads next to the spool. Slide the number of beads required for your first row right up to the knot.

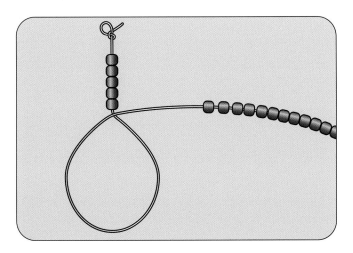

2 Keeping the beads next to the knot, make a loop with the wire. The head of the loop (the point at which the wires cross) should be a little way below the beads under your knot. This small length of wire forms the base wire of the petal. The loop itself should be about the length of your stem.

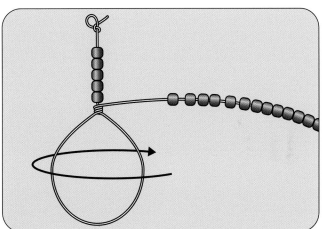

3 Once you have decided on the placement of the loop, use one hand to pinch the wires together and use the other hand to twist the loop round 4 or 5 times so that it is held securely in place. The base wire with your first row of beads and the knot should now be sitting directly above the loop pointing upward, while the spool wire is at a 90-degree angle to the right of your loop.

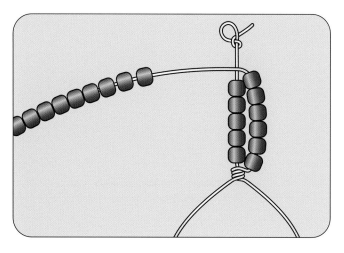

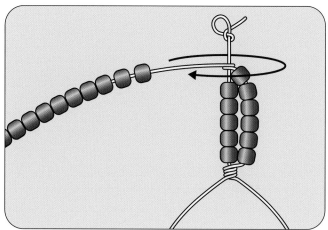

4 Add row 2 by sliding the required number of beads down the spool wire to the top of the loop. Make sure the row 1 beads are all pushed to the bottom of the base wire, directly on top of the loop. Adjust the spool wire so the row 2 beads sit along the right-hand side of the row 1 beads – they should fit snugly, so adjust the number of beads in row 2 if necessary. Wrap the spool wire over the top, round and back up to the front of the base wire so that the row 2 beads are held securely in place and the spool wire is now at the top of the petal.

5 For a round top to the petal, wrap the spool wire at a 90-degree angle to the loop and knot. For a pointed top, wrap the spool wire at a 45-degree angle. A pointed top will need slightly more beads in each row, so each row will sit higher than the previous row rather than wrapping neatly round it, but a pattern should provide a guide to this.

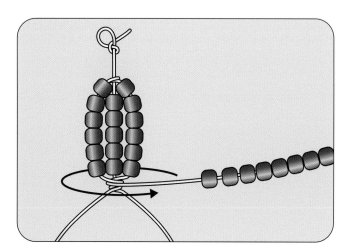

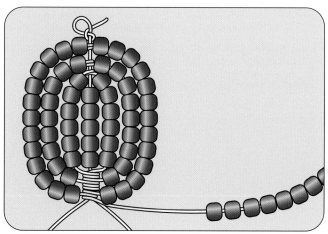

6 Repeat steps 4 and 5 to add row 3, this time working from the top to the bottom of the petal. Again, if you need a round bottom, wrap the spool wire at a 90-degree angle. If you need a pointed bottom, wrap it at a 45-degree angle.

7 Keep adding rows up the right-hand side and down the left-hand side until the petal is finished. Each subsequent row will need more beads so that it sits round the outside of the previous rows. As you work, keep adjusting the base wire so it remains as straight as possible and sits absolutely vertical to the loop that will be the stem.

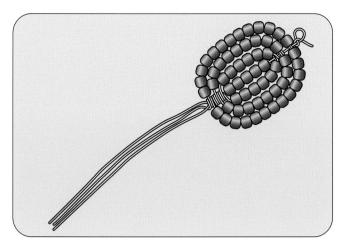

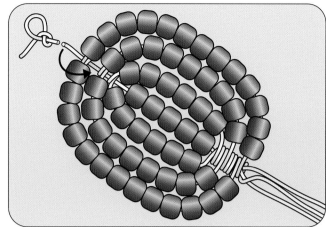

8 When you have finished your petal, the spool wire will be at the bottom of the petal. Cut it from the spool, leaving a long length and knotting the wire on the spool to prevent any beads falling off. Cut the bottom of the loop and smooth all three wires down to form a straight stem.

9 Trim the wire at the top of the petal about 6mm (¼in) from the petal and fold it down the back of the petal. This method of French beading creates petals and leaves that have a front and back, so be careful about choosing your wire colour and be aware of the right and wrong side of the petal as you assemble the flower.

Making a cone

To make a cone, begin in exactly the same way. The first row will be just 1 bead, then create at least two flat, round rows, and then begin shaping. Don't increase the number of beads in each row and, at the same time, pull the ends of the base wire downward so you begin to form a cone instead of a flat circle. This makes an excellent centre for a flower.

A pink lily made using the basic technique.

Three row crossover

This method is another development of the single loop and makes a slightly fatter petal that is ideal for small daisy-type flowers. Thread on enough beads at the start to complete the required number of petals.

Choosing the wire

Use wire that is approx 0.3mm diameter (US 28 gauge) and match the colour of the wire to the colour of the beads if it will show on the wrong side, so it will be less obvious.

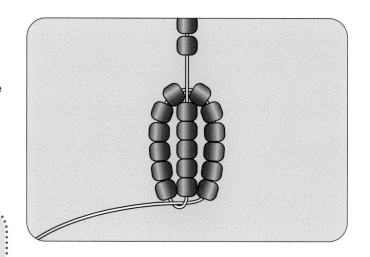

1 Make a single loop using 12 beads, curving the sides out so there is space in the centre. To add the single row of beads up the middle, push up five beads (as a general guide, the number of beads for the third row is just under half the number for the single loop). Holding the single loop with your left hand, use your right hand to guide the beads so they run up the centre front of the single loop. If they don't fill the gap completely, add another bead. If they sit too much above the top of the single loop, then take a bead away.

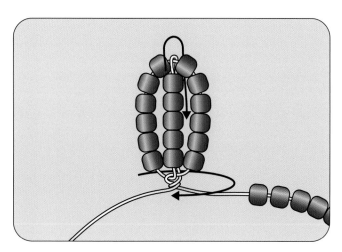

2 When the third row fills the gap in the single loop as neatly as possible, use the thumb and forefinger of your left hand to hold the beads in place. Using your right hand, pass the spool wire between beads 6 and 7 at the top of the single loop, pulling it snugly in place and down the back of the loop. Clamp the wire at the base of the petal between your right-hand forefinger and thumb and use your left hand to twist the petal to secure the beads in place.

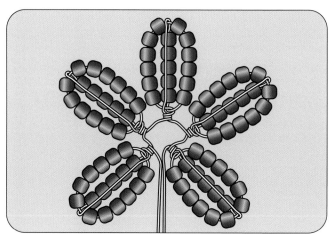

3 Make further petals by repeating steps 1 and 2. As you add each petal, leave a little over 6mm (¼in) of wire between each one. Note that these petals (or leaves) will have a right side (beads) and wrong side (wire down the back), so make sure you assemble them the right way around.

Four row crossover

This is a development of the single loop that makes a fatter petal, which can be used to make flowers like Stephanotis and Gerbera. Thread on enough beads at the start to complete the required number of petals.

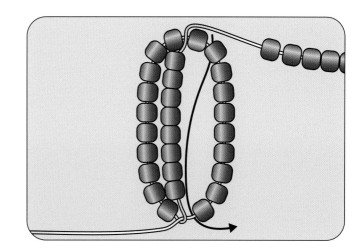

1 Make a single loop using 20 beads, curving out the sides into a broad shape so there is plenty of space in the middle. Make the third row, using 8 beads, and run it up the left-hand side of the gap in the centre of the single loop, leaving space on the right. As with the three row crossover, the number of beads used for the third row is usually just under half the number used in rows one and two, but adjust as necessary.

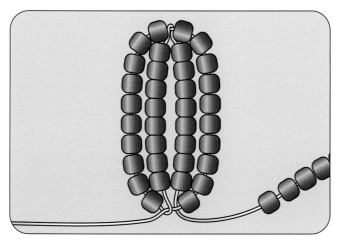

2 Pass the spool wire between the beads 10 and 11 at the top of the single loop. Slide another 8 beads along the spool wire so they run down the back on the right-hand side of the single loop to fill in the gap left in step 1. This fourth row should contain the same number of beads as the third row, but can be adjusted if you are having trouble filling the gap in the centre of the petal neatly.

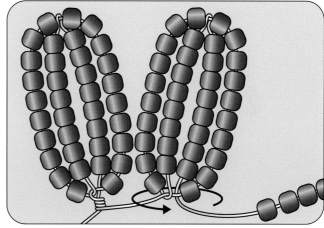

3 Use your left hand to ease the beads into place, holding the wires at the base of the petal with your right-hand forefinger and thumb. When you are satisfied that the beads are sitting correctly, twist the petal twice to finish it off. Repeat to add more petals, leaving enough space between the previous petal and the single loop of the next petal so the wire can be twisted twice over to make the new petal.

Single strands

An easy method to create a centre for your flower is to make a series of single strands of beads that can be bunched together like stamens.

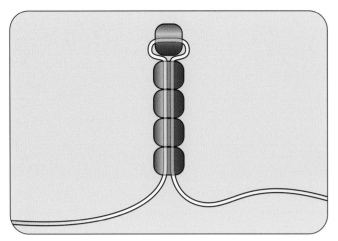

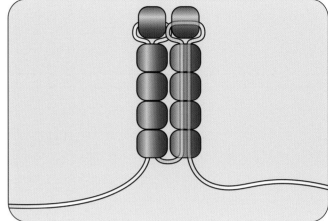

1 Cut a 30cm (12in) length of 0.3mm (US 28 gauge) wire and knot one end of it. Thread on five beads and slide them to about 10cm (4in) from the knot. Pass the end of the wire back through the first four beads and pull tight so that you have a strand of beads.

2 Thread another five beads onto one end and push them along the wire. Again, pass the end of the wire back through the first four beads and pull it tight, making sure that the second strand sits directly next to the first with no gap between.

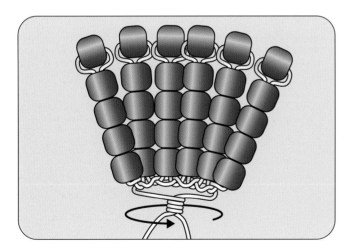

3 Continue adding strands in this way until you have the desired number. Bunch the strands together and secure them by winding the two ends of wire through the strands and then twisting them together to form a stem.

Forming a circle

Some patterns may call for the strands to be formed into a circle. Do this by bringing the two ends of wire together, then weave one of the ends over and under the base of each strand, moving halfway round the circle. This is exactly the same method as you used for forming a series of single loop petals into a flower.

Dragonfly pin

The enormous fairy-like opalescent wings of a dragonfly can be mimicked very successfully by using transparent glass beads in a technique that is based on French beading.

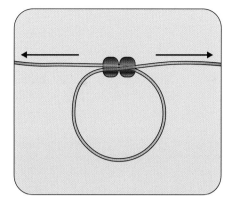

1 Cut 15cm (6in) of 0.3mm (US 28 gauge) wire, and thread on two size 7 beads. Thread one end of the wire back through the beads, creating a loop, and pull tight.

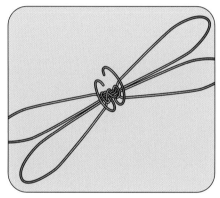

2 Thread the wire ends through a larger faceted bead, and then thread on six bugle beads.

3 Thread a seed bead on one wire, and pass the other wire through the bead the other way. Hold the wires in one hand, and twist the two ends together. Trim to 2.5cm (1in) in length, and slightly curl this end with round-nosed pliers.

4 With 0.6mm (US 22 gauge) wire, create a loop about 5cm (2in) in length. Twist the ends, and make another loop on the other side. Wrap the wire around itself in the centre, and make two more loops. Trim off any excess wire.

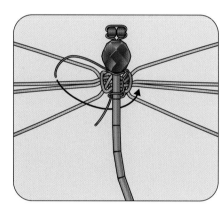

5 Place the body over the wing shape, and secure it by wrapping tightly just below the faceted bead with 0.3mm (US 28 gauge) wire.

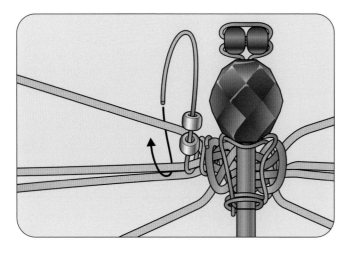

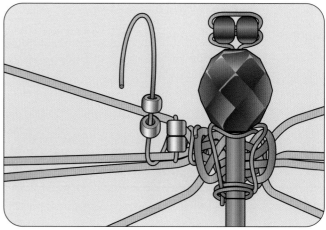

6 Cut a 50cm (20in) length of 0.3mm (US 28 gauge) wire, and secure it by wrapping around the wing case close to the body. Thread on two beads, and wrap the wire very tightly around one wing with the beads pushed to the top and only wire on the underside.

7 Hold the beads in place, and thread on two more. Continue wrapping seed beads all the way up the wing.

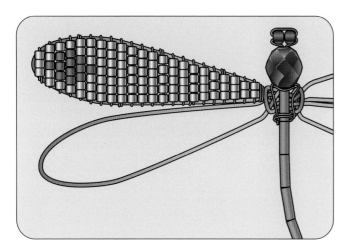

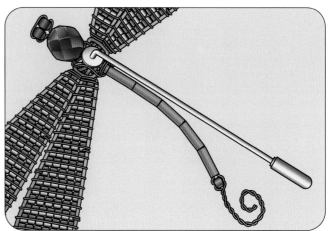

8 Occasionally wrap the wire around the 0.6mm (US 22 gauge) wire a few times to secure. Use different coloured beads to create the wing spots. At the tip of the wing, weave the wire on the back until all the beads are firmly held in place. Trim any excess wire, and repeat for the other three wings.

9 To make the dragonfly into a pin, glue it to the finding with epoxy glue, and leave it until it is completely set.

simple beaded wire shapes

One of the simplest ways to combine beads and wire is to thread the beads onto the wire and then twist the wire into the desired shape. Choose similar small beads for the main section, with a couple of larger beads to finish off the ends if you prefer.

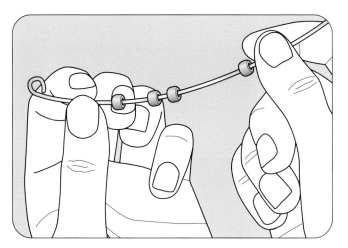

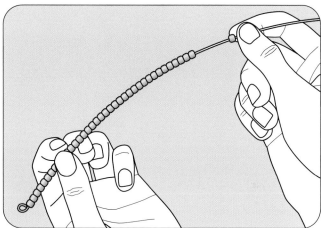

1 Cut a 60cm (24in) length of wire. Holding one end with pliers, twist the wire around to form a small loop. This will stop the beads from sliding off the end as you start to thread them onto the wire.

2 Continue to thread beads onto the wire, making sure there are no kinks to keep them from sliding on easily. Leave around 15cm (6in) of wire unbeaded at the end to allow for movement of the beads when the wire is being shaped in the next step.

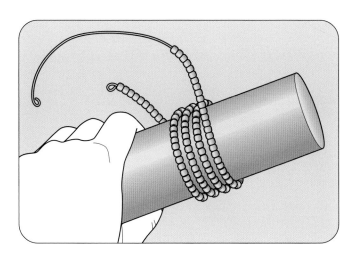

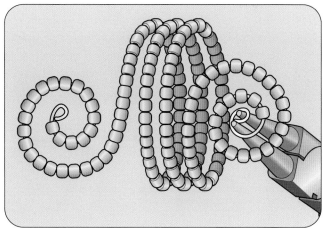

3 Mould the beaded wire into the desired shape – here it is being wrapped around a thick rod of dowel to create a coil. When you are happy with the result, gently ease the coil of beaded wire off the dowel.

4 Cut off most of the excess unbeaded wire then use the pliers to make a small loop at the end to secure the beads. Holding the loop firmly with the pliers, form the end of the beaded wire into a scroll. Repeat at the other end.

wirework with beads

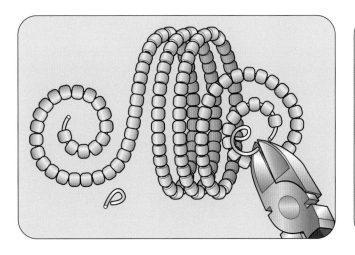

5 To replace the loop ends with larger end beads, snip off the end loops – being careful not to lose any beads – and straighten enough wire to accommodate the larger bead.

6 Fix the first end bead in place using epoxy glue. Repeat on the other wire end. Leave to dry thoroughly.

wire and bead panel

A simple prefabricated wire grid panel can be transformed by wiring beads into the openings in a regular pattern. Use larger beads that are a suitable size for the grid and work out a suitable design on graph paper first.

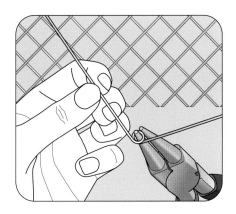

1 Carefully cut the wire grid with wire cutters to the size you need. To neaten the edges, cut a length of galvanized wire long enough to go all around the edge of the wire grid panel, with a little extra for corner loops. Use round-nosed pliers to form a small loop at each corner.

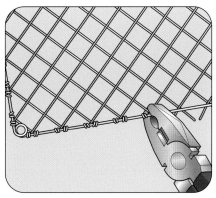

2 Bind the wire frame around the wire grid by bending the cut edges of the grating around the frame using sturdy pliers. Make sure it is secure and that all the grid wire ends are firmly bent around the frame.

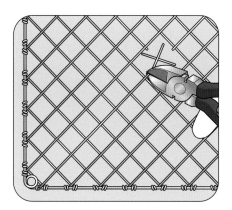

3 For larger bead shapes, cut out part of the grid so the shape will be suspended in the opening.

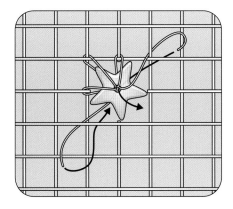

4 Thread a long length of fine beading wire through the centre hole of the large bead and wrap it around one arm of the grid above the opening and back through the centre hole again. Continue in this way around the opening, until the bead is securely suspended in the centre of the hole.

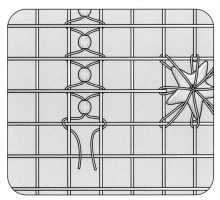

5 Smaller beads can be suspended in other openings in the grid, following a pattern worked out on graph paper beforehand. Thread two strands of fine wire through the centre of the bead then splay out the wire ends and wrap one round each corner of the square.

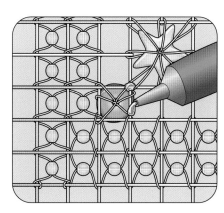

6 Large flat glass beads can be bound into position with a network of wires through the centre hole and then around the sides of the surrounding square. If the bead is quite heavy and hangs away from the wire grid, secure it tight against the edges of the opening with tiny dabs of epoxy glue.

making a beaded shape

By using beaded wire around a former, three-dimensional shapes can be achieved. Here the beaded wire is shaped using a bowl as a former to create a lacy beaded design.

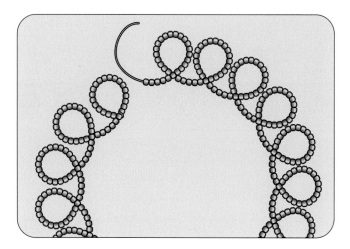

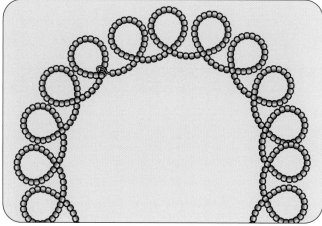

1 Thread seed beads onto a long piece of wire, leaving some wire unbeaded at the end to allow the beads to move when you bend the wire into shape. Count the number of beads required to make a petal shape – this will depend on how large you want the petals to be. Starting with one petal, loop and twist the wire to form a regular row of petals as a top edging.

2 When you have a sufficient length of edging to go around the top edge of the bowl, cut off any excess wire and use pliers to form a small loop at the end. Link this around the base of the first petal and squeeze closed.

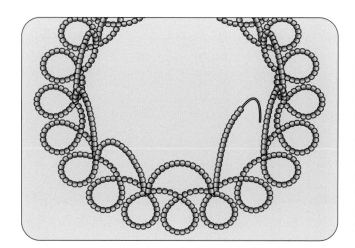

3 Thread beads onto another length of wire to form scallops between every alternate petal. Count the number of beads required to make each scallop – this will depend on how big each one is. Make a space between the beads at the end of each scallop and twist the wire around the neck of the petals to connect the scallops to the petal edging.

4 Form a circle of beaded wire to fit around the base of the bowl. Use pliers to form a small loop at each end of the wire and link them together (see page 125), squeezing the loops closed to secure.

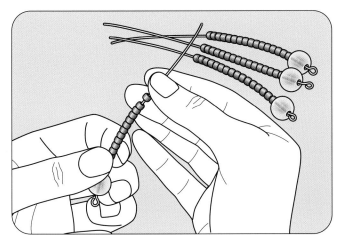

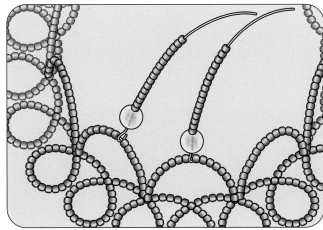

5 Cut lengths of wire to make the side struts to join the bottom ring to the top edging – you will need one strut for each scallop. Cut each wire 5cm (2in) longer than the depth of the bowl measured from the centre of the bottom of the scallop to the bottom ring. Use pliers to form a small loop at one end of each wire. Thread a larger bead onto each wire, then enough seed beads to reach to the bottom ring.

6 Hook the top loop of each wire strut onto the centre of a scallop, then squeeze the loop closed with pliers. Bend the other end of each strut slightly to keep the beads from falling off as you work.

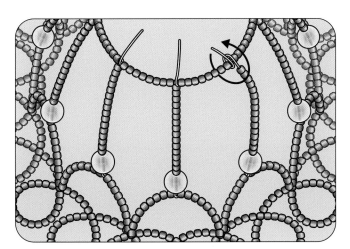

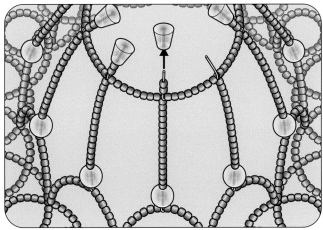

7 Loop the end of each strut around the beaded base ring at regular spaced intervals. You should be left with some unbeaded wire projecting below the bottom ring on each strut.

8 Thread a couple of seed beads onto one of the lengths of wire and then trim the excess wire leaving just enough to hold a larger conical bead as a foot – don't leave any wire protruding from the foot bead because it will cause scratches. Use epoxy glue to attach the conical bead to the wire. Repeat on all the other struts.

wire shapes
and hanging beads

By combining beaded wire with a range of different wire shapes, quite complex shapes can be achieved easily. Here the spirals and scrolls of wire are added to beaded lengths and highlighted with dangling beads.

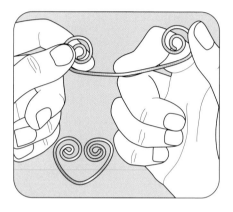

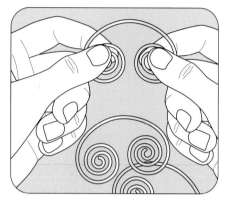

1 Cut eight 20cm (8in) lengths of 1.5mm (US 15 gauge) wire. Use pliers to form each wire into a heart (see page 124).

2 Cut thirty 25cm (10in) lengths of 1.5mm (US 15 gauge) wire and use pliers to form them into scrolls (see page 124). Make ten into short fat scrolls and twenty into more elongated scrolls.

3 Cut ten 33cm (13in) lengths of 1.5mm (US 15 gauge) wire. Form each length into a double-ended spiral (see page 124). Push the ends of the spiral together to form the back into a gentle curve.

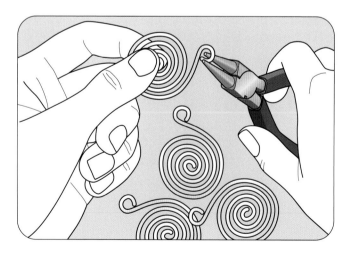

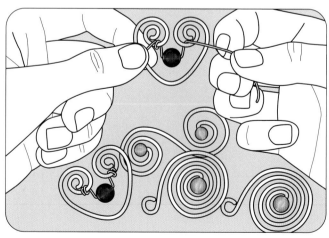

4 Cut eleven 28cm (11in) lengths of 1.5mm (US 15 gauge) wire and form each one into an open spiral (see page 125) approximately 4cm (1½in) in diameter. Bend the end of the wire into a loop in the opposite direction.

5 Use fine binding wire to suspend beads inside each heart shape. Insert beads onto the centre wire of the open spirals and short scrolls – you may have to cut off a little wire at the centre of the spiral to make room.

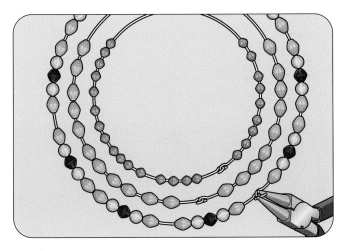

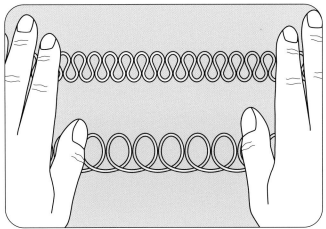

6 Cut 50cm (20in), 60cm (24in) and 68cm (27in) lengths of 1.5mm (US 15 gauge) wire. Thread approximately 30 large beads onto the longest piece, 20 large beads onto the medium piece and 25 small beads onto the shortest piece. Bend all three wires into circles, using pliers to join the ends (see page 125).

7 Make a flattened coil (see page 126) 60cm (24in) long and 2.5cm (1in) wide, using 1.5mm (US 15 gauge) wire. Use 1.5mm (US 15 gauge) wire to make a length of wiggly wire (see page 127), 58cm (23in) long and 2cm (¾in) wide.

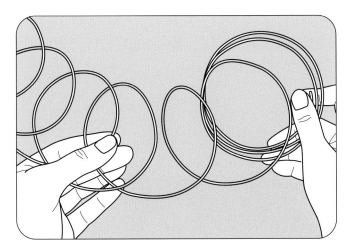

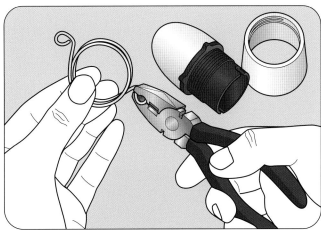

8 Coil some 1.5mm (US 15 gauge) wire around a 6cm (2½in) dowel or something of a similar diameter. Remove the coil from the dowel and extend the loops out flat, as shown, until you have a 10-petal flower shape. Use pliers to join the ends as before.

9 Cut a piece of 1.5mm (US 15 gauge) wire long enough to wrap around a lamp fitting two or three times. Wrap the wire around the fitting and use pliers to bend the ends out on opposite sides at a 45-degree angle. Cut the ends down to 1cm (½in) and use pliers to twist them into loops.

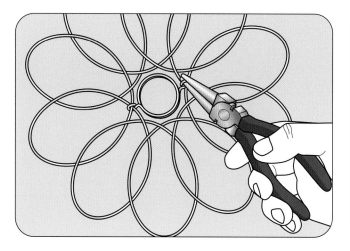

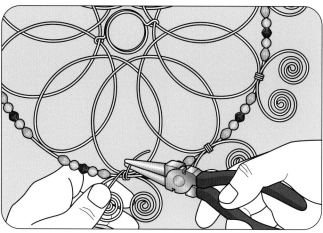

10 Position the wire lamp fitting in the centre of the flower made in step 8, connecting the links of the wire fitting to the petals and squeezing them closed to secure.

11 Place the largest beaded hoop around the petalled top section. Position the curved spirals made in step 3 at the tip of each petal. Arrange the beads on the hoop so there are an equal number between each spiral. Bind (see page 125) the spirals onto the hoop and the petal tip with short lengths of 1mm (US 18 gauge) wire.

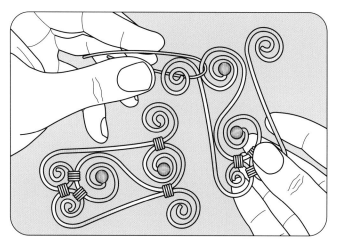

12 Place a short scroll between pairs of long scrolls, binding them together with 1mm (US 18 gauge) wire at the point where they touch.

13 Bind the medium-size hoop to the base of each curved spiral using 1mm (US 18 gauge) wire and spacing out the beads equally between each fixing point. Next bind the three-part scrolls made in step 12 around the medium-size hoop using 1mm (US 18 gauge) wire.

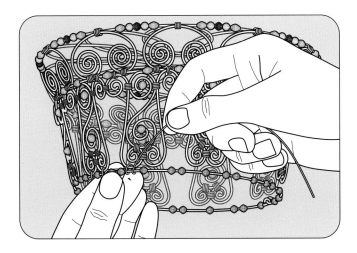

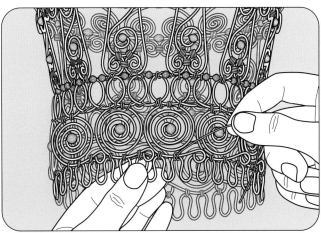

14 Using fine binding wire, attach the smallest hoop to the base of the three-part scrolls, again making sure the beads are spaced out equally between each fixing point.

15 Bind the flattened coil to the small hoop, and then attach the open spirals around the base of the coil with fine binding wire. Attach the length of wiggly wire beneath these spirals and bind together where they touch.

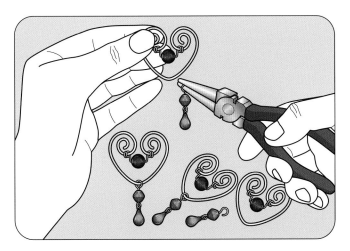

16 Cut eight 5cm (2in) lengths of 1mm (US 18 gauge) wire. Use pliers to form a hook at one end, suspend a droplet bead from this and then squeeze the hook closed. Thread a bead onto the remaining wire and form a loop at the top, cutting off any excess wire. Link one of these beaded wires onto the base of each heart and squeeze the loop closed.

17 Attach the beaded hearts around the bottom of the wiggly wire using jump rings (see page 80). Dangle more beads from any convenient point on the structure as desired.

bead looming, weaving and knotting

Using a loom to weave beads into long strips has its origins in Native American craft traditions and many bead looming designs were symbolic. Bead weaving is a completely different technique that does not require a loom – a needle and thread are used to attach beads to each other using a variety of stitches. And knotting is one of the simplest techniques, in which several threads are knotted or braided (braided) together to hold beads in place.

basic bead looming techniques

Looming produces a strong and neat piece of beadwork and is an easy technique to master; it is also a very fast way of creating bead cloth. It is done on a loom using two sets of threads: warp threads are attached to the loom and the weft thread is used for holding the beads and weaving under and over the warp thread.

Setting up a beading loom

There are many different models of loom so refer to your manufacturer's instructions for further details.

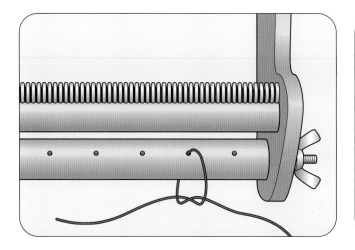

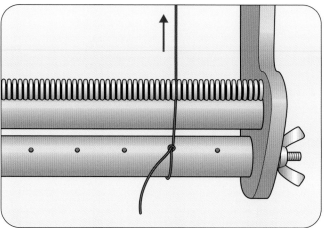

1 Tie one end of your thread through the hole, or to the screw or hook, on one side of the loom.

2 Pass the thread over the loom, matching the gaps in the springs or slots at each end.

Buying a bead loom

When choosing your loom, you will find there are many different types on the market, ranging from quite inexpensive kits to much more expensive versions. While a small loom does limit you to small pieces, it can be a good place to start for a beginner.

You can make your own loom – there are great instructions available on the Internet.

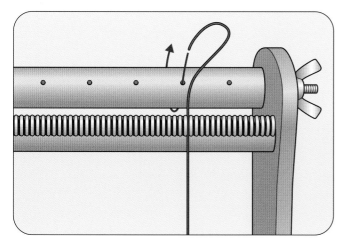

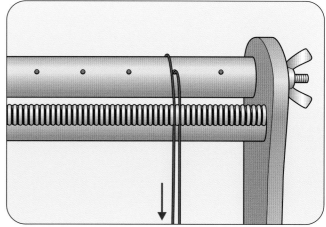

3 Wrap the thread through the hole, or around the screw or hook, on the other side of the loom, keeping the thread tension very firm.

4 Pass the thread back over the loom, going between the next space in the spring or slots. Continue until you have the correct number of warp threads, and tie off the last warp thread at the nearest hole, hook or screw.

Starting and finishing off

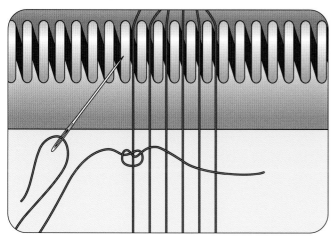

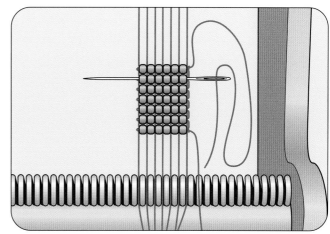

1 To start looming, tie the weft thread on to the left-hand outside warp with a secure knot. Leave a long tail.

2 To finish, tie a knot around the warp, then pass the needle up through the line of beads. Pass the needle down the next row, up the next, then trim. Repeat with the tail from the start of the thread.

Basic loom weaving

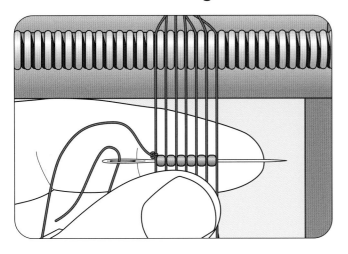

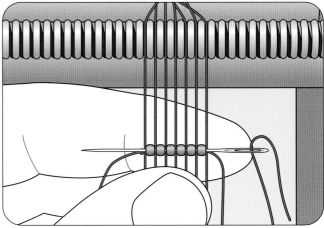

1 Thread on all the beads in the first row of the pattern in order, reading from left to right. Pass the needle under the warp threads, placing the beads so each one sits between two warp threads.

2 Support the beads carefully along your finger, and thread the needle back through the beads from right to left but passing the thread over the top of the warp threads. Pull the thread all the way through the beads.

Choosing beads and threads for looming

Always use beads of the same size when weaving; small beads will create a small design, large beads a bigger one but as long as they are all the same size in the design it doesn't matter which size you choose.

Delica beads have a subtle palette and distinctive shape and give a perfectly smooth finish – it's possible to create an almost photographic effect with them.

Chunky beads will give a more rustic, handmade effect.

Normal nylon thread is fine for basic beaded items, but for more serious projects and larger items a stronger thread may be required for the warp.

Adding thread

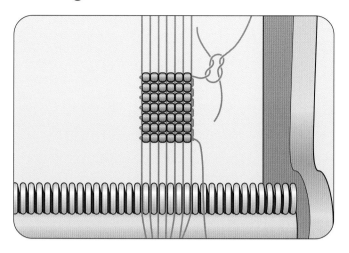

To add thread halfway through a project, weave the new tail back and forth through the loomed beads, exiting the last row in the proper direction for adding another line of beads. Tie the new thread to the old thread using a reef knot (see page 162).

Bead woven choker with a traditional hummingbird motif.

(see page 162)

Designs and colours

Designs are created by following a chart, which shows the placement of each colour bead in the design. Creating your own patterns is fun and easy with graph paper, or you can use one of the pattern-creation computer programmes designed for beadwork.

Cross-stitch patterns are also excellent when worked in beads because they are designed on a grid – but make sure you don't require too many different colours to complete the design.

basic bead weaving techniques

There are so many different bead-weaving stitches that it would be impossible to cover everything here, but these basic techniques will give you a first taste of what is possible.

Stopper bead

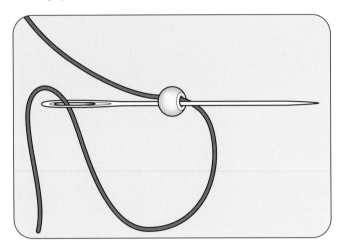 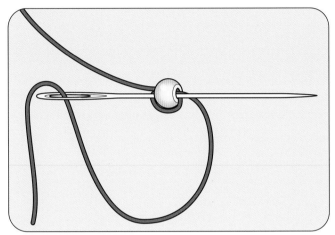

1 Thread on a small bead using a needle from right to left, and pass the needle back through the bead from right to left again, creating a loop.

2 Repeat once or twice for a firmer stop; be careful not to pass the needle through the thread strand, just through the hole in the bead.

Reef or square knot

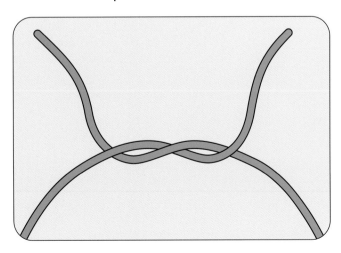 

1 Cross the left-hand thread over the right-hand thread, and wrap right around.

2 Cross the right-hand thread over the left-hand thread. Pull up through the hole. Tighten the knot.

Surgeon's knot

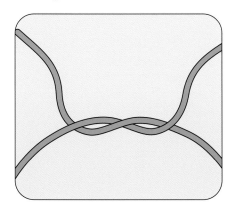

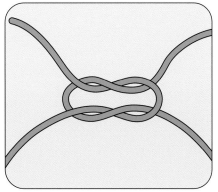

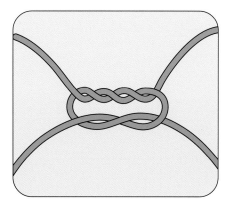

1 A stronger variation of the reef knot. Cross the left-hand thread over the right-hand thread, and wrap right around.

2 Now cross the right-hand thread over the left-hand thread, and pull up through the hole.

3 Wrap the right-hand thread end underneath, and pull up through the hole again.

Netting

Different numbers of beads can be used in each netted piece; these are instructions for a three-bead netting pattern.

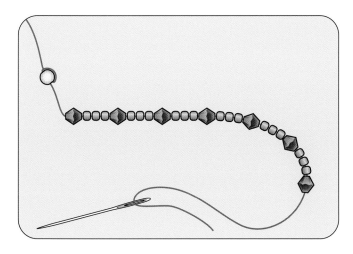

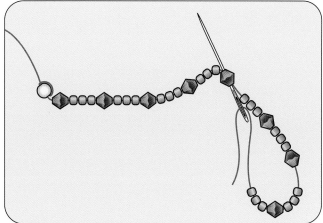

1 Fasten on a stopper bead; then thread on a bead of the first colour (A), three of the second colour (B), one A, three B, and so on to the length of your piece, ending with an A bead.

2 Thread on three B, one A, and three B, and then pass the needle through the third A bead of the first row.

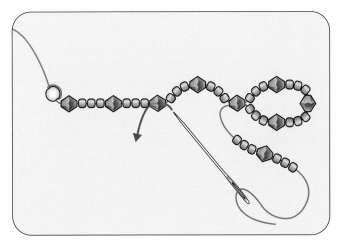

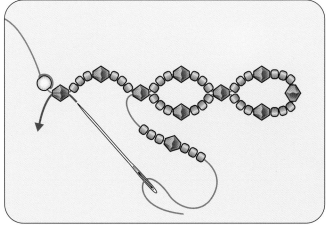

3 Repeat this sequence back down the row, taking the needle through every other A bead.

4 At the end add three B, one A, three B, one A, and three B and pass the needle through the first A bead below. Repeat from step 2 as necessary to the end.

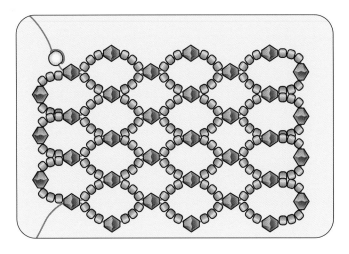

5 Carry on working up and down, working into alternate A beads on each pass, until the netting is the desired length.

 Choosing beads and threads for weaving

Seed beads in assorted sizes are the main type of bead used for bead weaving because they have no sharp edges.

Delicas in assorted sizes are popular for tighter stitches because they give a smooth, perfect interlocking weave.

Bicone crystals look fabulous woven using transparent nylon wire.

Choose beads with a large central hole, because in most designs the needle and thread has to pass through several times during the weaving process.

The usual thread used is a fine strong thread used by upholstery manufacturers, but any fine strong thread will do.

Use a very long, fine and sharp needle.

Spiral rope stitch

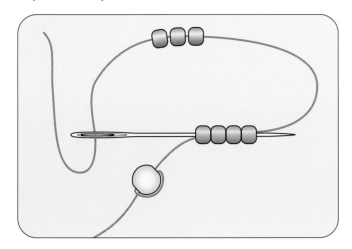

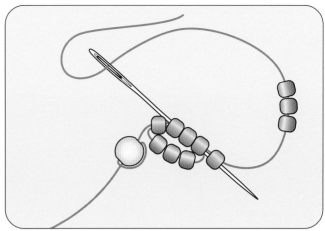

1 Thread a sharp beading needle with a length of thread. Place a stopper bead on the end of the thread by looping back through the bead. Thread on four size 10 seed beads for the core (A), then three in a contrasting colour (B). Thread the needle back up through the four A beads, creating a loop.

2 Thread on one A bead and three B. Pass the needle up through the top four A beads, but not through the bottom bead.

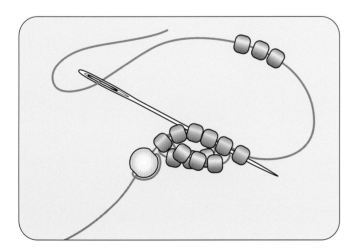

3 Repeat step 2, making sure the outside beads always lie either to the right or the left of the previous row, or the spiral will not build up properly. Continue until you have a rope the right length.

Necklace with spiral rope stitch sections.

Peyote stitch

Peyote stitch can be created as even or odd count and can be made flat or in a tube. These instructions are for flat even count peyote.

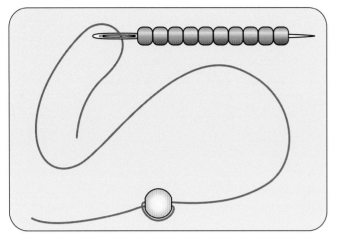

1 Thread a sharp beading needle with a length of fine beading thread. Place a stopper bead on the end of the thread by looping back through the bead. Thread an even number of contrasting beads in the pattern A, B, A, B, A, B, A, B, to the right width of your piece.

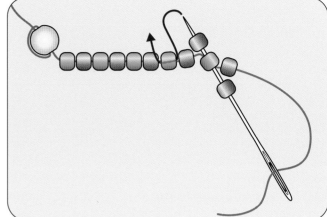

2 Add another bead, B, and pass the needle back down through the next to last bead, an A. Add another B bead and missing the next B bead along, pass the needle once more through the A bead. Repeat all the way down the row.

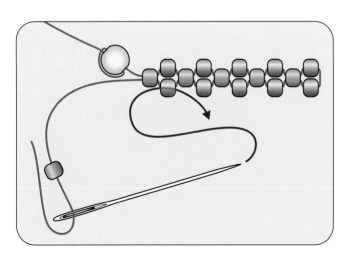

3 To make the third row, pick up an A bead, and pass the needle through the B bead. Repeat up the row, picking up A beads and going through Bs, keeping the tension firm. Continue from step 2 until the piece is the right size.

Peyote stitch

This tightly woven stitch is descended from the Native American bead stitch used to cover ceremonial regalia but has also been found on artefacts from Ancient Egypt. It is flexible in only one direction, unlike brick stitch, which looks very similar. Many variations of the stitch exist – even count peyote has an even number of beads in a row while odd count has an odd number, and it can be made flat, tubular or as a circular disk.

Attaching a thread

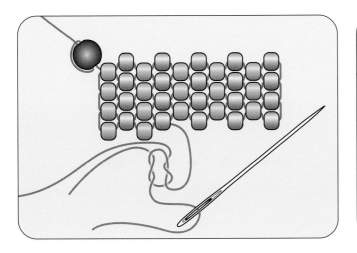

When you have about 7.5cm (3in) of thread left, cut a new length and tie a reef or surgeon's knot (see pages 162 and 163) close to the beads. Weave the end threads up and down in a zigzag pattern back through the work until they are secure, then trim.

Finishing a thread

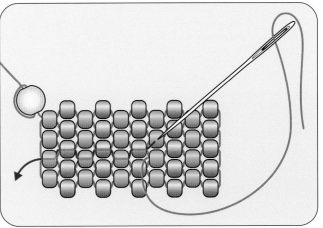

At the end of the work, weave the thread end up and down in a zigzag pattern back through the beads; when totally secure trim the end close to the beads.

Peyote stitch bracelet worked using silver-lined seed beads and with a diamanté clasp.

making a panel of bead looming

Looming doesn't have to be only about seed beads. Any beads can be used for weaving on a loom so long as they are all the same size – this example uses crystal beads with silver spacers.

Pattern chart

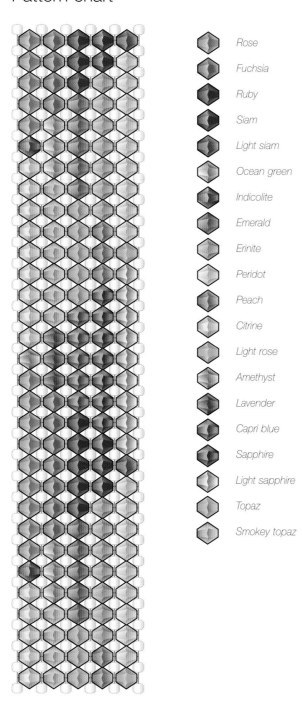

 Rose

Fuchsia

Ruby

Siam

Light siam

 Ocean green

 Indicolite

 Emerald

Erinite

 Peridot

Peach

 Citrine

 Light rose

 Amethyst

Lavender

 Capri blue

 Sapphire

Light sapphire

 Topaz

Smokey topaz

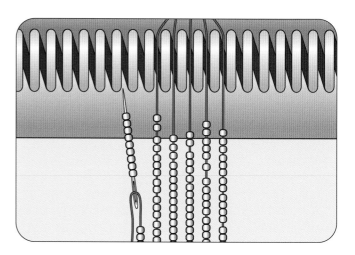

1 Cut 4m (4½yd) of thread and thread one end onto a needle. Thread up the bead loom, threading 30 silver seed beads onto each warp thread as you work and continuing until you have six beaded warp threads. Position the beads within the top weaving area.

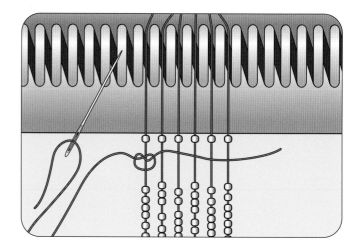

2 Push a seed bead from each thread to the top of the loom, and secure the weft thread below them, on the left-hand warp thread.

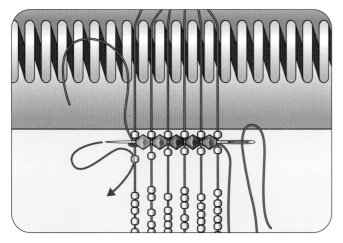

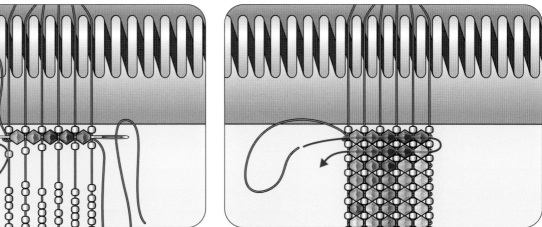

3 Thread on the crystals from the first row of the pattern chart, and secure by weaving the needle back. Push up another row of seed beads, and thread the needle down through the left-hand seed bead.

4 Continue threading crystals and pushing up rows of seed beads, following the pattern chart. When the design is complete, secure the weft thread with a knot and by weaving it back through the work.

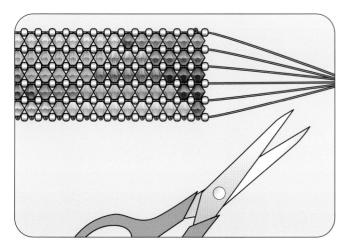

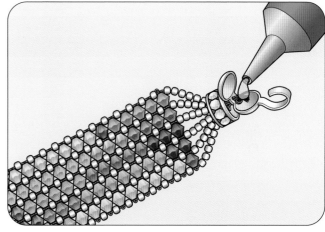

5 Remove your work from the loom by cutting the threads carefully, leaving equally long warp threads at each end.

6 On one side of the work, thread five seeds onto each warp thread and, using a wire needle, thread them all through a rondelle and a calotte end. Tie the threads securely with a reef knot and put a dab of glue on the knot.

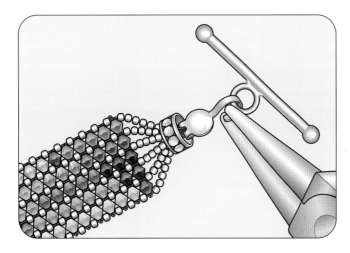

7 Close the calotte end with half-round or flat-nosed pliers, and then close the hook on the calotte onto the clasp with the round-nosed pliers. On the other side, attach the other part of the clasp in the same way.

Adding the clasp

The warp threads need to be brought together at each end of the panel of weaving to add the clasp. Try to choose a clasp that will enhance the overall design – a complex design only needs a very simple clasp. Always make sure the clasp is very securely added.

Swarovski crystal bracelet inspired by Art Deco.

adding a clasp to woven jewellery

There are two basic methods of adding a clasp to a panel of bead looming, depending on how wide your finished panel is.

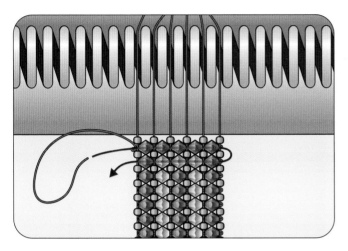

1 Set up the loom with the required number of threads, and weave up the pattern. Secure the weft thread with a knot and weave it back through the work.

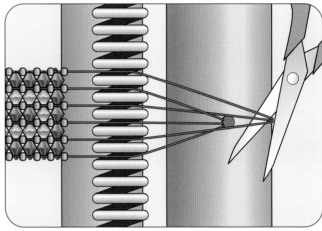

2 Next, cut the threads on the underside of the loom so that there are equally long ends of warp thread on each side of the woven piece.

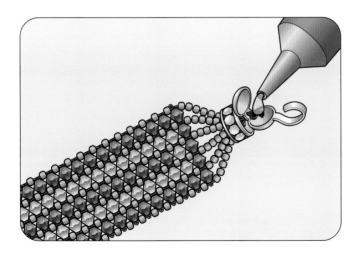

3 Thread seed beads onto the long ends. If gathering quite a wide panel into one calotte end, thread more beads onto the outer strands than on the inner ones, so they will come together in a neat triangle. Thread the ends through a decorative rondelle and then into a calotte end. Tie the threads securely with a knot and secure with a dab of glue.

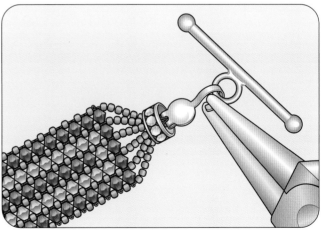

4 Close the calotte end with flat-nosed pliers. Close the loop at the top of the calotte onto the ring on the first half of your chosen clasp, using round-nosed pliers. Repeat at the other end with the other half of the clasp.

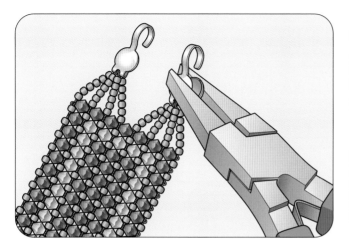

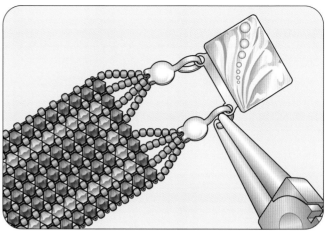

5 If the panel of bead weaving is very wide, it is better to use a multi-strand clasp. Divide the threads at one end into two equal groups – or more depending on how many rings the multi-clasp has. Add seed beads to each thread as described in step 6 on page 169. Thread one set of threads through a calotte end. Tie the threads securely with a knot and secure with a dab of glue. Repeat for the other set of threads.

6 Close each calotte end with flat-nosed pliers. Close the loop at the top of each calotte onto the rings on your chosen clasp using round-nosed pliers. Repeat steps 5 and 6 at the other end of the bead loomed panel.

The floral design of this bracelet is enhanced by the flower design clasp.

simple netting

This is a six bead netting design, which creates a very loose and stretchy net to enclose a large bead; you could try a tighter weave of three bead netting (see page 163) for a smaller, less ostentatious bead. Use delica beads, which are small enough not to overwhelm the main bead.

Pattern chart

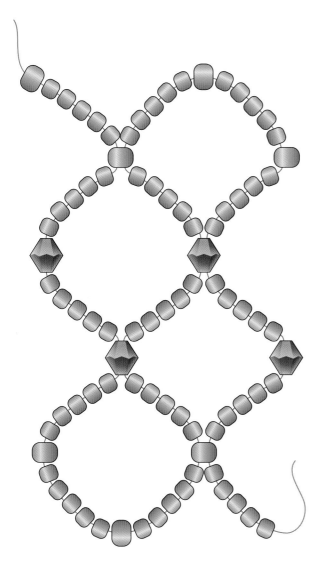

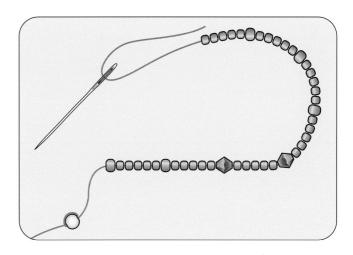

1 Cut 140cm (56in) of nylon thread, leaving a 7.5cm (3in) tail, and thread on a stopper bead. Thread on: one seed bead, five delicas, one seed, five delicas, one crystal, five delicas, one crystal, five delicas, one seed, five delicas, one seed, five delicas, one seed and five delicas.

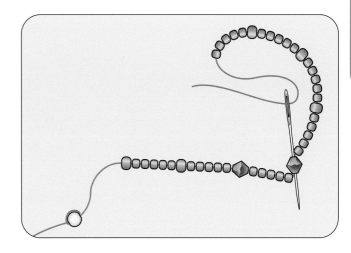

2 Pass the needle up through the second crystal, creating a loop of beads at the end of the string. Pull the thread tight.

 Delica

Seed bead

 Crystal

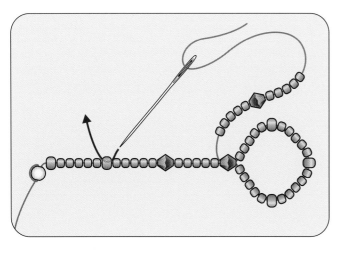

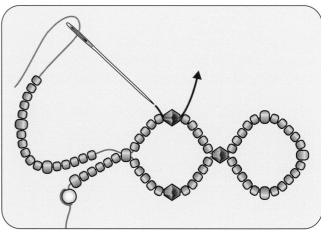

3   Add five delicas, one crystal and five delicas, and pass the needle through the second seed bead that you threaded.

4   Add five delicas, one seed, five delicas, one seed and five delicas. Pass the needle down through the top crystal.

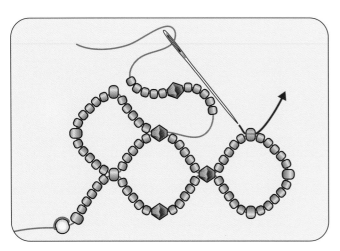

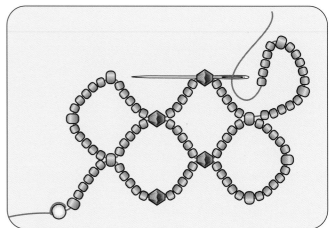

5   Add five delicas, one crystal and five delicas, and pass the needle through the bottom-right seed bead.

6   Add five delicas, one seed, five delicas, one seed and five delicas, and repeat from step 2.

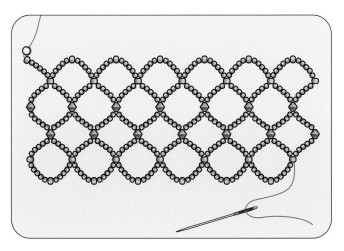

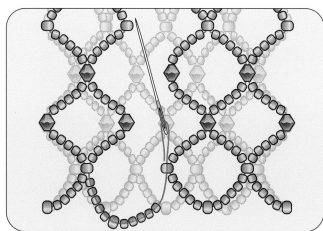

7 Repeat until you have made a length of netting large enough to enclose the bead. Place the net with the stopper bead at the top left-hand side, and the needle emerging from the bottom-right seed bead.

8 To join the net together into a tube, thread five delicas, one seed and five delicas, and pass the needle up through the bottom-left seed bead.

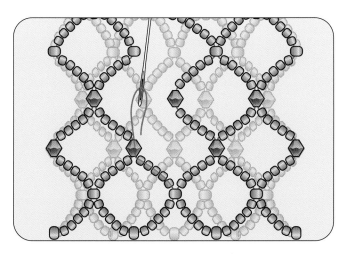

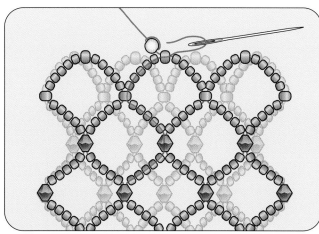

9 Thread on five delicas, and pass the needle through the last crystal threaded.

10 Add five delicas, and pass the needle through the first crystal threaded. Add five more delicas, and pass the needle through the opposite seed bead. Thread five more delicas, and pass the needle through the first bead threaded.

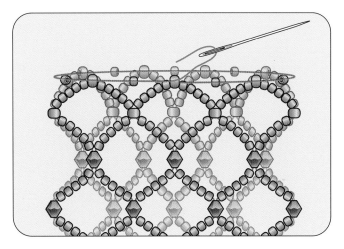

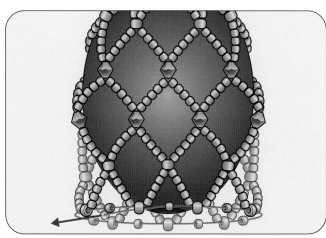

11 Add a delica and pass the needle through each top seed bead adding a delica between each. Pull tight and go around the circle again.

12 Weave the thread down the netting, emerging through a seed bead at the bottom. Repeat step 11, but before you pull tight, insert the bead. Weave all the ends up and down in the work, and trim when secure.

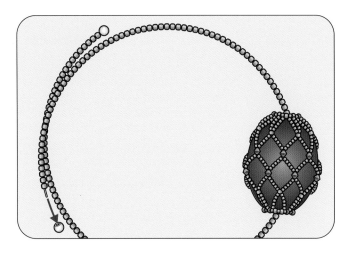

13 To make the netted bead into a choker, glue an end on the memory wire with epoxy glue (see page 133). Thread seed or delica beads halfway along, add the big bead and continue to thread seed beads. Finish by gluing another end onto the other end of the memory wire.

Bead netting

Bead netting looks very impressive but it is so simple to make once you understand the technique that even a beginner can master it quickly. It can be used in so many different ways – to cover large beads, plain bangles or Christmas baubles, or worked in a ring to make a bracelet or in a strip to create a necklace.

On a necklace, try varying the basic design by adding beaded lengths to each of the points on the bottom of the netting, to create a beaded fringe edge.

To make an unusual evening bag, try working a bead net bag over a plain fabric lining.

advanced netting

This spectacular Egyptian-style netting design is actually very straightforward to construct but is extremely time-consuming so be prepared to bead slowly and carefully, for a couple of hours at a time, over a week or two.

Pattern chart

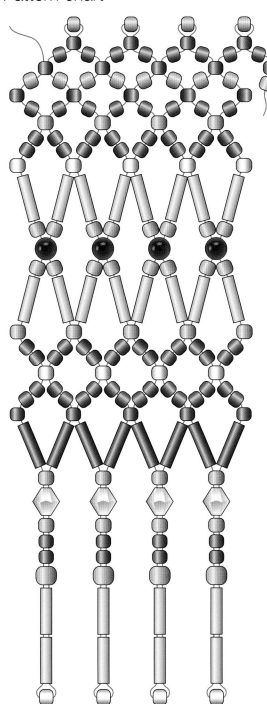

Colour code

Size 9 blue seed beads (b9)

Size 7 antique gold seed beads (ag7)

Size 7 bright gold seed beads (bg7)

Size 5 antique gold seed beads (ag5)

Blue bugles (bb)

Turquoise bugles (tb)

4mm lapis lazuli beads (ll4)

4mm green crystals (gc4)

Large lapis bead

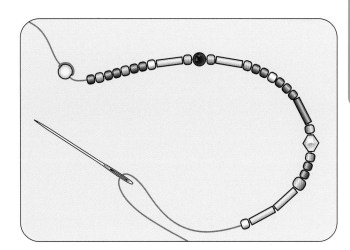

1 Cut a 2m (2¼yd) length of thread. Thread on a firm stopper bead and then thread on one b9, ag7, two b9, ag7, two b9, bg7, tb, ag7, ll4, ag7, tb, ag7, two b9, bg7, three b9, bb, ag7, gc4, ag7, two b9, ag5, two tb and bg7.

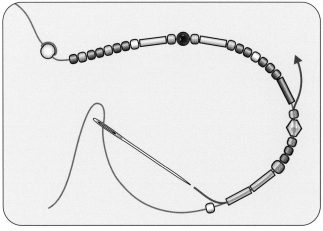

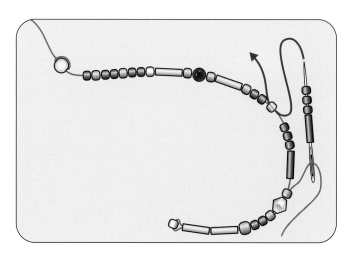

2 Use the bottom bg7 as a turning bead and thread the needle back up through the two tb, ag5, two b9, ag7, gc4 and ag7.

3 Thread on one bb and three b9 and pass the needle back up through the bg7 already threaded.

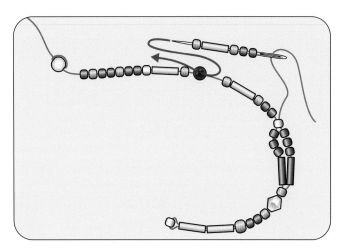

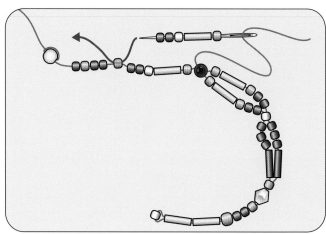

4 Add on two b9, ag7, tb, ag7 and pass the needle up through the ll4.

5 Thread one ag7, tb, bg7, two b9 and pass the needle up through the ag7.

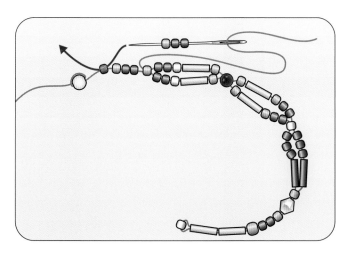

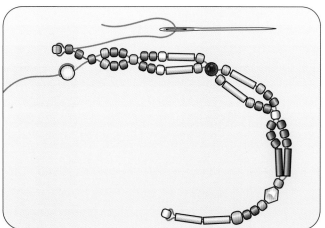

6 Add two b9 and one ag7 and pass the needle through the very first bead threaded, a b9.

7 Add two b9 and one ag7 and pass the needle down through the top b9 to make a picot edge.

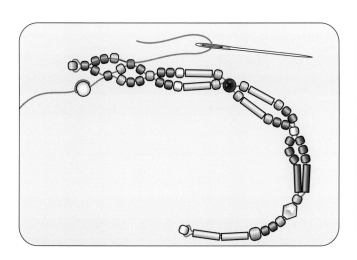

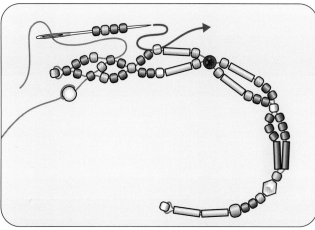

8 Thread two b9 and one ag7 and pass the needle through the next b9.

9 Add on one b9, ag7, two b9 and pass the needle down through the bg7.

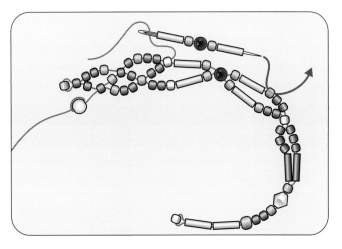

10 Add one tb, ag7, ll4, ag7, tb and pass the needle down through the ag7.

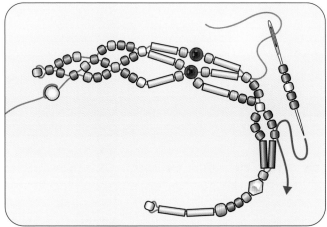

11 Thread two b9, bg7, two b9 and pass the needle down through the third b9.

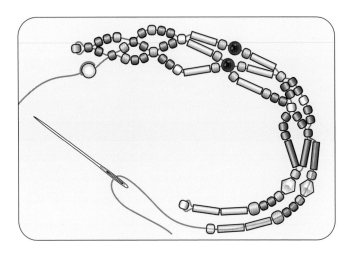

12 Thread on one bb, ag7, gc4, ag7, two b9, ag5, two tb, and a bg9.

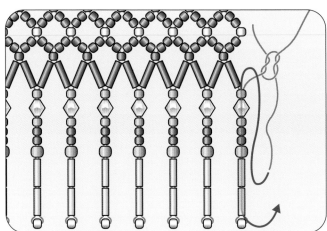

13 Repeat from step 2 until the netting is the length you require. When you have to add a new thread, tie a reef knot (see page 162) and leave the ends long to weave through the pattern later. You can do them all at the end, or you can neaten them as you go along if you prefer.

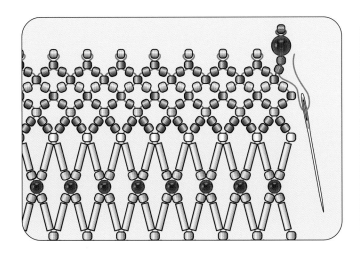

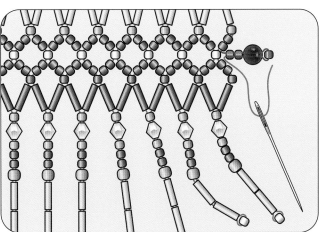

14 Finish your last row with the thread at the top of the necklace. To make the fastenings, thread on two b9 beads, one large lapis bead, and one b9. Using the last bead as a turning bead, turn and thread back through the lapis and the two b9.

15 Weave round the top circle of seeds, and go up and down through the lapis again to reinforce it. Weave the needle down to the next blue seed section, and attach another large lapis bead in the same way. Finish off the thread by weaving it very securely back through the work.

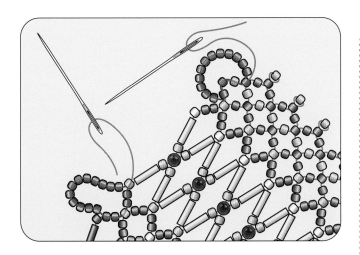

16 On the other side of the necklace, take off the stopper bead and thread on around 12 seed beads. Make a loop; attaching it up through the seeds you've already woven. Check the large lapis bead fits snugly through the loop – this will be your necklace fastening so make sure it won't slip out. Adjust the number of seeds as necessary. Go around the loop again for strength and weave down to the next blue seed section, attaching another seed loop in the same way. Finish off the thread by weaving it very securely back through the work.

Curving edges

To make this design into a necklace that sits nicely when worn, the top edge around the neck needs to curve much more tightly than the bottom edge that will lie over the shoulders. This is achieved by the design, with smaller gaps between the netting at the top than towards the bottom. The netting does naturally have some give just because of its construction, but do not stretch it too far or the beading thread will break.

making spiral rope jewellery

The spiral rope is so easy to stitch – all the impressive grading in size comes from simply using bigger beads in the centre section.

Bracelet

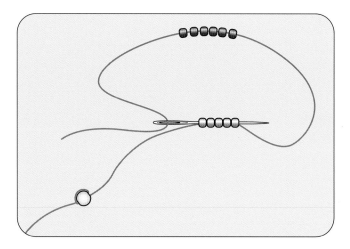

1 Cut and thread up a 140cm (56in) length of nylon thread. Thread a firm stopper bead leaving a tail of 15cm (6in). Thread five gold and six bronze seeds. To start the spiral rope pass the needle up through the five gold seeds.

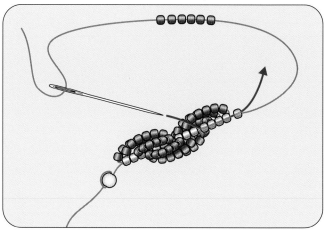

2 Thread a gold seed and six bronze seeds, and work a spiral rope stitch (see page 165) with one gold and six bronze seeds for 20 rows, passing the needle always through the top five gold beads.

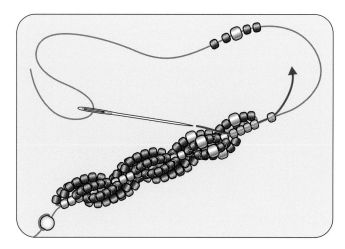

3 For the next section, thread on a gold seed, two bronze seeds, a small gold bead, and two bronze seeds. Pass the needle up through the top five gold seed beads as before. Work spiral stitch with this sequence for 10 rows.

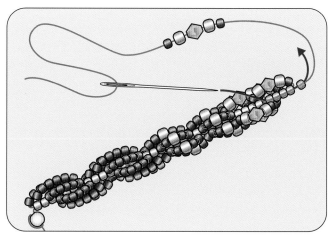

4 The next threading sequence is a gold seed, bronze seed, gold bead, crystal, gold bead, and a bronze seed. Pass the needle up through the top five gold seeds as before. Work spiral stitch with this sequence for 10 rows.

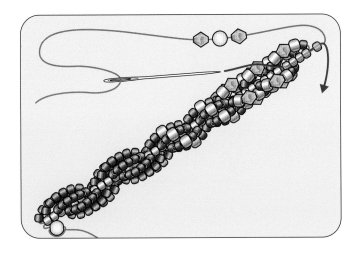

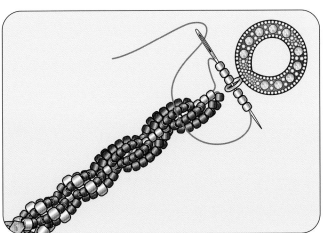

5 The centre section has no gold bead or bronze seeds – it is simply a gold seed, crystal, 4mm pearl, and crystal. Work spiral stitch with this sequence for ten rows. If you have to add thread, do so using a reef knot (see page 162) and weave the ends in.

6 Repeat the threading sequence and number of rows from step 4, then step 3, and finally step 2. To add a clasp, thread on three bronze seeds, the clasp, and three more seeds. Pass the needle around through the seeds and clasp once more for strength.

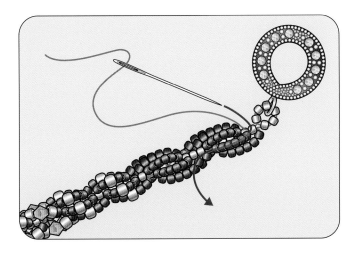

7 Weave the needle around and around, following in the path of the spiral rope stitches to secure the thread. Trim the thread when you feel it is secure. Unthread the stopper bead and add the clasp using this tail on the other side, securing and trimming as before.

An eye-catching bracelet made with spiral rope stitch.

odd count peyote stitch

The odd count peyote stitch is slightly more complicated than the even count version described in basic techniques on page 166. It takes a bit of practice, but it's worth persevering because it's so useful. It's also essential if you want a strip with a symmetrical pattern.

Choker

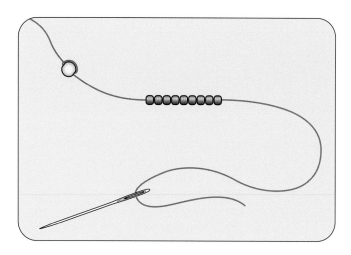

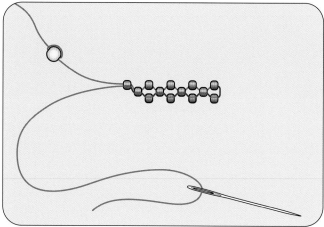

1 Using a 100cm (40in) length of strong nylon thread, place a stopper bead on the thread about 45cm (18in) from the end. You will return to this piece of thread to add the clasp. To begin the peyote stitch thread on nine delicas.

2 Add a tenth delica and weave the needle from right to left, through the eighth bead. Add a delica and pass the needle through the sixth delica. Add one more delica and pass the needle through the fourth delica. Add another delica, and pass the needle through the second and the first beads.

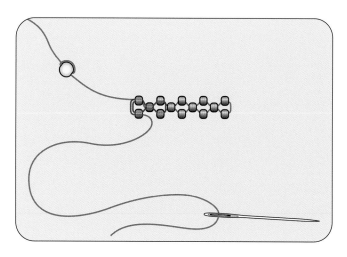

3 Thread on a delica (number 14), and pass the needle up from left to right through the second and third delicas of the original row. Pass the needle back down through numbers 13, two and one. Pass the needle from left to right through the last added bead (number 14). You will now have a ladder and are ready to start the third row.

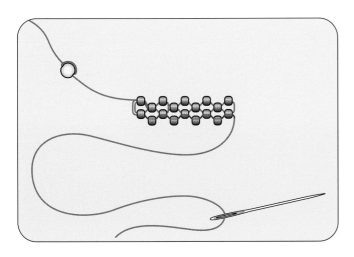

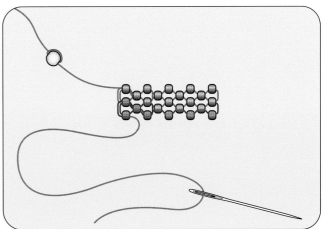

4 For the third row, weave a delica from left to right between each sticking out bead of the previous row.

5 Weave down from right to left to the last space (bead number 22). Pass the needle through the last two beads (numbers 15 and 14); add a bead and pass the needle left to right through 14 and 13. Pass the needle down from right to left through 17, 16 and 14, then back from left to right through 15.

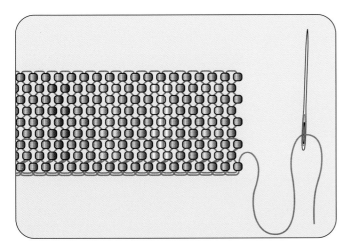

6 Repeat the bead-adding sequence from step 4, using the different coloured delicas to create the design.

7 To decrease the width of the band, finish the row so that you have four beads sticking out and the needle emerging from the end bead. Pass the needle from right to left through the last two beads of the previous row, and thread the needle back from left to right up through the last bead added.

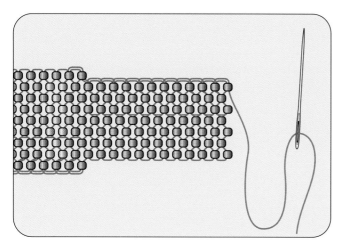

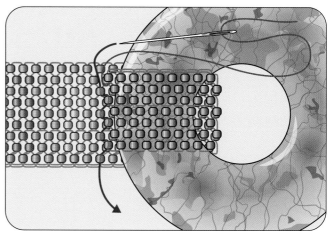

8 Continue weaving the thinner row in the same way to the length you need. When you finish the last row, be sure to leave the thread end nice and long.

9 The narrower section of the band can be threaded around the edge of a decorative ring. Attach it back onto the main band like a zip by weaving the beads together with the long thread end. Secure the thread by weaving back in a zigzag through the work and trim.

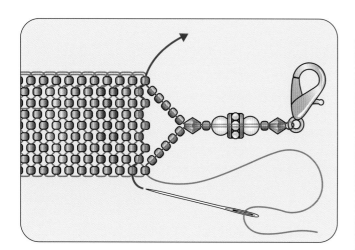

10 To add a clasp to the other end of the strap, unthread the stopper bead and thread on five delicas, crystal, delica, pearl, rondelle, pearl, delica, crystal, clasp or jump ring and then go back down through all the beads to the second crystal. Add five delicas and weave your thread through the bottom delica and around securely through the work, and trim. Attach the other part of the clasp in the same way.

Reinforcing the clasp

The beading leading up to the clasp is the weakest point in this design if it is left with just a single thread running through most of the beads. To reinforce it, after you have taken the thread through the main part of the work once, take it back around all the beads up to the clasp and back down again. Then secure the thread end as normal, at the end of the main panel.

frilled edge peyote stitch jewellery

This glitzy peyote stitch bracelet is made using silver-lined seed beads and with an unusual three-dimensional frilled edge.

Bracelet

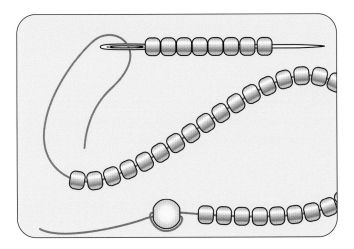

1 Cut 100cm (40in) of nylon thread, and thread on a stopper bead about 40cm (16in) from the end. Thread the needle with the other end, and pick up 80 seed beads.

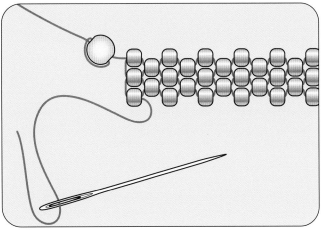

2 Pick up another seed bead, and work peyote stitch (see page 166) down the length of the row. Work two more rows of peyote up and down. If you run out of thread, add more.

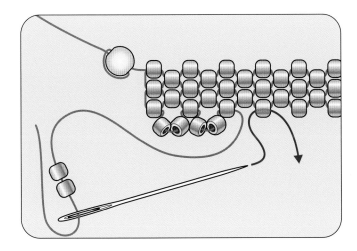

3 Continue with another row of the stitch, but pick up and add two beads in each gap instead of just one. This will create a frilled edge on one side, so keep the tension tight but expect it to twirl all over the place.

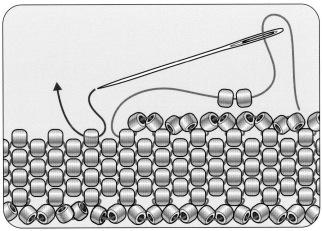

4 Thread the nylon thread up and down along the top edge of the weave, and work a row of peyote along the non-frilled edge. Make the frill on this side as described in step 3. Finish with the thread emerging from one corner.

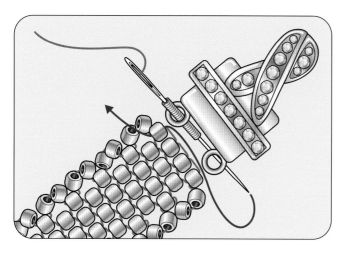

5 Thread a piece of gimp and pass it through one end of the clasp. Thread back through a seed bead and work the needle up and down, zigzagging through the seeds until it is totally secure. Repeat for the other corner of the weave and the other hole of the clasp.

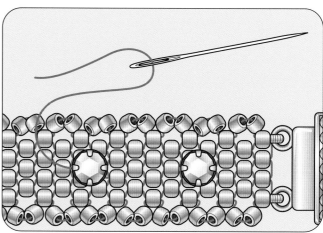

6 For extra glitz, weave the needle down the seeds, and sew on a crystal in the centre of the strip, sewing straight through the seeds. When it's totally secure, weave down 1cm (½in) passing the needle through the beads and sew on another crystal – repeat for a third sparkle.

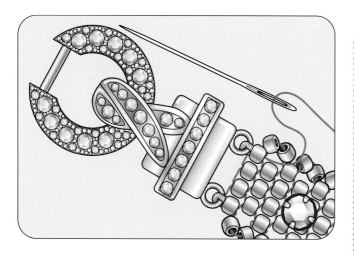

7 Finally attach the other end of the clasp, with another row of crystals stitched at this end of the bracelet in exactly the same way.

Silver-lined beads

This type of bead is made of transparent glass or crystal – which may be clear or coloured – but the hole through the middle of the bead is lined with a metallic silver coating that reflects the light for additional sparkle. Many different shapes of beads are available as silver-lined, including seed beads, delicas, bugle beads, square and disk beads. The hole can also be lined with metallic gold, or with a bright colour for a different effect.

knotting

Knots are not only used to join two cords together or to hold beads in place – the knots can also be used as a decorative technique to create beaded items. Macramé is a way of making textiles using knotting instead of weaving – this section has a simple version of it but macramé designs can be extremely complex.

Simple knotting

Hemp is such a fabulous natural fibre – it's strong and has a great texture and is perfect for knotting. Here it is combined with beading thread.

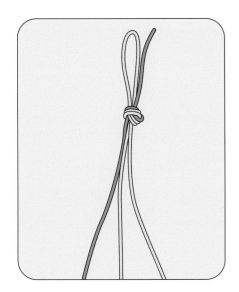

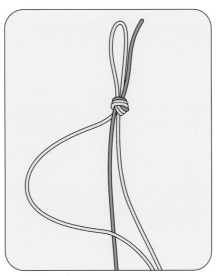

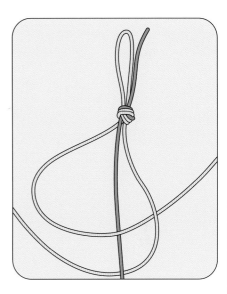

1 Find the centre of the hemp yarn, add the end of the bead thread, and tie an overhand knot (see page 91) to secure all three together. Leave the hemp in a loop so that you can attach the ends to a hook or nail, making the knots easier to tie.

2 Arrange the threads so you have a hemp strand each side of the bead thread. Make the left-hand hemp thread into a small loop and cross it above the bead thread. Hold firmly with your thumb and finger where the two threads cross.

3 Make a loop with the right-hand hemp thread, crossing over the left-hand hemp thread tail, then passing under the central bead thread.

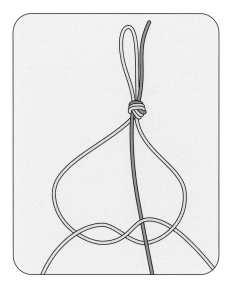

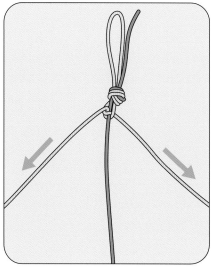

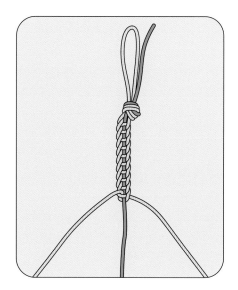

4 Now thread the right-hand hemp up through the loop on the left-hand side. The hemp strands will now have changed sides and the bead thread will be caught through the centre of the knot.

5 Gently pull the knot until it is firm but not tight. Practise a bit until you find the correct tension – just like knitting, everyone will knot differently.

6 Repeat from step 1 until you have 10 knots. The cord will begin to gently spiral clockwise. Try to keep all the knots the same size and firmness to create a smart uniform piece.

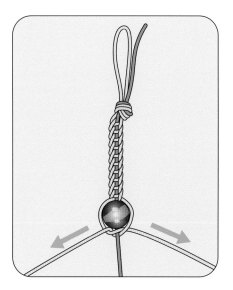

7 Thread a tiger's eye bead onto the central bead thread, and pass the hemp either side to work a knot directly under it, holding the bead in place. Continue knotting another 10 times and then add a green aventurine bead. Continue knotting and threading beads in sequence: picture jasper, tiger's eye, green aventurine, goldstone, malachite, picture jasper, carnelian, picture jasper, malachite, goldstone, green aventurine, tiger's eye, picture jasper, green aventurine, tiger's eye.

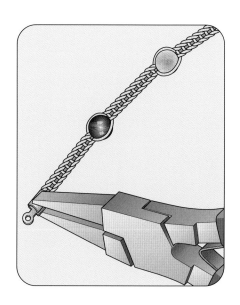

8 Finish with ten knots of spiral and then knot the threads together. Remove the loop from the hook and trim both ends 6mm (¼in) from the knot. Put a dab of glue on one end, and place in a cord end (see page 86). Repeat on the other side.

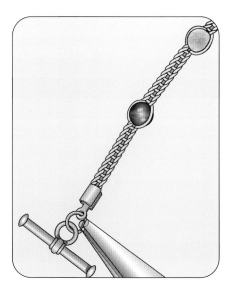

9 Attach the T-bar clasp using a jump ring (see page 80).

Experimenting with materials

The hemp used for this choker with the natural stone beads gives it a rather rugged, outdoor, masculine look. The same piece made using rubber cords instead of hemp and plain silver beads would look quite futuristic – and if you made it with fluffy textured knitting yarn and bright crystals it would look very light and feminine. Many designs can be changed completely just by choosing different materials, so time spent considering exactly what to use at the start is one of the most important parts of the design process.

Hemp cord combined with natural stone beads.

Macramé

The decorative square knots of macramé are simple to make once you get into the rhythm and it is very easy to add beads as you work.

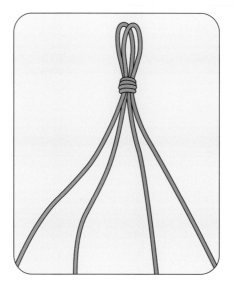

1 Cut two cords each about 60cm (24in) long, fold in half and knot the cords together just below the loop.

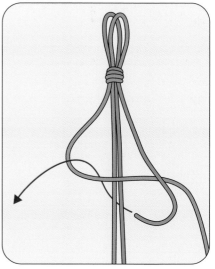

2 Bring the left cord over the two middle cords. Then bring the right cord over the left cord, under the two middle cords and through the loop formed by the left cord. Pull the right and left cord until the knot tightens.

Components

Items from hardware stores can make unusual and interesting 'beads'. Hex nuts are often made of shiny brass and they already have a central hole so they are ideal for threading. They come in a range of sizes, too. So for unusual bead ideas, check out the small components at your local hardware store and think creatively.

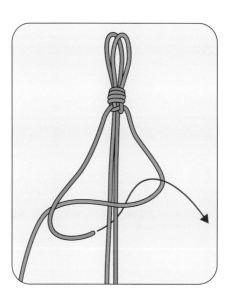

3 Bring the right cord over the two middle cords. Then bring the left cord over the right cord, under the two middle cords and through the loop formed by the right cord. Pull the right and left cord until the knot tightens. This completes one square knot.

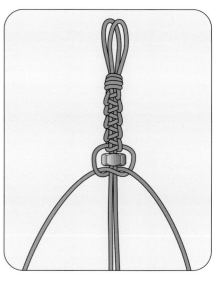

4 Tie around eight square knots, then introduce a bead (or try a bead substitute, such as a hex nut), by threading it onto the two middle cords. Tie another square knot beneath to hold the bead in place. Alternate beads and square knots spaced along the length of the cord.

Braiding

Braiding with beads and string or cord has been used to create friendship bracelets by cultures all over the world. There are hundreds of different designs and techniques – far too many to cover them all here – but here is a selection to try.

Three-strand braid with side beads

This simple design is just a braid with beads added at either side, but the final result is very effective.

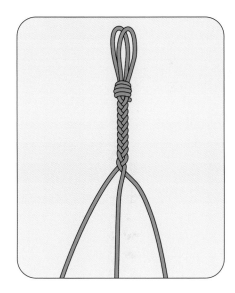

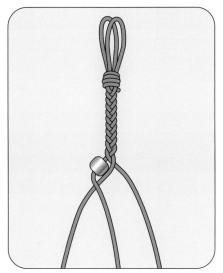

1 Cut three equal lengths of linen cord or hemp. Fold the ends over and tie a knot about 1cm (½in) down from the loops. Snip off any excess short ends close to the knot, leaving three long strands. Start braiding the strands.

2 After 2.5cm (1in) or so, thread a bead onto the outer left strand. Push the bead against the base of the braid, and cross the left strand over to the middle to hold the bead in place.

3 Now thread another bead onto the outer right strand. Push it to the base of the braid and cross the right strand over to the middle to hold the second bead in place.

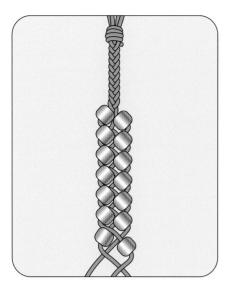
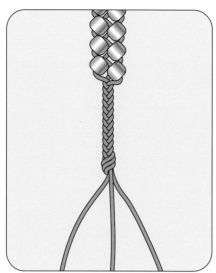
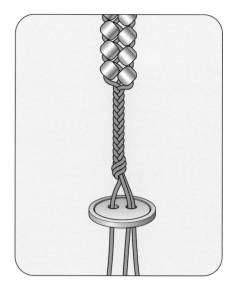

4 Keep a finger at the base of the braid, holding the beads in their place and keeping the braid tight. Continue threading on beads before each strand is crossed over.

5 Finish the bracelet with another 2.5cm (1in) or so of braided cord to match the beginning, and measuring it against the wrist if it is to be a bracelet. Tie a knot and trim the end.

6 For an unusual fastening, thread on a two-hole button to slip through the starting loop. Thread two strands through one hole of the button and one strand through another. Secure the ends with another knot below the button.

Section of beading in a braided natural string bracelet.

Three-strand braid with centre beads

This variation on the three-strand bracelet has the beads added down the centre. The instructions give a longer bracelet than normal, which can be wrapped around the wrist several times. Add a clasp as described on page 190, or just knot the ends.

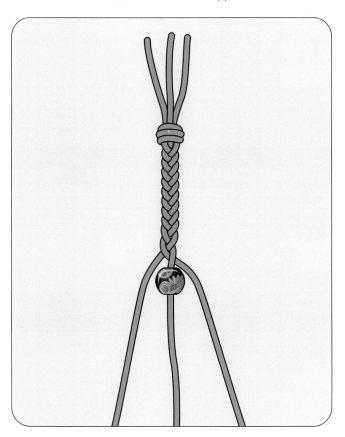

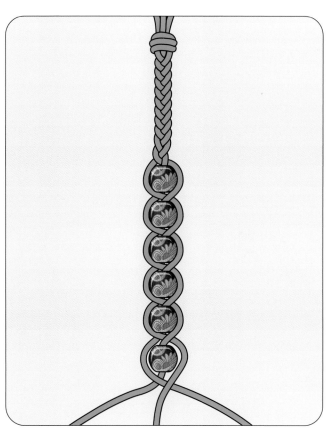

1 Cut three 65cm (26in) lengths of linen cord or hemp. Secure the ends together with a knot. Start braiding the strands. To begin adding the beads, thread the first bead onto the centre strand.

2 Braid the two side strands over beneath the bead as normal. Don't pull them too tight or the bead will pop forward. Continue until you have the length required, then knot the strands.

beaded chevron

The chevron, or arrow, design is usually worked in several coloured threads to create chevron stripes, but can be beaded for a different look. Here we have used coloured strands to make it clearer what is happening, but beads will look just as good on a single colour chevron.

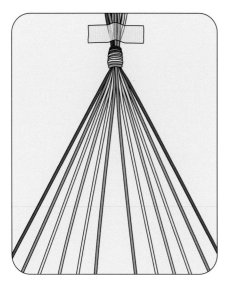

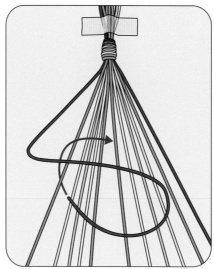

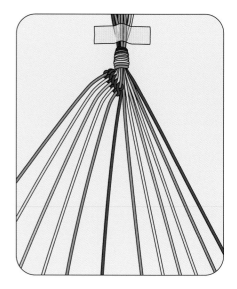

1 Start by cutting several strands of embroidery thread each about 60cm (24in) long – if you are making a coloured chevron design you need two strands of each colour. Combine the threads and tie a knot, leaving at least 7.5cm (3in) of tail above the knot. Tape the knot to a flat surface or pin it to a cushion. Separate the strands – if using colours arrange them in a mirror-image order so the two outside strands are the same colour and so on moving inwards.

2 Start on the left side with the first strand (shown here in red) and make a forward knot on the second strand by creating a 4-shape over the second strand (shown here in orange), looping the first strand under and back through the opening.

3 Pull up and to the right to tighten. Repeat the same knot on the second strand again. Continue knotting the first strand over the next colour to the right each time – remembering to make two knots on each strand – until the first strand is in the middle. This is one half of the chevron pattern.

Chevron designs

This chevron can be created with any even number of threads – you need a pair of each strand, one on each side. The more strands you start with, the wider the finished chevron will be. A variation of the design is to continue working across the threads in one direction rather than from each side – this will create diagonal stripes instead of a chevron, but can be beaded in the same way.

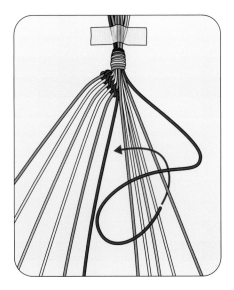

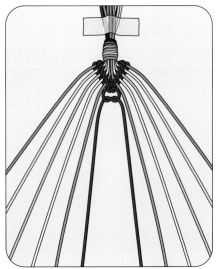

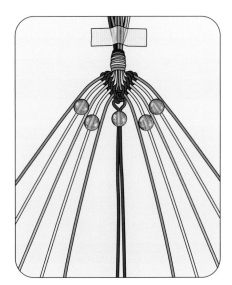

4 Now pick up the outermost strand on the right side (shown here in red) and make a backward knot, creating a reverse 4-shape over the second strand to the left, looping under and back through the opening. Pull up and to the left to tighten.

5 Continue knotting towards the left – remembering to make two knots on each strand – until the outermost strand is in the middle. Tie a knot twice with the two middle strands to connect the two halves. The first chevron row is complete.

6 To add the beads, take five beads; skip the first strand, put a bead on the second strand, skip the third strand, put a bead on the fourth strand, skip the fifth strand, put a bead on the two centre strands, skip the eighth strand, put a bead on the ninth strand, skip the tenth strand, put a bead on the eleventh strand, skip the twelfth strand.

7 Repeat steps 2 to 5 to make as many rows of chevron as you like, then repeat step 6 to add another row of beads. Keep repeating this sequence until the strip is the length you want it. Finish with a knot and either braid the strands at each end, or add a clasp as explained on page 190.

beaded knitting and crochet

Adding beads to knitting and crochet is very easy once you know a few simple techniques. The beads can either be added into the stitch as you work, or added later as a surface decoration.

choosing beads

There are a couple of things to bear in mind when buying the beads. Firstly, the hole in the bead must be large enough for a double strand of yarn to pass through and secondly, the bead must not be too heavy for the yarn. This means in bead-sizing terms about a size 6, but always take a needle (see Threading Beads onto the Yarn on page 202), and a length of the yarn to the store and check whether or not the hole is big enough. This is also an excellent opportunity to see how the yarn and the bead look together.

Using a heavy bead on a fine yarn will cause the stitches, and possibly the whole garment, to stretch. It is probably also a good idea to avoid fragile beads that might break during washing and wearing, or those that have sharp edges (such as cut glass) that could damage the yarn. Before you start a large piece of work, make a small sample using the beads and the yarn you have chosen. Establish how the beads will affect the tension (gauge), whether they will snag or fray the work, and whether or not they are washable, colourfast or liable to damage.

– Wooden beads are light and strong, but if they are dyed they may fade with washing and any varnish may flake off. However, wooden beads – even when varnished – have a matte look that will suit a project with a homespun or ethnic look.

– Plastic beads are light and durable and can be found in a variety of colours and shapes, sometimes simulating materials such as glass, metal or ceramic. The only problem is that they can melt – and sometimes at surprisingly low temperatures.

– Bone beads tend to come only in shades of cream, in limited shapes and are very expensive. However, if you are planning to use the bead as a main feature of the project, they could be worth considering.

– Glass beads are available in a vast range of colours and a variety of shapes and will add a glamorous note to a project. Although they can shatter this should only be considered a problem if they are applied so densely that they have very little yarn around them to cushion them.

– Metal beads can give a project vintage charm or a hi-tech look but, like metal buttons, they will tarnish. It is often recommended that metal buttons are removed before washing, but this is completely impractical for metal beads incorporated into the fabric.

– Ceramic beads can look great, but they do not wash well: they may survive the laundry once, but not regularly.

choosing colours

The beads you choose will not only add sparkle and texture – they may well also have an affect on the colour of the yarn used. These swatches show the effect of different colour beads on pieces of knitting that have the same colour background.

In the swatch on the top left the colour of the pink yarn is intensified by the presence of the red beads. This is because pink is derived from red.

In the swatch on the top right the blue bead appears slightly more lilac, while in that at bottom left the green bead appears more yellow. Both colours of bead also appear to have drained the pink yarn of some of its vibrancy.

When a lilac bead of similar value to that of the pink yarn is used in the bottom right swatch, neither element seems to dominate because both contain equal amounts of red.

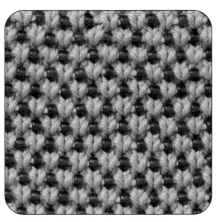
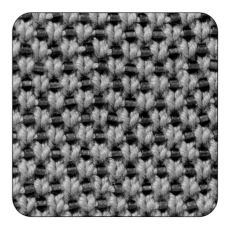
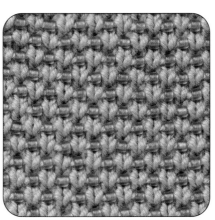
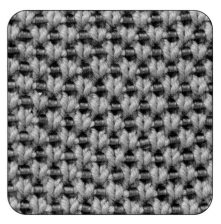

Washing beaded fabric

Beads can add a lot of weight to your fabric when used in large amounts, so do make sure you use a sturdy yarn that will withstand washing and wearing. It is not a good idea to wash a beaded knitted or crochet fabric in the washing machine, both because the weight of the beads may pull the yarn out of shape when wet and because the action of the machine my damage the beads. Instead, wash by hand using a mild detergent and be very careful that the beads do not cause threads to snag. When drying, avoid a rigorous spin in the machine and dry flat where possible.

threading beads

The first step in both knitting and crochet beading is to get the beads onto the yarn. For this you will need a strong sewing thread and a fine sewing needle – a yarn needle will be far too large to thread beads. It is essential that all the beads needed for the design are threaded onto the yarn before you begin to work – although if you are using a very large number of beads you may have to thread them onto the yarn in sections. Lay a piece of craft felt or a fine flannel over a saucer or small bowl to hold the beads, because threading from the palm of your hand or a slippery flat surface can be troublesome.

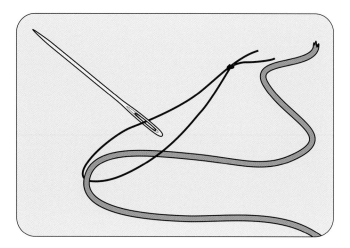

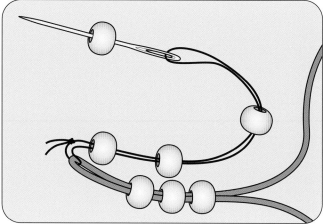

1 Thread the needle with a short length of sewing thread and knot the ends to form a loop. Move the knot so that it falls on one side of the loop of thread. Put the tail end of the yarn through the loop of thread.

2 Pick up the beads with the needle, slide them down the thread and onto the yarn. The first few beads may be a bit tricky, but so long as the beads are large enough, threading will become easier.

Beading sequence

When threading beads onto yarn to follow a chart design (see page 211), first thread on the bead closest to the top left-hand corner of the chart. Follow the row along to the right-hand side, threading on the correct beads as they appear on the chart. Follow the next row from right to left, threading on the correct beads. Continue until you reach the bottom right-hand corner of the chart. This means that when you work the chart, following it from bottom right to top left as normal, the beads will be on the yarn in the correct order.

knitting techniques

There isn't a lot to learn in knitting – just casting on, knit and purl stitch, and casting off. Almost all the other knitting techniques are variations of these basics. It is simple to add beads and a basic sweater design can be made glamorous by a row of beading around the cuff or edge of the collar.

Making a slip knot

To cast on you need a starting point and this is the slip knot. The slip knot will always count as the first cast on stitch in knitting.

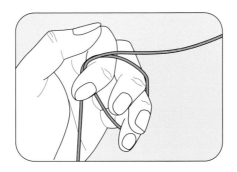

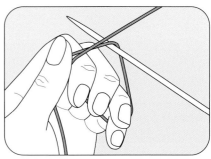

1 Hold the working (ball) end of the yarn in your right hand and wrap it around the fingers of your left hand.

2 Put the tip of a knitting needle, held in your right hand, through the loop around your fingers.

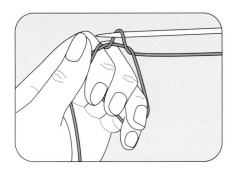

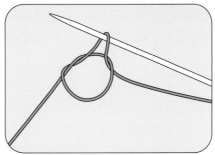

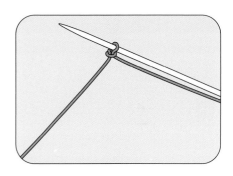

3 Wrap the working end of the yarn around the needle and pull the needle, and the yarn wrapped around it, through the loop around your left hand.

4 Keeping the yarn on the needle, slip the loop off your left hand.

5 Pull gently on the ends of the yarn so that the loop tightens around the needle.

Tight cast on

With all the cast-on techniques that follow, do not cast on too tightly. If your stitches are not moving freely along the needle as you make them, try using a larger needle.

Cable cast on

This technique involves using two knitting needles and gives a firm edge that looks good with stocking (stockinette) stitch.

Placing the needle

If you find it difficult to push the right-hand needle between the stitches in step 6, try putting it through before you tighten the previous stitch. With the needle in place, pull the last stitch made tight, then work the next stitch.

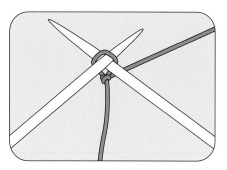

1 Make a slip knot about 15cm (6in) from the end of the yarn. Hold the needle with the slip knot in your left hand and the other needle in your right. With the working end of the yarn in your right hand, put the tip of the right-hand needle into the stitch on the left-hand needle.

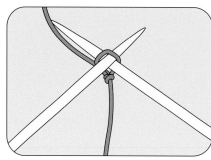

2 Bring the yarn in your right hand under and around the point of the right-hand needle.

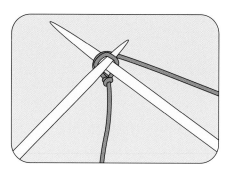

3 Pull the yarn taut so that it is wrapped around the tip of the right-hand needle.

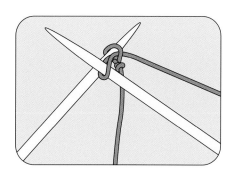

4 Bring the tip of the right-hand needle, and the yarn wrapped around it, through the stitch and towards you.

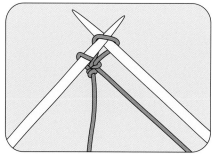

5 Pull gently until the loop is large enough to slip it over the tip of the left-hand needle. Take the right-hand needle out of the loop and pull the working end of the yarn so that the loop fits snugly around the left-hand needle.

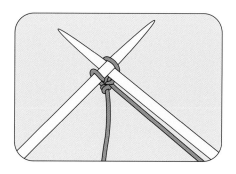

6 To cast on all the other stitches, put the tip of the right-hand needle between the last two stitches instead of through the last one. Then repeat steps 2–6 until you have the required number of stitches on the left-hand needle.

Thumb cast on

The thumb technique uses one knitting needle and your thumb and produces an edge that has elasticity.

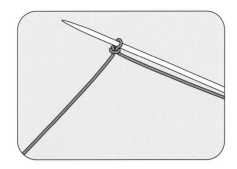

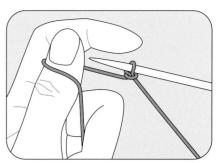

1 For this cast on you firstly need to pull enough yarn from the ball to make all the stitches; approximately 2cm (¾in) per stitch is needed. Measure out the correct amount of yarn then make a slip knot (see page 203).

2 Hold the ball end of the yarn and the needle in your right hand. Hold the other end of the yarn (the measured length) in the palm of your left hand. Move your left thumb behind and under the yarn, so that the yarn is wrapped from front to back around your left thumb.

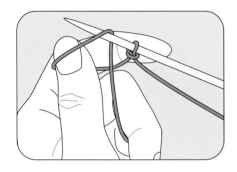

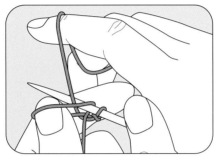

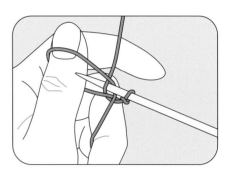

3 Insert the tip of the needle into the loop on your thumb.

4 Wrap the yarn in your right hand under and around the tip of the knitting needle.

5 Bring the needle, and the yarn wrapped around it, through the loop around your thumb and towards you to make another stitch on the needle.

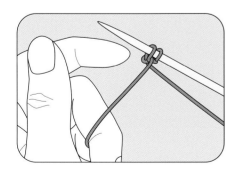

6 Slip your thumb out of the loop and pull the two ends of yarn away from the needle in opposite directions. Repeat steps 2–6 until you have cast on the number of stitches required.

Choosing a technique

Although cable cast on produces a firmer edge than thumb cast on, in most instances it doesn't matter which one you use. If you don't already have a favourite cast on technique, try both and use the one that feels most comfortable to work.

Casting (binding) off

Once you have completed your piece of work you need to finish the stitches so you can take out the needles without the knitting unravelling. These steps are for casting (binding) off knitwise; casting (binding) off purlwise is essentially the same, but you work purl stitches.

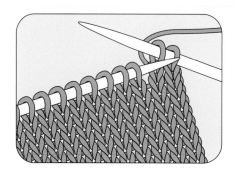

1 Knit the first two stitches in the usual way (see opposite), so you now have two stitches only on the right-hand needle.

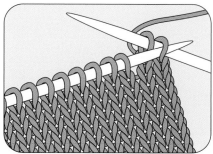

2 Slip the tip of the left-hand needle into the first stitch you knitted onto the right-hand needle. Lift it over the second stitch you knitted and drop it off the needle. You now have only one stitch on the right-hand needle.

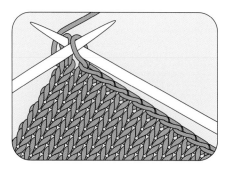

3 Knit another stitch from the left-hand needle and then pass the previous stitch you knitted over it. Continue in this way until you have one stitch remaining on the right-hand needle.

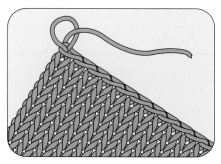

4 Cut the yarn leaving a 15cm (6in) tail to sew in later. Put the cut end through the remaining stitch and pull it tight to secure.

Slipping stitches

When you need to move a stitch from the left-hand needle to the right-hand needle without actually knitting or purling it, then you must slip it.

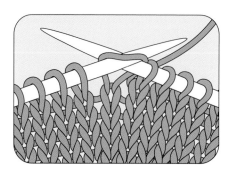

1 To slip a stitch knitwise, from front to back, put the tip of the right-hand needle into the next stitch on the left-hand needle and slip the stitch over onto the right-hand needle.

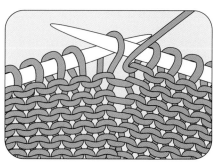

2 To slip a stitch purlwise, from back to front, put the tip of the right-hand needle into the next stitch on the left-hand needle and then slip the stitch over onto the right-hand needle.

Basic knit stitch

When you knit, you transfer stitches from the left-hand needle to the right-hand needle. When you come to the end of the row, you put the needle with the stitches on into your left hand and work on the reverse side of the project to work the next row.

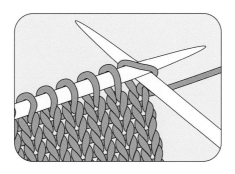

1 From front to back, insert the tip of the right-hand needle into the first stitch on the left-hand needle.

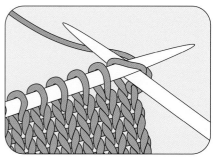

2 Bring the yarn you are holding in your right hand under the tip of the right-hand needle.

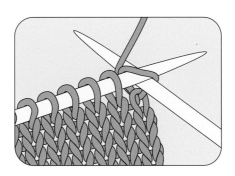

3 Wrap the yarn over the needle.

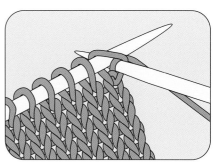

4 Bring the tip of the right-hand needle, and the yarn wrapped around it, through the stitch on the left-hand needle.

5 Pull the loop of yarn through to make a new stitch on the right-hand needle.

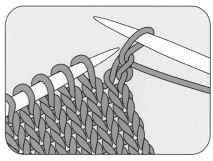

6 Slip the original stitch off of the left-hand needle. The knitted stitch is now complete.

Tension (gauge)

Tension (gauge) is given in a pattern as the number of stitches and rows within a 10cm (4in) square of the fabric. If you are not knitting to the same tension as given in the pattern your item will come out a different size. You can't change how you knit easily, so to adjust the tension change the needles. If you have too many stitches/rows in your measured square your tension is too tight – use larger needles. If you have fewer stitches/rows in your square your tension is too loose – use smaller needles.

beaded knitting and crochet

Basic purl stitch

Most patterns use a combination of knit and purl stitches, so once you have mastered the purl stitch you are able to go forward and try any design.

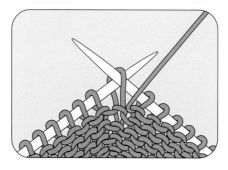

1 For purl stitch, you need the yarn at the front of the work as shown. From back to front, put the tip of the right-hand needle into the first stitch on the left-hand needle.

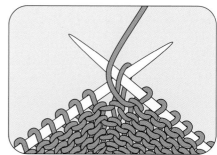

2 Bring the yarn forward and then take it up over the tip of the right-hand needle.

Knitted fabric

Most beading is worked on stocking (stockinette) stitch fabric, in which rows are alternately knitted and purled. This gives a smoother surface with V-shape stitches on the right side and a more bobbly surface with interlocking loops on the wrong side.

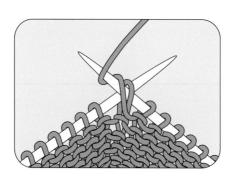

3 Wrap the yarn under and around the tip of the needle.

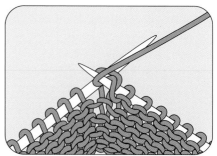

4 Bring the tip of the right-hand needle, and the yarn wrapped around it, backwards through the stitch on the left-hand needle, making sure that this stitch remains on the needle.

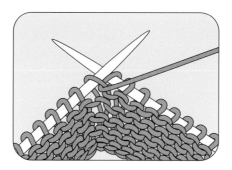

5 Pull the loop completely through the stitch, creating a new stitch on the right-hand needle.

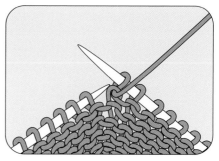

6 When it's safely through, slip the original stitch off the left-hand needle. The purl stitch is now complete.

adding beads
to knitted fabric

The two most commonly used bead knit techniques are slip stitch beading and knitted-in beading. With both these techniques the bead can be added on either the knit or the purl stitch.

Slip stitch beading

This is the simplest and most often used beading technique, though beads can only be placed on every alternate stitch and row. Generally slip stitch beading will not affect your tension (gauge), so you can add beads to an existing plain pattern.

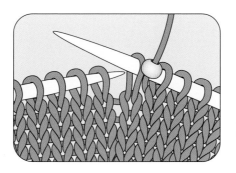 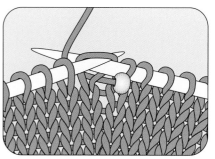

1 Knit to the position of the bead. Bring the yarn forward between the needles and slip a bead down the yarn to sit right in front of the work. Slip the next stitch onto the needle purlwise.

2 Take the yarn between the needles to the back of the work, making sure the bead stays in front of the slipped stitch. Knit the next stitch quite tightly to hold the bead in place.

Purling beads

Beads can be placed on a purl row using the slip stitch technique by taking the yarn to the back, sliding the bead down, slipping the next stitch knitwise, then taking the yarn to the front again.

Detail of slip stitch beaded motif.

Knitted-in beading

This technique, which is also known as close beading, allows you to place a bead in every stitch on every row. However, if you bead an item heavily you may affect your tension (gauge) and will certainly affect the drape of the finished project.

Placing beads with knit stitch

Use this technique to place a bead on the right side of the work while working a knit row.

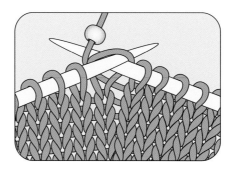

1 Knit to the position of the bead. Put the tip of the right-hand needle into the next stitch, wrap the yarn around it and slide the bead down to the needles.

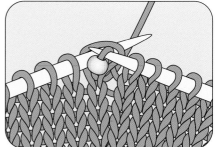

2 Knit the stitch, making sure that as you pull the loop of yarn through, the bead comes with it to the right side of the work.

Wriggling beads

With knitted-in beading you will find that the beads try to wriggle their way through to the back of the work. To help prevent this, before you work the next row push all the beads down to sit at the bottom of their stitches, then keep an eye on them as you work the next row.

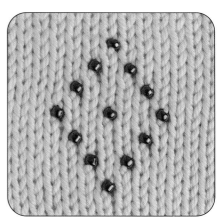

Detail of knitted-in beaded motif.

Placing beads with purl stitch

Use this technique to place a bead on the right side of the work when working the purl row.

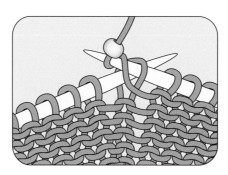

1 Purl to the position of the bead, Put the tip of the right-hand needle into the next stitch, wrap the yarn around it and slide the bead down to the needles.

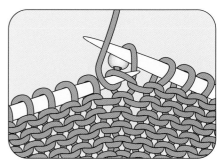

2 Purl the stitch, making sure that as you pull the loop of yarn through, the bead comes with it to the right side of the work.

Following a chart

You can take beading one step further and introduce different colour beads to make a more intricate design. The thing to remember when using more than one colour of bead is that you have to thread them onto the yarn in the right order. The bead that is threaded on last will be the one that is knitted first, so you need to follow the chart backwards (see page 202).

To knit this chart you would have to thread the beads on in the order given below, starting from the top left of the chart.

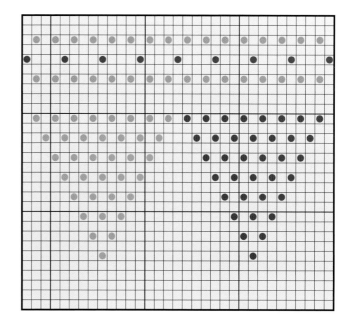

 Grey (A)

● Brown (B)

● Red (C)

Thread the beads onto the yarn in the following sequence to knit this chart.

16 C
8 B
16 C
8 B
8 A
7 B
7 A
6 B
6 A
5 B
5 A
4 B
4 A
3 B
3 A
2 B
2 A
1 B
1 A

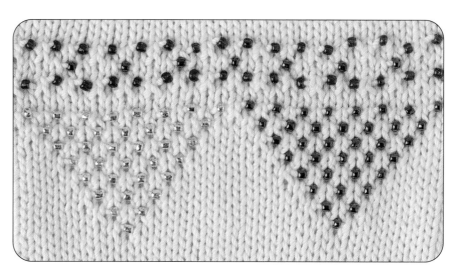

This swatch has been knitted following the chart above.

Fair Isle beading

True Fair Isle traditionally has only a maximum of two colours per row, but that tradition is often broken. To avoid the dense mass of stranded threads at the back of a Fair Isle, particularly one with more than two colours, substitute beads for one of the colours.

bead motif patterns

A selection of charts for beaded motifs on knitting, all worked on stocking (stockinette) stitch. These motifs can be added when working any large enough piece of plain knitting. Choose beads to suit the colour of the yarn and the overall project.

Heart beaded motif

The beaded motif here is 13 stitches wide, with 2 extra stitches allowed on each side (which are not shown on the chart).

Thread 40 beads onto the yarn.

Using the beaded yarn, cast on 17 sts.
Row 1: Knit.
Row 2: Purl.
Beginning with a RS row, work rows 1–20 from chart, placing beads as indicated.
Next row: Purl.
Next row: Knit.

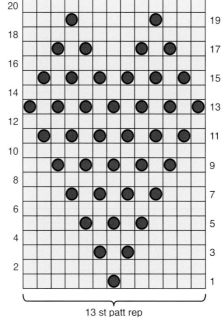

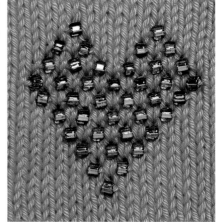

Beaded heart motif worked from the chart.

Star beaded motif

The beaded motif here is 13 stitches wide, with 2 extra stitches allowed on each side (which are not shown on the chart).

Thread 37 beads onto the yarn.

Using the beaded yarn, cast on 17 sts.
Row 1: Knit.
Row 2: Purl.
Beginning with a RS row, work rows 1–18 from chart, placing beads as indicated.
Next row: Purl.
Next row: Knit.

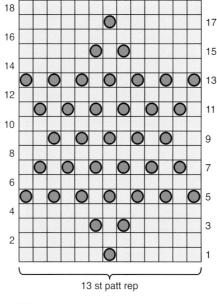

13 st patt rep

 Unbeaded stitch

Bead

Beaded star motif worked from the chart.

Triangles beaded motif

The beaded motif here is 47 stitches wide, with 2 extra stitches allowed on each side (as shown on the chart).

Thread 180 silver beads onto the yarn.

Using the beaded yarn, cast on 51 sts.

Row 1: Knit.

Row 2: Purl.

Beginning with a RS row, work rows 1–28 from chart, placing beads as indicated.

Next row: Purl.

Next row: Knit.

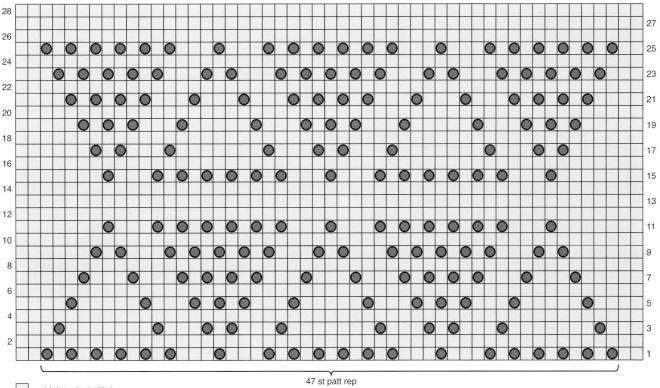

47 st patt rep

☐ *Unbeaded stitch*

⬤ *Bead*

Checking the chart

Compare the chart with the text before you begin, because patterns sometimes show information in slightly different ways. The two charts on page 212 do not show the extra unbeaded stitches on either side of the beaded section, but the chart above and the one on page 214 do show them.

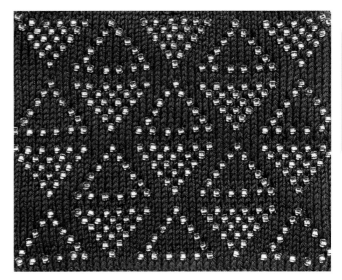

Beaded motif (opposite) worked from the chart.

Seed heads beaded motif

The beaded motif here is 20 stitches wide, with 8 extra stitches allowed, 3 on one side and 5 on the other.

100 green beads (A)

94 pink beads (B)

72 turquoise beads (C)

Thread the beads onto one ball of the yarn in the following order:

4B, 9C, 5B, 1C, 1B, 1C, 1B, 1C, 2B, 1C, 1B, 1C, 1B, 1C, 2B, 1C, 2B, 1C, 2B, 1C, 2B, 1C, 2B, 1C, 1B, 1C, 2B, 1C, 1B, 1C, 2B,1C, 4B, 11A, 4B, 1A, 6C, 1A, 3C, 1A, 4B, 1A, 1B, 1C, 1B, 1C, 1B, 1C, 1B, 1A, 1B, 1C, 1B, 1C, 1B, 1C, 1B, 1A, 1B, 1C, 2B, 1C, 1B, 1A, 1B, 1C, 2B, 1C, 1B, 2A, 1B, 1C, 1B, 1C, 1B, 2A, 1B, 1C, 1B, 1C, 1B, 2A, 1B, 1C, 1B, 2A, 3B, 50A.

Using the beaded yarn, cast on 28 sts.

Row 1: Knit.

Row 2: Purl.

Beginning with a RS row, work rows 1–87 from chart.

Next row: Purl.

Next row: Knit.

Placing the design

The pattern instructions will tell you when to begin working the chart so the beaded motif falls in the correct place. You can add a beaded motif to a plain pattern, but you will have to work out when to begin working the chart to get the motif where you want it. The unbeaded stitches on either side of a motif allow for multiple repeats – they are there so the motifs will be spaced out slightly. On the seed heads chart there are more unbeaded stitches on one side to allow for the asymmetrical design of the motif.

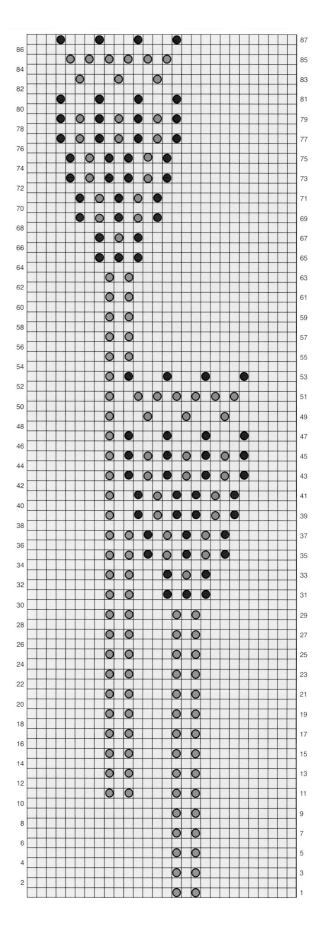

Beading on individual stitches

This is a good method of adding the occasional bead or a forgotten bead in a bead sequence. However, its appearance differs from that of slip stitch beading in that the bead holes lie up and down the knitting and the bead does not stand proud of the knitted surface. The bead is equally visible on the right and wrong sides.

At the position of the bead, thread the stitch through the bead using either a crochet hook or a needle and thread. Return the loop to the left-hand needle and knit or purl the stitch as usual.

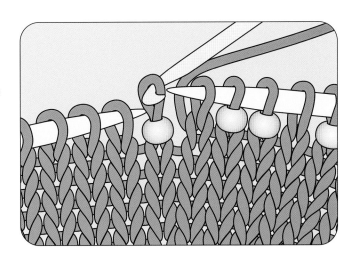

Beading on a second yarn

You can thread tiny beads onto fine yarn or thread and work the project with both fine and main yarn. If a contrasting or complementary colour is used the fine yarn can be a design feature as well as carrying beads, although check the yarns have similar laundering requirements. If a matching colour is used the fine yarn can be almost invisible.

When you reach the position of a bead, leave the main yarn at the back of the work. Bring the fine yarn to the front and slide a bead down to the stitch. Work the stitch in the main yarn, then take the fine yarn to the back of the work. Continue working in both yarns until you reach the next stitch to be beaded.

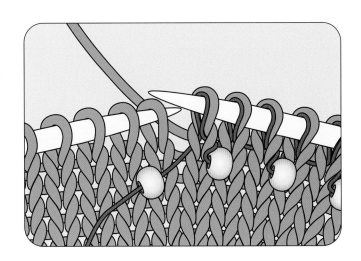

Adding beads between stitches

This is a useful method of beading on garter stitch (all rows knit) without any slipped stitches distorting the regular waves of the stitch pattern. Beads can only be added on alternate rows and the yarn is very visible. This method can also be used to bead on reverse stocking (stockinette) stitch (when the smooth side is the wrong side) with beads positioned between every bead on every row. On knit rows, position the beads as described below and on purl rows slide a bead up the yarn to sit next to the last stitch, then purl the next stitch.

With the yarn on the right side, work to the position of a bead. Slide a bead along the yarn, up tight against the last stitch, and work the next stitch.

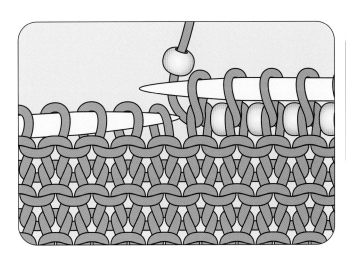

edge beading

The cast-on or cast- (bound-) off edge can also be decorated with beads. In addition to its decorative qualities, the right bead will help to create a firm edge, the weight will reduce curl on a stocking (stockinette) stitch edge, or it will highlight the knit stitch on a ribbed edge. However, edges with more than one row of beads can be weighty and cumbersome and make the rest of the knitting awkward. The weight can also easily distort the shape of a project.

Beaded cable cast on

Thread beads onto the yarn. Place a slip knot on the left-hand needle. Position a bead behind the knot. Insert the right-hand needle into the loop. *Knit, drawing the bead through with the loop. Put the loop onto the left-hand needle and slide the bead to the front so it sits against the knot. Slide a bead up the yarn, insert the right-hand needle between the last stitch and the slip knot and repeat from *.

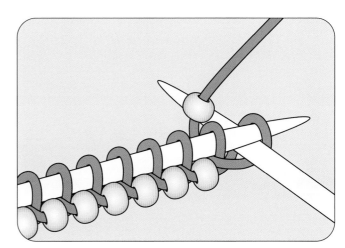

Beaded thumb cast on

Thread the beads onto the yarn and push them beyond the position for the slip knot, which will be the first stitch. Work the cast on with the beads on the length of yarn coming from the ball, and leaving the tail without any beads. Before each new stitch, push one bead up against the last stitch then work as usual. There are several variations of this cast on, including having beads on the tail and pushing them up to the last stitch, and a frill with beads on both sections of the yarn.

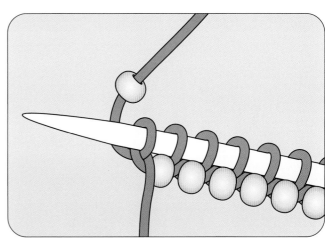

Beaded cast (bind) off

Cut the yarn to four times the width of the row from the last stitch. Thread the yarn with sufficient beads to work the row, minus two. Work one stitch. *Push a bead up against the back of the knitted fabric, work the next stitch and draw the bead through the stitch with the loop. Pass the first stitch on the right-hand needle over the last one. Repeat from * to the last stitch. Work the last stitch without a bead and cast (bind) it off.

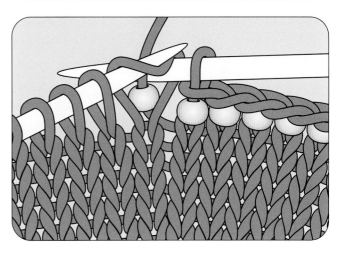

Beaded fringe

Beads make fringing a little more special and the weight of the beads can help the fringe to drape well. Beaded fringes can be added to the edges of both knitting and crochet in exactly the same way.

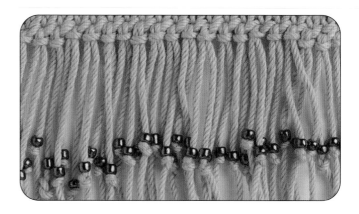

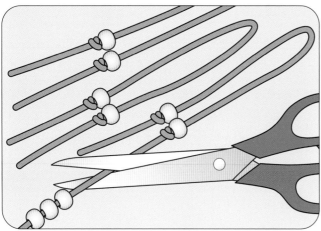

1 Thread the beads onto the yarn as for knitted beading (see page 202). Cut the yarn to the lengths required for the fringe, with two beads on each length. Knot each end of each length to stop the beads from falling off.

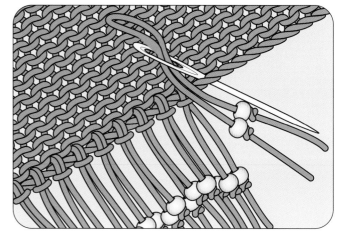

2 Fold the length of yarn in half and put the folded end through a large-eyed tapestry needle. Take the needle and the folded end of the yarn from front to back through the fabric, just above the edge.

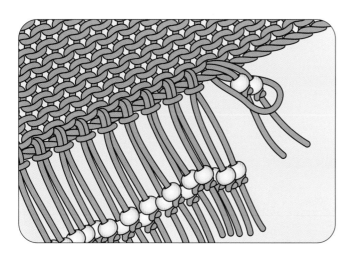

3 Slip the needle off the yarn. Tuck the cut ends through the loop and pull it tight. After you have finished the fringe, trim the ends level if necessary.

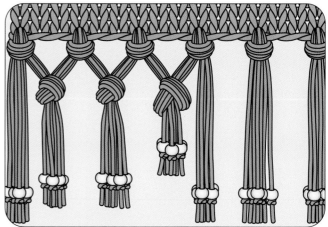

4 For a more complex beaded fringe you can also knot the strands in various ways. Work a simple beaded fringe but space the individual tassels slightly further apart. Split each tassel in half and knot each half to half of the adjacent tassel.

adding beading with embroidery

Working embroidery stitches on knitted fabric is generally easy because the stitches and rows act as a grid, helping you to space the embroidery stitches evenly. However, getting the tension of the embroidery right (so that the fabric is not puckered up or the embroidery stitches too baggy) can take a bit of practice. Remember that embroidery will stop knitted fabric stretching, so don't embroider collars or cuffs if you have to stretch them to get the garment on. The embroidery stitches shown here can be used to add detail and colour to a simple project, lifting it to another level. See pages 244–264 for how to work a selection of beaded embroidery stitches.

Starting and stopping

To start embroidery on a knitted fabric, do not knot the end of the yarn as it will probably just pull through the fabric. Instead, weave the needle and yarn back and forth through a few knitted stitches on the back of the fabric, underneath the area that will be covered by the embroidery stitches. To fasten off after finishing the stitching, either weave in as before or, if the stitch permits, weave the end into the back of the embroidery, being careful not to pull it too tight and so distort the stitching on the right side of the work.

Knitting with embroidered chain stitching, a satin stitch flower with added beads and lazy daisy flowers with bead centres. Individual beads have also been added using slip stitch beading.

Decoration including appliquéd ribbon, a crochet motif with beads stitched on and chain stitch paisley motifs with added beads. The background knitting has also been felted after knitting.

beaded edge patterns

Some basic patterns for different beaded edges, which will allow you to add beading to any suitable knitting project.

Beaded frill

The beads used here are slightly wider than a stitch, so when they are positioned on every stitch using the thumb cast on method, they produce a pronounced frill.

Cast on twice as many stitches as required for the body of the work, using the beaded thumb cast on method (see page 205) and placing a bead on every stitch.
Next row: [K2tog] rep to the end of the row.
Work in chosen stitch pattern.

Beaded loops

A bracelet of looped beads inspired this swatch, which has the beads worked on the edge of a knitted fabric. Of course, the beads do not have to be on an edge, but could be in a band across the middle of a project, as a vertical strip, or as single stitches.

Thread beads onto the yarn and cast on using the thumb method (see page 205).
Work 2 rows of k1, p1 rib.
Row 3 (RS): [K1, yf, slide 7 beads to the base of the right-hand needle, p1tbl, k1] rep to the end of the row.
Row 4: [P1, purl into the loop of the st below the next st and place it onto the left-hand needle, p2tog] rep to the end of the row.
Rep the last two rows twice more.
Alternatively, row 4 can be just purled to give a flatter edge.

Beaded buttonhole

This little detail won't always be visible, it will mean working a larger buttonhole to accommodate the button, and it may be slightly fiddlier to use, but you will know it is there. Worked in a contrasting colour, it will sparkle provocatively at the keen observer. These instructions are to make a buttonhole on stocking (stockinette) stitch.

Row 1 (RS): K to the position of the buttonhole and cast (bind) off using the beaded cast (bind) off method (see page 217). K1 with bead (see page 210) after the cast (bind) off and k to the end of the row.

Row 2: P to the position of the cast- (bound-) off sts, use the thumb loop method (see page 205) to cast on the sts, passing the yarn to between your thumb and the needle before the last stitch is cast on, and p to the end of the row.

Row 3: K to just above the buttonhole, k1 with bead into the front of the cast-on sts and k to the end of the row.

A stronger buttonhole

Beading the cast on makes the buttonhole stronger. The thumb loop cast on makes the buttonhole look closed rather than gaping, as it would with a cable cast on.

Bead weaving with a second yarn

The weaving technique is used to secure a second yarn threaded with seed beads to the knitted fabric. This will inevitably catch and is not practical for a project that will receive constant wear. This swatch is worked in stocking (stockinette) stitch using the main colour only (without the beaded thread), except for the first and last stitches of every row.

Thread the beads onto the embroidery thread.

Multiple of 6 sts + 2 sts

Row 1 (RS): K1 [beaded thread yf, k3, beaded thread yb, k3] rep to last st, k1.

Row 2: P1 [p3, beaded thread yf, p3, beaded thread yb] rep to last st, p1.

Rep rows 1–2 as required.

Beaded i-cord

Beading stiffens an i-cord, but this is perfect for bag handles and edgings that do not require flexibility. This feature can also be used to help maintain a shape or form that has a tendency to sag, such as cushion edgings or hats. Thread the beads onto the yarn and use the slip stitch method (see page 209).

Cast on 5 sts.

Rows 1–3: K3, do not turn work and rep, starting with first st on the right again.

Row 4: K2, PB, k2.

Row 5: K.

Row 6: K1, PB, k1, PB, k1.

Row 7: K.

Rep rows 4–7.

Knit tightly

The first knitted stitch can become rather baggy as the i-cord grows, so it is important to pull the yarn across firmly in step 3 and to knit the first stitch tightly.

Beaded i-cord.

Knitting abbreviations

cm	centimetre
in	inch
K	knit
k2tog	knit two stitches together
mm	millimetre
P	purl
PB	place bead
p2tog	purl two stitches together
rep	repeat
RS	right side of work
st/sts	stitch/stitches
st st	stocking (stockinette) stitch
tbl	through the back of the loop/s
WS	wrong side of work.
yb	yarn back
yf	yarn forward
*	repeat instructions between * as many times as instructed
[ ]	repeat instructions between [ ] as many times as instructed

crochet techniques

There are a few more basic crochet stitches than there are in knitting, but once you have learned the principle of the crochet technique the more complicated stitches are just variations. The first stitch is a slip knot, just as in knitting (see page 203).

Tensioning the tail

If you do not create a tension on the tail end of yarn you will find that you are attempting to crochet in mid air. The tension of the tail is regulated by the left hand.

Use the middle finger and thumb of your left hand to pull gently on the tail end of yarn by pinching it just below the hook.

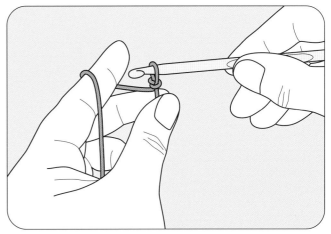

Foundation chain

Crochet nearly always starts with a series of chain stitches. These stitches form the basis of the work and are equivalent to the 'cast on' used in knitting. Chain stitches are also used to take the hook to the correct height at the end of a row in preparation for the following row. You may find that you struggle to keep an even tension (gauge) at first, but it is important to keep the chains even and not to make them too tight or loose. With practice this becomes easier.

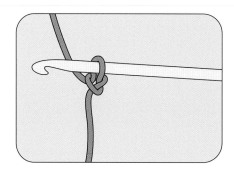

1 Place a slip knot on the hook and hold it in the right hand. Hold the yarn in the left hand, using your preferred method, and at the same time keep a good tension on the tail end of the yarn. With the yarn sitting to the reverse of the hook, turn the hook so that it is facing away from you.

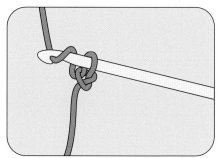

2 *Push the crochet hook against the yarn then rotate the hook in an anti-clockwise direction in order to catch the yarn around the hook, finishing the step with the hook facing down.

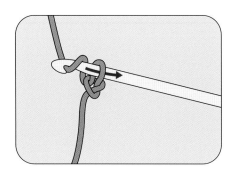

3 Draw the yarn through the slip knot or the loop on the hook. Note that the fingers tensioning the tail end of the yarn (see page 223) are not shown in steps 1–4 to keep the diagrams clear and simple, but the yarn should be kept under tension at all times.

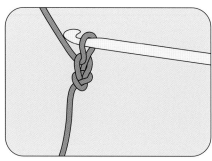

4 Rotate the hook in the opposite direction so that the hook is left facing up and the new stitch is resting on the hook.

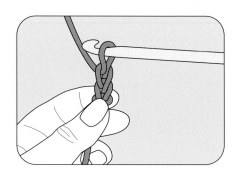

5 Continue to work from * in step 2 to create more chain stitches. You will need to reposition the tensioning fingers of your left hand every couple of stitches to ensure a good tension on the yarn.

Avoiding too tight chain stitches

When making chain (or subsequent stitches) you must make sure that each stitch is taken up onto the thicker part of the hook before starting the next one. If you work your stitches on the thinner part of the hook they will become tight, and you will struggle to place your hook into them on subsequent rows.

Turning chain

When creating crochet fabric in rows or rounds, before you commence your chosen stitch you will need to make a chain long enough to take you to the height of your next row. When working on a flat piece of crochet, the chains created at the end of a row are referred to as turning chains. The turning chain is usually counted as the first stitch of the row.

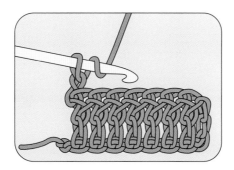

Double crochet (US single crochet)
1 chain.

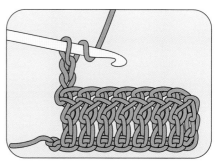

Half treble (US half double crochet)
2 chain.

Treble (US double crochet)
3 chain.

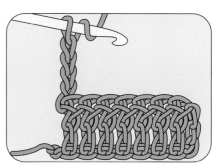

Double treble (US treble)
4 chain.

Working into the foundation chain

To create a crochet fabric, stitches are worked into the foundation chain to create the first row. Subsequent rows are then usually worked into the top of the previous row. The first row can be a little tricky because you will be working into the foundation chain and not into stitches.

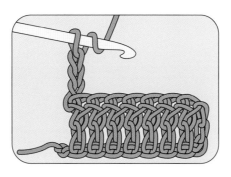

1 When working into the foundation chain, you can choose whether to place your hook into the top side of the chain, thus working over just one yarn.

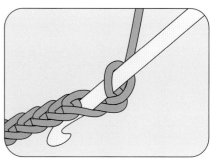

2 Or you may decide to place your hook into the lower part of the chain, thus working over two yarns.

Double crochet
(US single crochet)

This is probably the most commonly used crochet stitch; it is hard-wearing and durable and the fabric produced has a dense, sturdy feel.

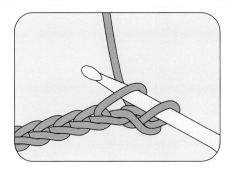

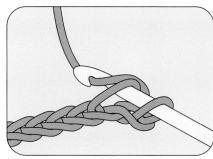

1 To work the first row, make a foundation chain to the required length, adding 1 chain to allow for turning. Insert your hook into the second chain below the hook.

2 *With the hook facing forward, pass the hook under the yarn so that this crosses over the hook.

3 Rotate the hook anti-clockwise until it faces down, in order to catch the yarn. Draw the yarn through the chain stitch so that there are two loops on the crochet hook.

4 By rotating the crochet hook as before, catch the yarn again and draw the yarn through both loops on the crochet hook.

5 One complete double crochet (US single crochet) stitch has been made. To continue, place the hook into the next foundation chain and repeat from * in step 2.

Rows of double crochet (US single crochet).

Treble (US double crochet)

This stitch produces a more open and softer fabric. The stitches produced appear like posts leading up from the previous row, and because it produces these longer stitches this is quite a speedy stitch to complete once it has been mastered.

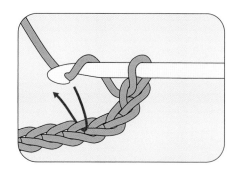

1 To work the first row, make a foundation chain to the required length, adding 3 chain to allow for turning. Wrap the yarn around the hook (from back to front) once. Insert the hook into the fourth chain below the hook.

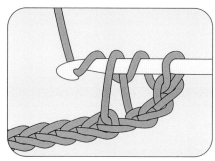

2 *With the hook facing forward, pass the hook under the yarn so that it crosses over the hook. Rotate the hook anti-clockwise until it faces down in order to catch the yarn.

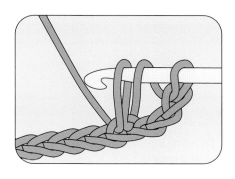

3 Draw the yarn through the chain stitch so that there are three loops on the crochet hook.

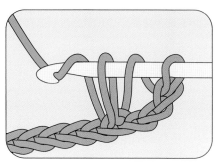

4 By rotating the crochet hook as before, catch the yarn again.

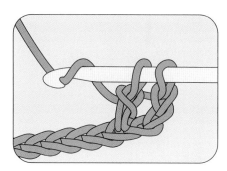

5 Draw the yarn through two loops on the crochet hook. Catch the yarn again and draw through the two remaining loops on the crochet hook.

6 One treble (US double crochet) made. Here the turning chain is counted as a stitch, so two stitches have been created. To continue, wrap the yarn around the hook, place the hook into the next foundation chain and repeat from *.

Rows of treble (US double crochet).

Double treble crochet (US treble)

This stitch is often used in conjunction with other stitches when making variegated patterns or motifs.

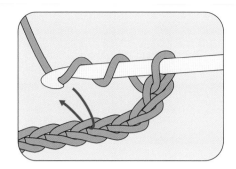

1 To work rows, make a foundation chain to the required length, adding 4 chain to allow for turning. Wrap the yarn around the hook twice; insert the hook into the 5th chain from the hook.

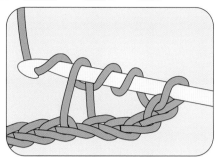

2 *With the hook facing forward, pass the hook under the yarn so that it crosses over the hook. Rotate the hook anti-clockwise until it faces down in order to catch the yarn.

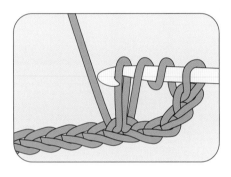

3 Draw the yarn through the stitch so that there are four loops on the crochet hook.

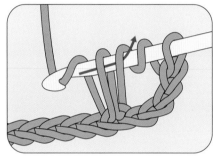

4 By rotating the crochet hook as before, catch the yarn again and draw through two of the loops on the crochet hook.

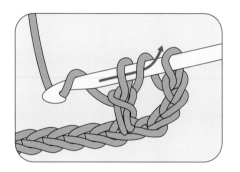

5 Catch the yarn again and draw through the next two loops on the crochet hook.

6 Catch the yarn again and draw through the remaining two loops on the crochet hook.

7 To continue, wrap the yarn around the hook twice, place hook into next chain, or as indicated by pattern instructions, and repeat from *.

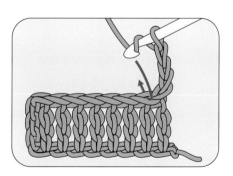

8 At the end of the row, chain 4 stitches and turn. The first double treble is worked into the second stitch to the left of the turning chain (penultimate stitch of the previous row). At the end of the row work the final stitch into the top of the turning chain of the previous row.

Beaded crochet cushions.

Rows of double treble crochet (US treble crochet).

Other stitches

Other crochet stitches are worked using the same basic technique; the difference is in how many times the yarn is wrapped around the hook and drawn through loops on the hook. The more times the yarn is wrapped the longer the stitch will be, and the more open the final fabric.

working in the round

Many crochet motifs are created by working in the round, which often means that there is no need to turn your work at the end of each row, so that you constantly have one side of the work facing you. To start your circular motif, you need to create a base of chain stitches to work around.

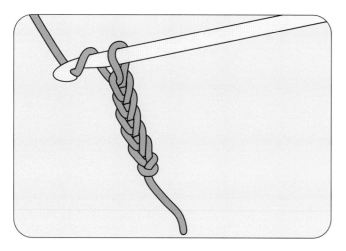

1 Make the required number of chain; the more chain that are made at the start, the larger the hole at the centre of the motif will be.

2 Join the chain using a slip stitch: to do this, insert the hook into the first chain made after the initial slip knot.

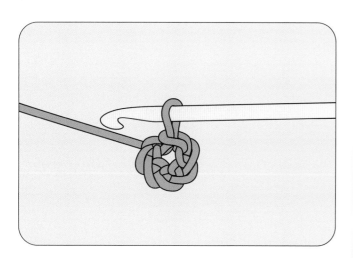

3 Wrap the yarn around the hook and bring through all loops on the hook. Tighten by pulling gently on the yarn.

adding beads to crochet fabric

Crocheting with beads is an age-old art that was particularly popular in the 18th and 19th centuries, when ladies made intricate crochet purses using very fine thread and tiny glass beads. Adding beads and sequins to your crochet can be really effective and is a relatively easy technique to achieve. Beads and sequins can be used in conjunction with one another to create some really exciting effects and can be placed randomly or to a predefined graph pattern.

Placing beads with double crochet (US single crochet)

You need to place beads when you have the wrong side of the fabric facing you, because they come out on the reverse. Think ahead, because you may need to turn your work to get a bead on the right side of your work.

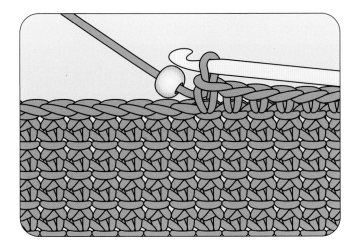

1 Work to where a bead is required. Slide the bead along the yarn so that it sits against the right side of the fabric. Put your hook through the next stitch.

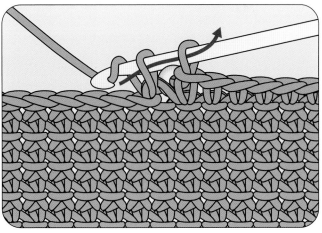

2 Wrap the yarn around the hook and bring it through the stitch. Wrap the yarn around the hook and complete the stitch, holding the bead in place while you do so.

beaded knitting and crochet

Bangle covered in beaded crochet.

Groups of beads

You can achieve some really nice effects by grouping more than one bead together. To do this, work as on page 231 but bring a group of beads (say 3 or 4) in place of a single bead.

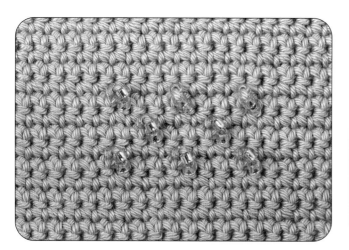

1 Double crochet (US single crochet) with several groups of beads.

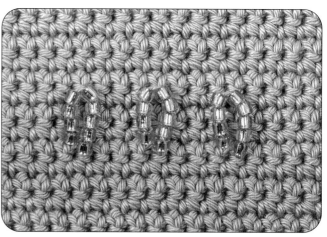

2 Bead loops worked on a background of double crochet (US single crochet).

Placing beads with treble crochet (US double crochet)

Again you need to place beads when you have the wrong side of the fabric facing you, because they come out on the reverse. Think ahead because you may need to turn your work to get a bead on the right side of your work.

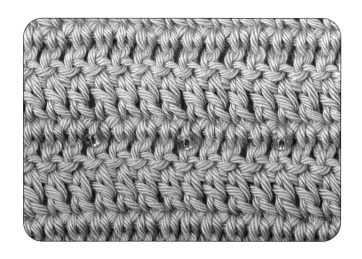

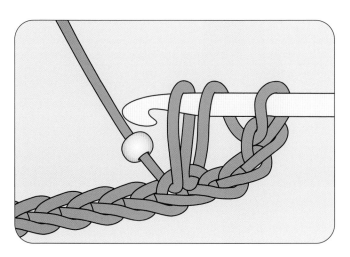

1 Work to where a bead is required. Wrap the yarn around the hook. Insert the hook into the next stitch and draw through the stitch so that 3 loops remain on the hook.

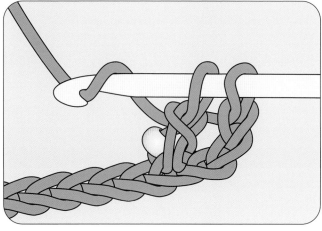

2 Slide the bead along the yarn so that it sits against the right side of the fabric. Complete the stitch, holding the bead in place while you do so.

Keeping beads in place

When placing beads within this stitch they could push through to the wrong side of the work because the stitch is fairly open. Make sure you make the stitch nice and tight each time you add a new bead.

Placing beads within a chain

This method also requires you to place the bead when you have the wrong side of the fabric facing you, because they come out on the reverse. Think ahead because you may need to turn your work to get a bead on the right side of your work. When placing beads or sequins within the chain they could push through to the wrong side of the work, so make sure you make the chain nice and tight.

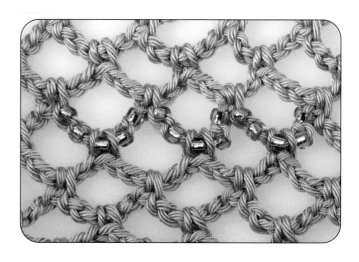

1 Work a chain until a bead/sequin is needed. Slide the bead/sequin along the yarn so it sits next to the hook.

2 Complete the chain by wrapping the yarn around the hook beyond the bead/sequin and draw it through the stitch.

Enlarging the hole

The holes in identical beads are not always exactly the same, particularly with smaller beads. If the hole in a bead is a little too small or has slightly roughened edges you may be able to enlarge or smooth it with the tip of a round needle file.

Adding beads with a crochet hook

This is a great technique for when you want to add beads to crochet without pre-threading them onto the yarn. The technique is a little fiddly, but is a fantastic method for adding beads as you go along. You will need a really tiny metal crochet hook to thread the beads onto the stitch. This method can be used for all crochet stitches, but it is more effective on those where the stitch is not too long.

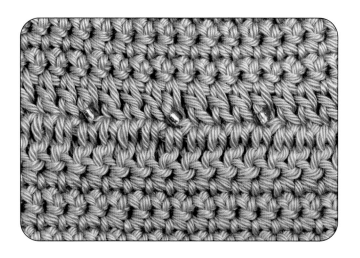

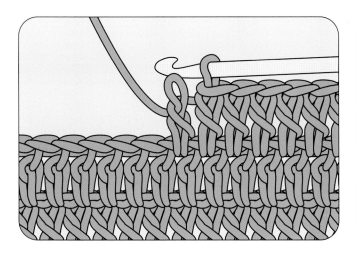

1 Work to where a bead is needed. Work the next stitch to the point where 2 loops remain on the hook. Carefully slip the yarn loop from your crochet hook, making sure not to pull on the yarn end to unravel.

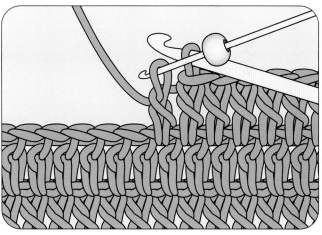

2 Push a bead onto the small crochet hook and catch the yarn loop with this hook. Push the bead from the crochet hook and onto the yarn loop.

3 Slip the yarn loop back onto the crochet hook and complete the stitch.

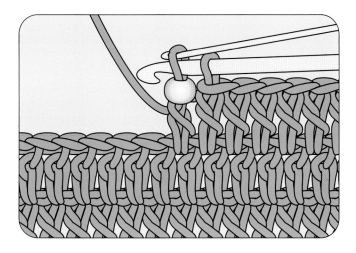

Following a chart

On a crochet chart, a bead is usually represented by a circle, sometimes shaded, over the top of the stitch symbol. Read the row where a bead is to be placed from left to right and the alternate row from right to left – this is because beads are placed when working a wrong side row.

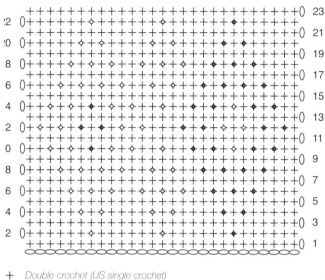

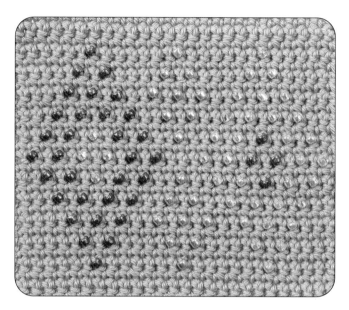

+ *Double crochet (US single crochet)*
○ *Chain*
◆ *Pink bead*
◇ *White bead*
◇ *Blue bead*

Most commonly used stitch symbols

Below is a chart showing the symbols for the most commonly used stitches.

Chain ○

Slip stitch ●

Double crochet (UK)
Single crochet (US) +

Half treble crochet (UK)
Half double crochet (US) T

Treble crochet (UK)
Double crochet (US)

Double treble crochet (UK)
Treble or Triple crochet (US)

Treble treble crochet (UK)
also referred to as Triple treble
Double treble (US)

Loop stitch

Recognizing groups of stitches

You may notice that some symbols are grouped to form 'V' shapes. These indicate a group of stitches that need to be worked into the same stitch or space. They will increase the number of stitches over a given distance.

The stitch symbols below indicate that either 2, 3, 4 or 5 stitches should be worked into one stitch or space on the previous row. Some may denote a special stitch, such as a Shell Stitch.

bead motif patterns

A couple of simple charts for beaded motifs on crochet, along with a beaded loop stitch and a beaded Granny Square. The motifs can be added when working any large enough piece of double crochet. Choose beads to suit the colour of the yarn and the overall project.

Star motif

Thread 24 beads onto the yarn.

Using 3mm hook work 19ch + 1 turning chain.

Row 1: 1dc into 2nd ch from hook, 1dc into each ch to end, turn. (19 sts)

Row 2: 1ch, 1dc into each ch to end, turn.

Row 3: 1ch, 1dc into each of first 9 sts, bead 1, 1dc into each st to end, turn.

Row 4: As row 2.

Row 5: 1ch, 1dc into each of first 8 sts, bead 1, 1dc into next st, bead 1, 1dc into each st to end, turn.

Row 6: As row 2.

Row 7: 1ch, 1dc into each of first 3 sts, [bead 1, 1dc into next st] 3 times, 1dc into next st, [1dc into next st, bead 1] 3 times, 1dc into each st to end, turn.

Row 8: As row 2.

Row 9: 1ch, 1dc into each of first 4 sts, bead 1, 1dc into each of next 9 sts, bead 1, 1dc into each st to end, turn.

Row 10: As row 2.

Row 11: 1ch, 1dc into each of first 6 sts, bead 1, 1dc into each of next 5 sts, bead 1, 1dc into each st to end, turn.

Row 12: As row 2.

Row 13: As row 9.

Row 14: As row 2.

Row 15: As row 7.

Row 16: As row 2.

Row 17: As row 5.

Row 18: As row 2.

Row 19: As row 3.

Work row 2 twice more.

Break off yarn.

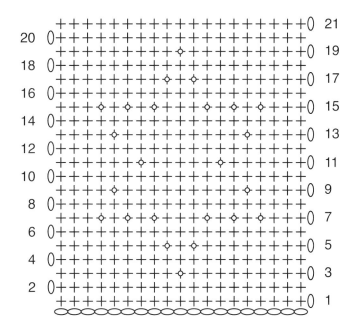

+ Double crochet (US single crochet)
⬭ Chain
♦ Bead position

Beaded star motif worked from the chart.

Heart beaded motif

Thread 12 beads onto yarn.

Make 13ch + 1 turning chain.

Row 1: 1dc into 2nd ch from hook, 1dc into each ch to end, turn. (13 sts)

Row 2: 1ch, 1dc into each st to end, turn.

Row 3: 1ch, 1dc into each of next 6 sts, bead 1, 1dc into each st to end, turn.

Row 4: As row 2.

Row 5: 1ch, 1dc into each of next 5 sts, bead 1, 1dc into next st, bead 1, 1dc into each st to end, turn.

Row 6: As row 2.

Row 7: 1ch, 1dc into each of next 4 sts, bead 1, 1dc into each of next 3 sts, bead 1, 1dc into each st to end, turn.

Row 8: As row 2.

Row 9: 1ch, 1dc into each of next 3 sts, bead 1, 1dc into each of next 5 sts, bead 1, 1dc into each st to end, turn.

Row 10: As row 2.

Row 11: As row 9.

Row 12: As row 3.

Row 13: As row 7.

Work row 2 another 3 times.

Break off yarn.

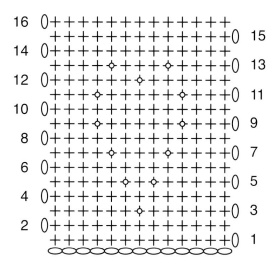

+   *Double crochet (US single crochet)*

⬭   *Chain*

✧   *Bead position*

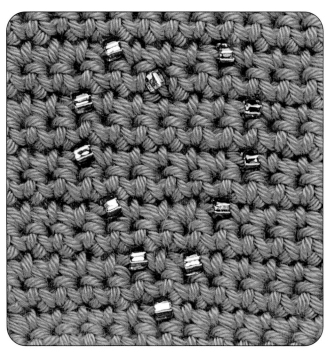

Beaded heart motif worked from the chart.

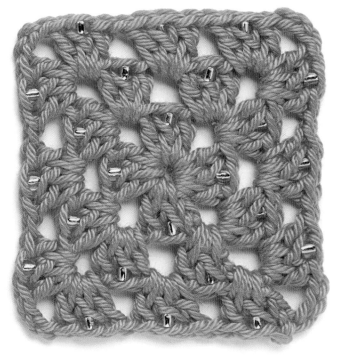

Beaded Granny square worked from the chart.

Granny square motif

Thread 24 beads onto the yarn.

Work 4ch, join ends together with ss to form a ring

Round 1: 6ch (counts as 1tr and 3ch), *[1tr, 1beadtr, 1tr] into ring, 3ch; rep from * twice more, 1tr, 1beadtr into ring, join with ss into third of 6-ch at beg of round. Ss into first ch3sp.

Round 2: 6ch (counts as 1tr and 3ch), [1tr, 1beadtr, 1tr] into first ch3sp, *1ch, [1tr, 1beadtr, 1tr, 3ch, 1tr, 1beadtr, 1tr] into next ch3sp; rep from * twice more, [1tr, 1beadtr] into first ch3sp, ss into third of 6-ch at beg of round. Ss into ch3sp.

Round 3: 6ch (counts as 1tr and 3ch), [1tr, 1beadtr, 1tr] into first ch3sp, *1ch, [1tr, 1bead tr, 1tr] into next ch1sp, [1tr, 1beadtr, 1tr, 3ch, 1tr, 1beadtr, 1tr] into next ch3sp; rep from * twice more, 1ch, [1tr, 1beadtr, 1tr] into next ch1sp, [1tr, 1beadtr] into first ch3sp, ss into third of 6ch at beg of round.

Break off yarn.

Loop stitch with bead

Foundation chain: multiples of 1 + 1.

Special Abbreviation: Loop Stitch (WS facing) = wrap yarn around left index finger to make a loop, insert hook into next st, draw through both threads of the loop; yarn over hook, draw through all loops to complete stitch.

Note: Beads need to be threaded onto the yarn before starting the pattern and should be incorporated into each loop.

Row 1: 1dc into 3rd ch from hook, 1dc into each ch to end, turn.

Row 2: Ch1 (counts as 1dc), skip 1 st, Loop Stitch into each st to end, 1dc into top of tch, turn.

Row 3: Ch1 (counts as 1dc), skip 1 st, 1dc into each st to end, 1dc into top of tch, turn.

Repeat Rows 1 and 2 to required length.

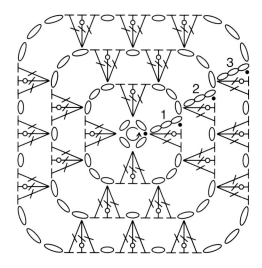

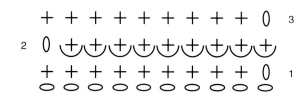

+ Double crochet (US single crochet)
O Chain
± Bead position

+ Double crochet (US single crochet)
O Chain
• Slip stitch

Ⱦ Treble crochet (US double crochet)

Ⱦ Bead position

Beaded loop stitch.

beaded edge patterns

Beads can add a lovely bit of sparkle to even the plainest piece of crochet. Remember that beads are crocheted into the fabric with the wrong side facing, so it may be an idea to do a base row along the edge of the piece first.

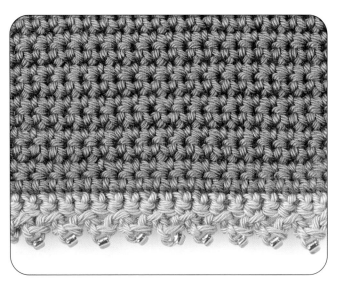

Placing a bead at the tip of a picot

Working from right to left along the edge of the fabric, work a foundation row of double crochet (US single crochet) stitches into the edge of the fabric. Work out how many beads are needed for the picot edge by dividing the stitch count by 2.

Foundation chain: Multiple of 2 sts.
Note: Beads need to be threaded onto the yarn before starting the pattern.

Row 1: Insert hook into back of first stitch on foundation row and work a slip stitch into it. *Make 3 ch, insert hook into back of third chain from hook (first of 3-ch just made) and work a slip stitch into it, 3ch catching a bead into chain on second of 3-ch, miss 1 st, ss into following st; rep from * to end of row.

Three-beaded edge

Working from right to left along the edge of the fabric, work a foundation row of double crochet (US single crochet) stitches into the edge of the fabric. Work out how many beads are needed for the edge by multiplying the stitch count by 3.

Foundation chain: Multiple of 3 sts.
Note: Beads need to be threaded onto the yarn before starting the pattern.

Row 1: 1dc, *slide 3 beads up to top of yarn, catch yarn beyond beads and complete the st; rep from *.

A selection of beaded crochet flowers.

Beaded loops

Working from right to left along the edge of the fabric, work a foundation row of double crochet (US single crochet) stitches into the edge of the fabric. Work out how many beads are needed for the edge by multiplying the stitch count by 3.

Foundation chain: Multiple of 3 sts.
Note: Beads need to be threaded onto the yarn before starting the pattern.

Work as for 3-beaded edge, using any number of beads to create the loops. Here we have used a varying number to create uneven loop lengths.

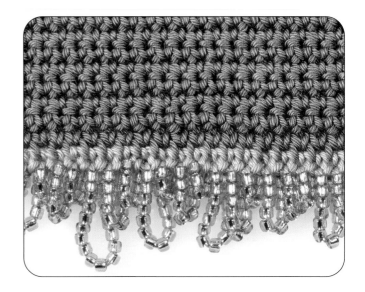

Beaded dash

Foundation chain: Multiple of 2 sts + 1 st (add 1 st for base chain).
Special Abbreviation: beaded-dtr = yrh, insert hook into next st, yrh, draw loop through, slide bead along yarn to base of hook, yrh, draw yarn through 2 loops, slide bead along yarn to base of hook, yrh, draw yarn through rem two loops.
Note: Beads need to be threaded onto the yarn before starting the pattern.

Row 1 (RS): 1tr into 2nd ch from hook, 1tr into each ch to end.
Row 2: 3ch (counts as 1 dtr), *1 beaded-dtr into next tr, 1 dtr in next tr; rep from * to end, turn.
Row 3: 1ss into front loop of each st to end of row.
Fasten off.

Crochet jewellery

The beaded dash and the beaded edgings on this and the previous page can be worked as separate pieces and made up into jewellery. The beaded dash could be an ideal alternative to knotting or braiding beads (see pages 189–195) into a bracelet, for instance.

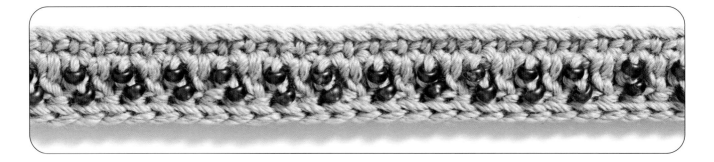

Crochet abbreviations

ch	chain
cm	centimetre
dc	double crochet (US single crochet)
dtr	double treble (US treble)
in	inch
mm	millimetre
PB	place bead
rem	remaining
rep	repeat
RS	right side of work
ss	slip stitch
st/sts	stitch/stitches
tch	turning chain
tr	treble (US double crochet)
WS	wrong side of work
yrh	yarn round hook
*	repeat instructions from * as many times as instructed
[ ]	repeat instructions between [ ] as many times as instructed

Crochet trims

Beaded crochet trims or motifs are very versatile – they can be stitched onto knitting or used to decorate sewn items just like purchased braid or motifs. If you make you own, you can choose the exact yarn colour and the beads to suit the item.

beaded embroidery

Many embroidery stitches can be worked to incorporate beads with very little change to how the basic stitch is worked. Single beads or strings of beads can be stitched onto fabric as highlights, or areas of fabric can be closely covered in beads using embroidery filling stitches.

choosing fabric and thread

Most types of fabric are suitable for beading – even patterned or embroidered fabrics can have beads added to highlight areas of the design. The fabric needs to be heavy enough to support the beads but not too stiff, which will make it difficult to work. Stretch fabrics can be beaded, but may need lightweight interfacing on the back to support the beads. Be aware of the laundering requirements for fabric, thread and beads – washing may not be an option for very complex beading or fabrics that shrink, but some beads may not stand up to dry cleaning chemicals very well.

If working embroidery stitches part of the stitching thread will show so use a standard embroidery thread. There are various types available, but stranded thread offers the option to use fewer strands for a finer thread when working with small beads. When sewing on single beads or couching, most of the thread will be covered by the bead itself, so you can use ordinary hand sewing threads.

choosing beads

Most types of beads can be used in beaded embroidery, as long as the hole is large enough to accommodate the thread. Avoid beads that are very large or heavy – except perhaps at the hem – because they may pull the fabric out of shape, or even pull a hole. Check that the beads you want to use do not have sharp edges anywhere that may cut the thread. As with knitted and crochet fabrics, plastic beads may melt if the item needs to be pressed and some wooden beads may not be colourfast.

As a general guide, use smaller beads with sewing than you would with knitting and crochet because the threads used tend to be finer – although this is by no means a hard-and-fast rule and using unexpected combinations often gives a more interesting result.

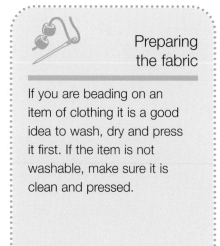

Preparing the fabric

If you are beading on an item of clothing it is a good idea to wash, dry and press it first. If the item is not washable, make sure it is clean and pressed.

starting off

These basic embroidery skills are used with all the stitches. Embroidery thread is usually thicker than normal sewing cotton, but the stranded type – which consists of six strands twisted together – can be used as it is or separated down into fewer strands if you need a thinner line.

Threading by hand

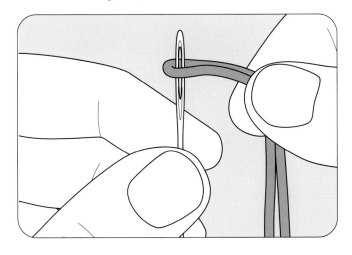

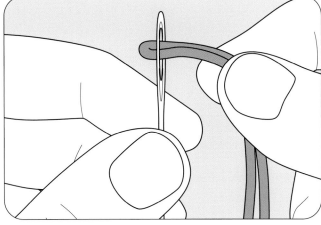

1 Double the thread a short distance from the needle and then fold it around the needle eye as shown.

2 Push the folded thread through the needle eye, holding the needle steady as you do so.

Threading with a needle threader

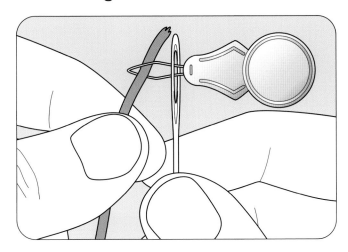

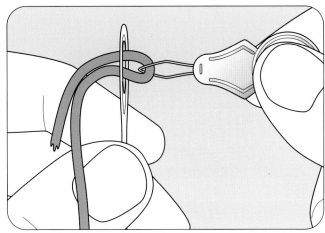

3 If using a needle threader, push the wire loop through the needle eye and then put the end of the embroidery thread through the wire loop.

4 Carefully pull the wire loop with the inserted thread back through the needle eye until the thread end is clear of the needle eye.

Using a hoop

When beading motifs you may find it easier to use an embroidery hoop to hold the fabric taut as you work.

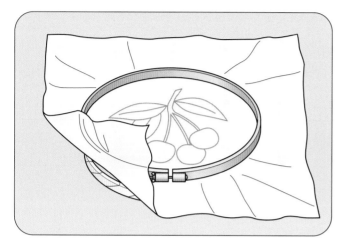

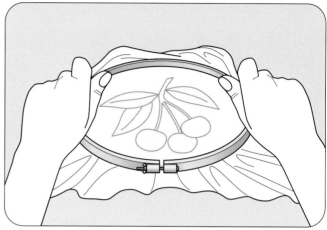

1 Bind the smaller ring with cloth tape and place it under the fabric. Place the larger ring over the fabric, centring the area you want to bead.

2 Push down on the larger ring. Pull the fabric around the edges until it is taut in the ring and then tighten the screw on the outer ring to hold everything in place.

Fastening the thread end

There are several different methods of fastening the thread end and which one you choose is up to you, although it may also depend on which embroidery stitch you are working.

Overstitching

Pull the threaded needle through the fabric from the back to the front, leaving a tail at the back 4cm (1½in) long. Begin stitching, holding the thread end at the back of the work so it is secured by the stitching. Trim off excess thread.

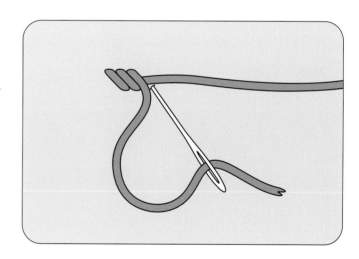

Knotting the end

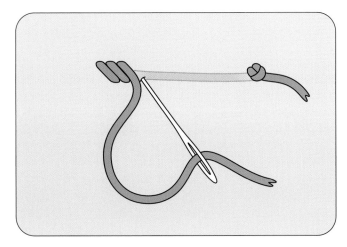

Make a knot at the end of the thread and pull the threaded needle through the fabric from front to back about 4cm (1½in) to the right of the first stitch. Bring the needle up to the front, working the stitches over the thread at the back. When the thread is secure, cut off the front knot and pull the tail to the back.

Waste knot

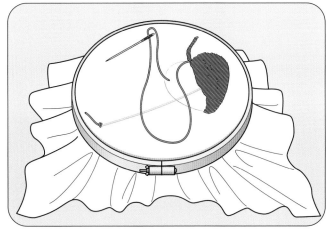

Make a knot at the end of the thread and pull the threaded needle through the fabric from front to back about 15cm (6in) away from the area of work. Bring the needle up to the front and work the stitches. To finish, cut off the knot and weave the tail into the back of the work.

Changing threads mid row

Come up at A. With a new thread in a new needle, come up at C. Hold the thread as shown, go down at B with the old thread and fasten off. Continue with the new thread.

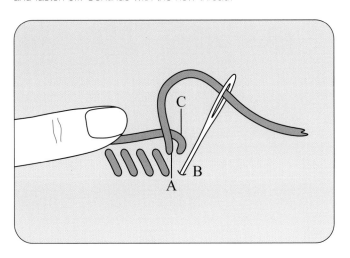

Finishing off

To finish a length of thread, take the needle and thread through to the back of the fabric and weave it in and out of three or four adjacent stitches. Pull the thread through the stitches gently.

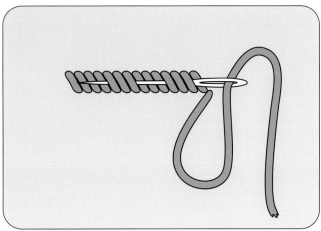

Basic stitching technique

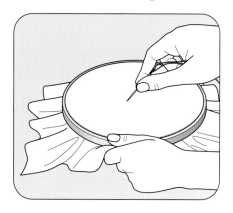

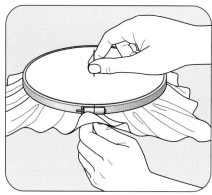

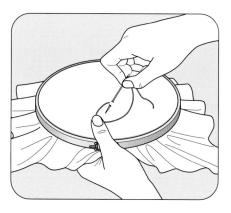

1 The stab method helps to give your stitching an even tension. Hold the hoop firmly and use a stabbing motion to prick the fabric surface with the needle.

2 Bring the needle to the back of the fabric, pulling the thread through gently. Then repeat the stabbing motion to come up on the right side of your work as shown.

3 When working looped stitches, use your non-stitching thumb to hold and guide the thread around the needle as you work. This will help to prevent the thread tangling or knotting.

Sewing single beads

To sew on a single bead, come up through the fabric and the bead, and then take the needle back down into the fabric close to the bead. Take a stitch under the fabric to the next bead position and repeat.

Couching

To sew several beads at once, come up through the fabric and thread a few beads onto the needle. Go down into the fabric at the end of the row of beads and take a small stitch to secure. To couch the line of beads, come up at A, over the thread between two beads, and down at B. Repeat every three or four beads.

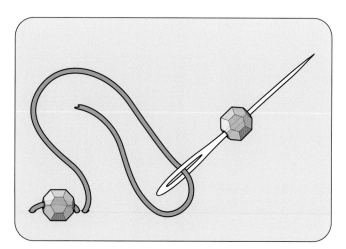

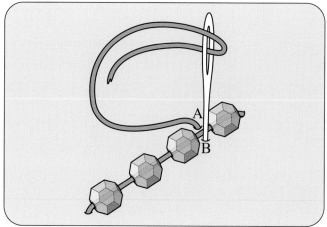

beaded embroidery stitches

The following are a few examples of embroidery stitches with beading added to show some possibilities. A specialist embroidery book will give additional stitches, most of which can have beads added either while working the stitch or by adding them afterwards.

Lines of beads

These stitches are ideal to create borders or to add a line of beading to highlight around the edges of a motif.

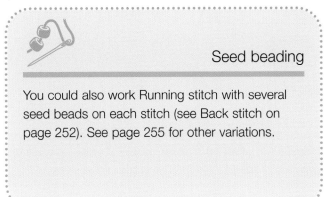

Seed beading

You could also work Running stitch with several seed beads on each stitch (see Back stitch on page 252). See page 255 for other variations.

Running stitch

This stitch can be worked as a single line or as rows of lines to fill an area. If worked as rows of lines, the stitches can be arranged in columns (perhaps with a different colour bead for each column) or staggered to create a brickwork pattern.

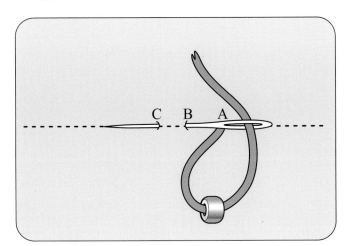

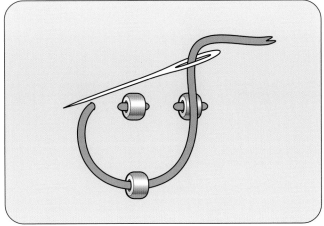

1 Come up at A and add a bead to the thread. Go down at B and then up at C. Pull the thread through gently so the fabric does not pucker.

2 Continue stitching in this way – the stitches and gaps between can be the same size, or can vary in size to create different effects.

Back stitch

This stitch can be used to create a continuous line of beading, either as a straight line or around curving shapes.

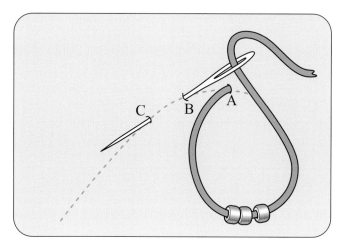

1 Bring the thread through at A and pick up three seed beads. Go down at B and then up at C. Pull the thread through gently so the fabric does not pucker.

2 Pick up another three seed beads and go down again at B and then up at D. Pull the thread through gently.

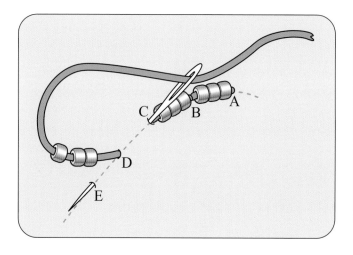

3 Pick up another three seed beads and go down again at C and then up at E. Continue in this way, picking up three beads for each stitch.

Trying options

Experiment with different effects – you could bead each stitch in a different colour, or add a slightly larger bead as the middle one of the three.

Feather stitch

On this stitch you need to pick up an even number of seed beads for each V-shape loop, and make the stitch at the base of the V between the two centre beads. See page 254 for variations on this stitch.

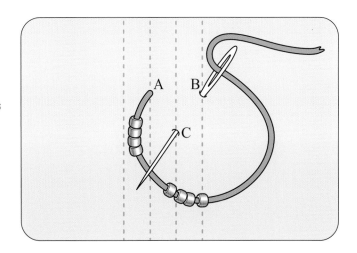

1 Come up at A and thread on eight seed beads. Go down at B and up at C, carrying the beaded thread under the needle point from left to right so the needle falls between beads four and five.

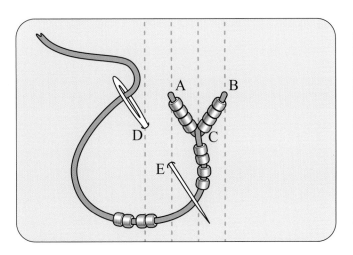

2 Bring the needle through at C and thread on another eight seed beads. Go down at D and up at E, carrying the beaded thread under the needle point from right to left so the needle falls between beads four and five.

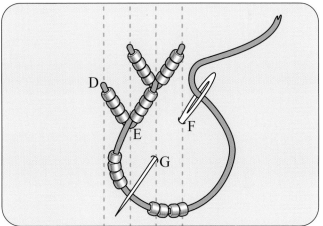

3 Carry on in this way, working V stitches on alternate sides and threading on eight seed beads for each stitch. If you make longer stitches you may need more than eight beads, but don't make the stitches too long.

Double feather stitch

A variation of Feather stitch, this stitch creates more feathery branches. Again you need to pick up an even number of seed beads for each V-shape loop and carry the beaded thread under the needle point each time so the needle falls in the middle of the group of beads.

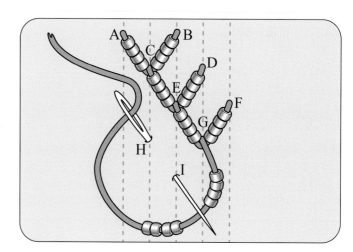

1 Come up at A and thread on eight seed beads. Go down at B and up at C (between beads four and five) taking the thread over the stitch, thread on another eight seed beads, go down at D and up at E taking the thread over the stitch, thread on another eight seed beads, go down at F and up at G taking the thread over the stitch, thread on another eight seed beads. Now begin working back across by going down at H and up at I.

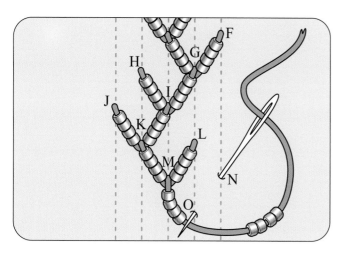

2 Follow the lettering sequence to make two V-shape stitches to the left and then make two to the right again, each time picking up eight seed beads. Try to keep the V-shapes an even size – it helps to draw five parallel lines in an erasable marker before you begin, so you have guidelines to keep the stitching straight.

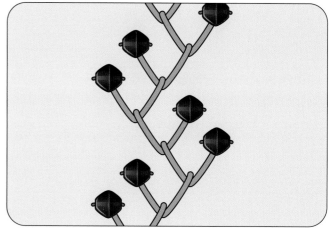

3 An alternative way of beading Double feather stitch is to work the stitch without any seed beads and then to stitch a small bead at the end of each outer arm. This single bead can be slightly larger and more ornate than the seed beads because it does not have to fit onto the embroidery thread.

Cordonnet stitch

Also known as Whipped running stitch, this stitch can be beaded in several ways to achieve different effects.

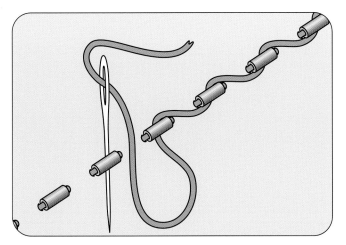

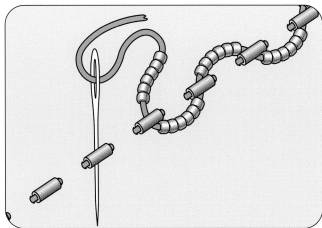

1 Work a row of Running stitch (see page 251), threading a single bugle bead onto each stitch as you work. Choose a bead that is about the same length as the stitch for best results. Using a thread that contrasts with the bead colour, whip in and out of each stitch as shown. Alternatively, the running stitch can be left plain and the whipping thread seed beaded.

2 As another option, bead both threads by working the Running stitch with bugle beads and threading seed beads onto the whipping stitch. Here the whipping is also worked in a slightly different way – in step 1 it was worked down through each stitch, while here it is worked down through one stitch and up through the next alternately.

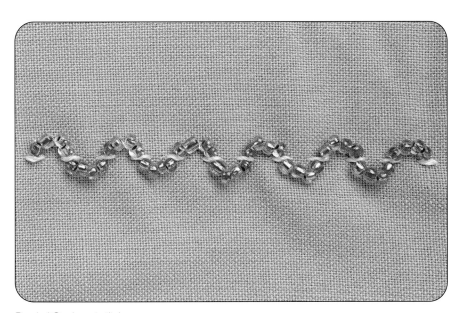

Beaded Cordonnet stitch.

Blocks of beading

These stitches can be used to fill in areas of fabric with beading in a decorative pattern.

Seed stitch

This filling stitch, which is also known as Speckling stitch or Seeding stitch, just consists of tiny straight stitches, usually of an even length, that are placed randomly at contrasting angles.

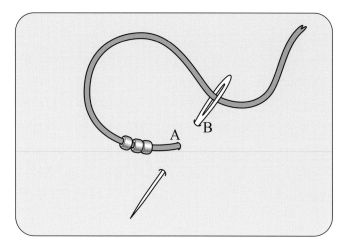

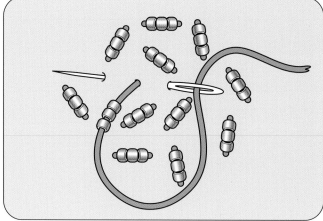

1 Bring the thread through at A and pick up three seed beads. Go down at B and then up where you want the next stitch to start. Pull the thread through gently so the fabric does not pucker.

2 Pick up another three seed beads for each stitch and work the stitches at random angles to fill the motif shape or background area.

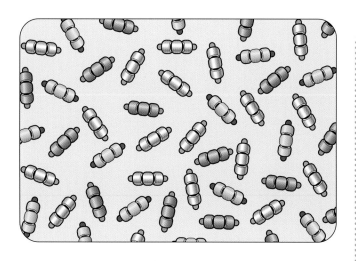

3 As a variation, you can work over the area using different threads in turn, with different colour beads on each strand.

Watching the weight

Remember that beads can be quite heavy – particularly glass beads – and even seed beads can add weight if there are enough of them. Try to place areas of close beading where they will not be able to pull the fabric out of shape.

Beading at the hem is a wonderfully decorative way of preventing the hem from blowing upwards and will help a garment hang well.

Darning stitch

Also known as Tacking stitch or Damask stitch, this stitch is best worked with seed beads, with three or four threaded onto each stitch depending how long you want to make it.

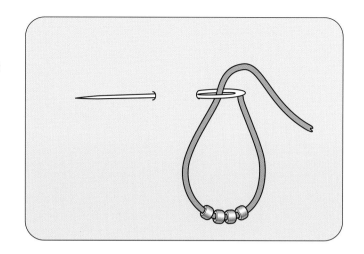

1 Thread the needle in and out of the fabric to create a single row of horizontal straight stitches, threading three or four seed beads onto the thread for each stitch. Work from right to left, keeping the stitching even.

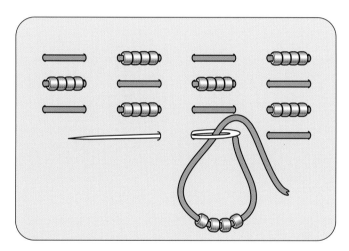

2 Rows of stitching can be worked parallel to each other so the stitches sit in columns – and you can either bead every stitch or every other stitch to achieve different effects. Try working alternate rows or columns in different colour beads.

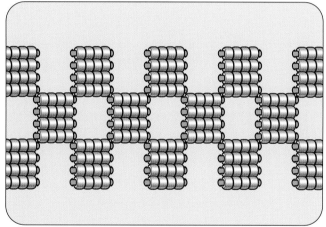

3 Blocks of close stitching could also be staggered to create a basket weave effect. Again, you could bead each block or leave some unbeaded – but be aware of the weight of many beads in one small area.

Basket satin stitch

Also known as Basket filling stitch, this is a variation of Darning stitch in which the blocks of stitching are worked at right angles to each other.

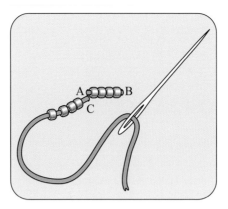

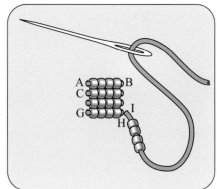

1 Come up at A and thread on four seed beads. Go down at B and up at C, threading on another four seed beads for the next stitch.

2 Complete four stitches, threading on four seed beads for each stitch to make a block of horizontal straight stitches, finishing by going down at H. Come up again at I and thread on four seed beads ready to work the next block.

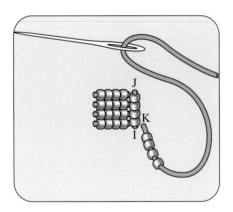

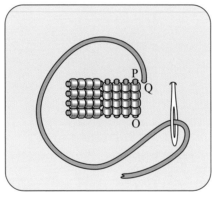

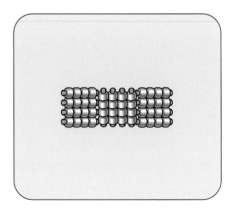

3 Repeat the block of four stitches, this time working them vertically. Keep the stitches evenly spaced.

4 Make the last stitch of the block by coming up at O, threading on four beads and going down at P. Come up again at Q and thread on four seed beads ready to work the next horizontal block.

5 Work alternate horizontal and vertical blocks. On the next row, stagger the blocks so a vertical block comes below a horizontal one and vice versa. Make sure the stitches are of equal length to keep the blocks regular.

Cloud filling stitch

This trellis stitch is traditionally used in crewelwork embroidery but can be adapted very easily as a beadwork stitch. Make sure the bead has a large enough hole to accommodate the thread, which goes through most beads twice.

Creating the lattice

The beads in the lattice can be the same colour as the thread so they just add texture, or they can be in a contrasting colour.

Choose small to medium beads – large beads will overpower the stitching.

The spacing of the beads will set the size of the lattice, which needs to be reasonably open but not set too widely apart.

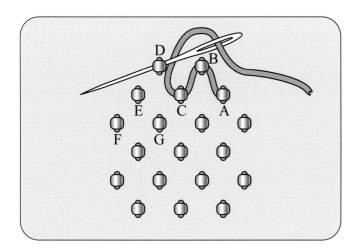

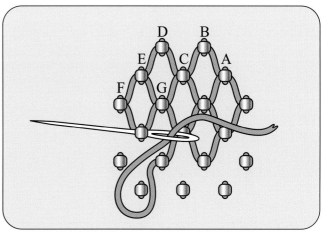

1 Stitch on small beads spaced out in staggered rows as shown. These beads can be sewn on with ordinary sewing thread, which is finer, because it does not need to show and this will leave more space for the double strand of embroidery thread to create the lattice. Using embroidery thread, begin to weave up and down under the beads as shown.

2 Continue weaving backwards and forwards across each row to complete the lattice. Do not pick up the background fabric when weaving under the beads.

Bead highlights

Single beads can also be used at key points on
an embroidery stitch to add sparkle or texture.

Blanket stitch

This stitch is generally used as an edging, but can be worked in
the middle of the fabric as a decorative stitch. It can be beaded
in several ways.

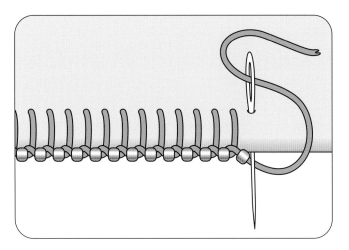

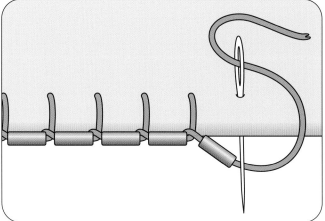

1 To work the basic stitch, bring the thread out of the fabric
at the edge. Go back down vertically the distance the
vertical bars are to be and then bring the needle under the fabric
until the tip is past the edge. Take the thread under the tip of the
needle to create the horizontal bar and pull the needle through.
To add a bead on the horizontal bar, thread on before making the
vertical stitch and push it into position before taking the thread
around the tip of the needle.

2 As an alternative, each horizontal bar can hold one bugle
bead, creating a line of beading that can be particularly
effective along an edge. Push the bead into position before taking
the thread under the tip of the needle.

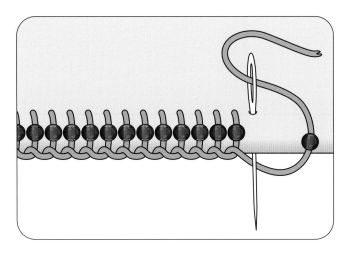

3 Another alternative is that each vertical bar can hold one
bead that will sit on the surface. Take the thread under the
tip of the needle, holding the bead to one side. Push the bead
into place as you complete the stitch.

Chevron stitch

This stitch is made up of two diagonal lines worked in opposite directions and joined across top and bottom with small horizontal stitches, which can easily be beaded. The instructions here are for using single bugle beads on the horizontal stitches, but you could substitute several seed beads on each stitch.

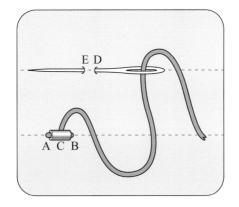

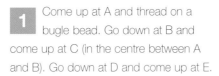

1 Come up at A and thread on a bugle bead. Go down at B and come up at C (in the centre between A and B). Go down at D and come up at E.

2 Thread on a bugle bead. Go down at F and come up at D (in the centre between E and F) ready to begin the next diagonal stitch down.

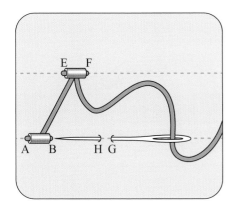

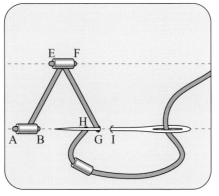

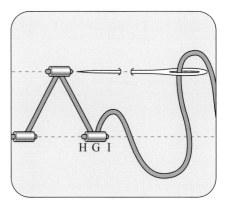

3 Cross down and insert at G and then come up at H.

4 Thread on a bugle bead. Go down at I and come up at G (in the centre between H and I) ready to begin the next diagonal stitch up.

5 Repeat the stitching sequence along the row. As an alternative, the diagonal stitches can also be threaded with seed beads.

Combining stitches

For a more complex design you can combine several different embroidery stitches, all beaded or a mixture of beaded and unbeaded stitches. Bead highlights also look great added to fabric motifs – see page 269 for an example.

beaded embroidery

Zigzag stitch

This stitch is made up of alternate upright and diagonal stitches, which need to be worked in two passes. Draw guidelines to keep the stitching straight.

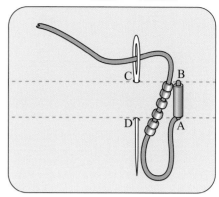

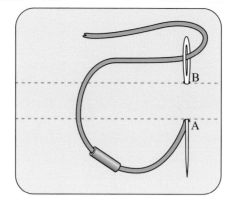

1 Come up at A, thread on a bugle bead, go down at B and then come back up at A. Pull the thread through gently so the bead sits against the fabric.

2 Thread on up to six seed beads (depending on the length of the stitch) and then go down at C to make the diagonal stitch and up at D, directly below C.

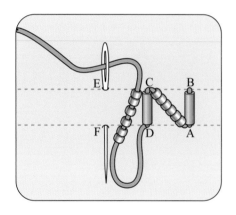

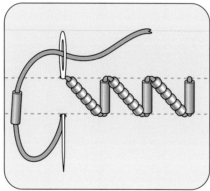

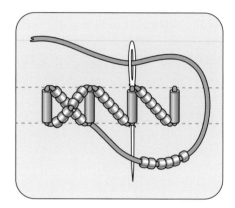

3 Repeat steps 1 and 2, threading on a bugle bead for all the vertical stitches and a number of seed beads for each diagonal stitch.

4 Continue right to the end of the line to form a zigzag pattern as shown. This part of the stitch could also work as a stand alone beading design.

5 On the return slope the diagonal stitches in the opposite direction, threading on seed beads as before, but taking the vertical stitches through the fabric behind each bugle bead.

Fly stitch

This very simple single stitch, which is also known as Y stitch or Open loop stitch, can be scattered at random, or worked in lines or in staggered rows, either horizontally or vertically.

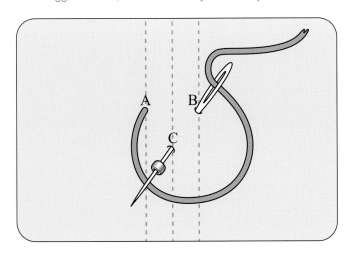

Extra beads

For additional interest the arms of the V-shape stitch could also be seed beaded – see Feather stitch on page 253. Also consider just adding a bead to the tip of each arm – see the alternative version of Double feather stitch on page 254.

1 Come up at A, go down at B and come up again at C, keeping the needle over the top of the working thread. Thread on a small bead.

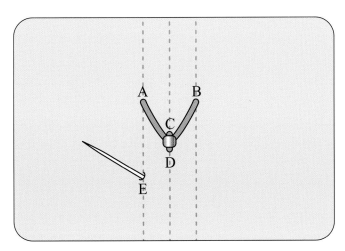

2 Go down at D, forming a small straight stitch holding a bead to tie down the loop. Come up a short distance away to begin the next stitch.

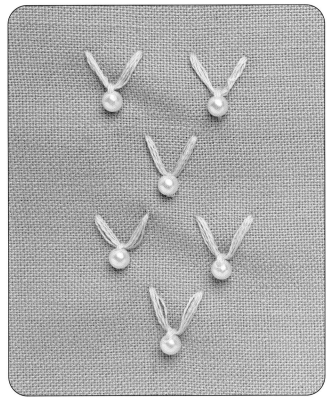

Sample of beaded Fly stitch.

Guilloche stitch

This stitch looks complex but is worked in several easy stages. It is based on architectural ornamentation and is used to create a decorative band. As in Cordonnet stitch (see page 255) the whipping threads could also be seed beaded.

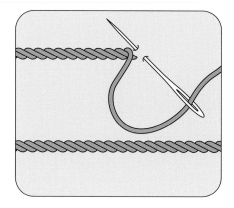

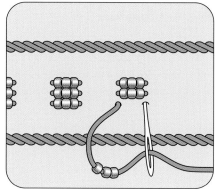

1 Work two parallel lines of stem stitch as shown, using unbeaded embroidery thread – although you could also add a single seed bead to each stitch for some extra sparkle.

2 Between the lines, work evenly spaced vertical bands, each made up of three small horizontal straight stitches holding three seed beads. Alternatively, you could thread a single bugle bead on each stitch. Keep the beading fairly loose to allow room behind for the whipping threads.

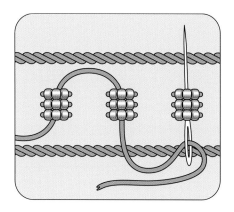

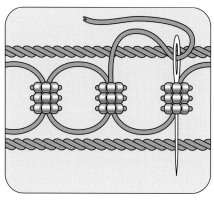

3 Lace the first whipping thread through the vertical bands, alternately up and down as shown. Be careful not to pick up the background fabric behind the beads.

4 Repeat in the opposite direction. If you choose, you can use a contrasting colour thread for extra interest in the design.

5 Traditionally, a French knot is stitched in the centre of each circle of the design, but this can be replaced with a single small bead in each space.

beaded fringing

Embroidered fabrics can be edged with beaded fringing in different designs, ranging from simple bead strings to quite complex designs.

Simple bead fringing

Beaded fringes can be long or short, colourful or muted; it depends on your project and the effect you want to achieve.

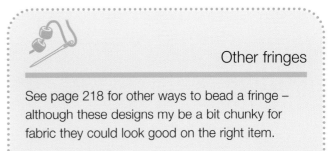

Other fringes

See page 218 for other ways to bead a fringe – although these designs my be a bit chunky for fabric they could look good on the right item.

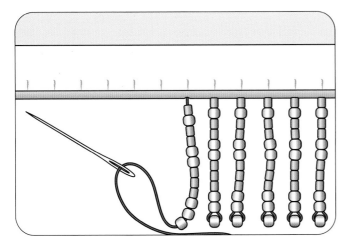

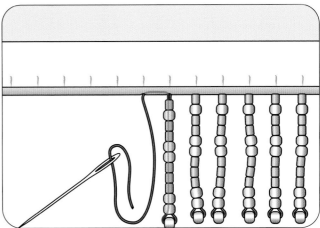

1 Cut a strip of low tack tape the length of the edge to be fringed and make evenly spaced marks along one edge to establish the distance between each strand of fringe. Stick the tape to the reverse of the fabric. Bring the needle out through the edge of the fabric at the first marked point. Pick up the beads for one strand of fringe.

2 Skipping the last bead so it becomes an anchor bead (see page 87), take the needle back up through the remaining beads. Pull until the first bead sits next to the edge of the fabric. Take the needle through the fabric to the next marked point and repeat the process. Fringing grows surprisingly quickly, so a fringed edge can be achieved quite fast.

Coral fringe

This wonderful fringe is called coral or branching fringe and creates a dense texture very quickly.

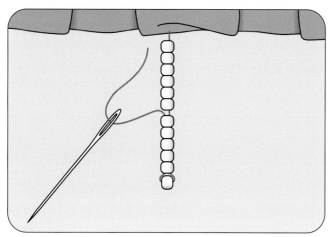

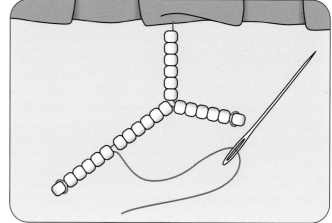

1 Thread up a needle with 90cm (1yd) of thread and make a couple of stitches at one bottom corner edge of the hem edge to secure. Thread on about 12 size 10 seeds. Use the bottom bead as an anchor bead (see page 87), and pass the needle up through five beads.

2 Thread on around 12 more seeds. Once more use the last bead threaded as an anchor bead, and pass the needle back up through five of the beads above it. Make a final branch in the same way.

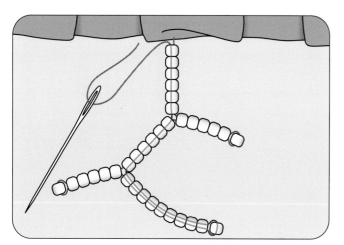

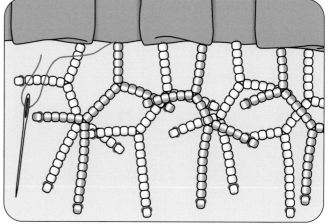

3 On the final branch, pass the needle all the way up to the top of the stem, bypassing the branches, and pull until the beading is firm but not too tight or the strand will not hang correctly. Make a stitch at the top to secure; then move on to another spot 1cm (½in) away, passing the needle along inside the fabric edge.

4 Make another stitch to secure, and make a second fringe strand. Continue all the way along the edge, varying the length and quantity of the branches on some of the strands. Finish off the thread at the end.

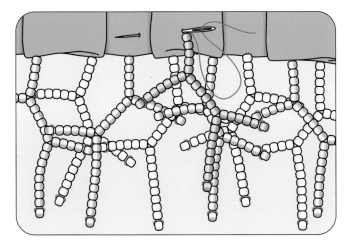

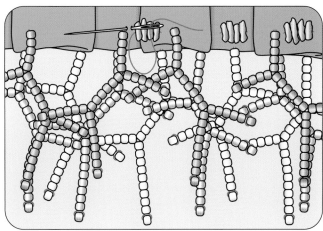

5 For the second row of the fringe, continue creating branches in exactly the same way about 1cm (½in) above the first row, but use delicas and colour-lined beads. Be careful not to sew through to the back of the fabric – keep the stitching between the layers of the hem.

6 To create coral clumps so the fringe is more visually a part of the fabric edge, thread on about four coral twigs and make a stitch to secure them on the fabric edge between two strands. Repeat between each pair of strands.

The technique of coral fringing can also be used to create stunning jewellery.

beaded embroidery

Pattern fringe

This fringe is almost as easy and fast to work as the simple fringe on page 265, but the beading creates an interesting and elegant design.

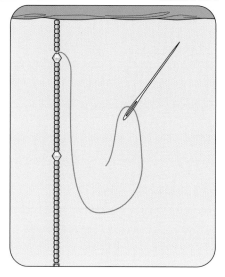

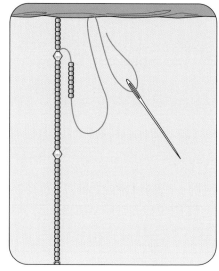

1 Bring the needle through the edge of the hem where the trim is to start. Pick up seven seed beads, one crystal bead, 20 seed beads, one crystal, 24 seed beads. Skip the last bead so it becomes an anchor bead and take the needle back through the last groups of beads, bringing it out above the first crystal bead.

2 Pick up eight seed beads and then, from front to back, make a tiny stitch through the hem 1cm (½in) along from where the first strand of the fringe emerges.

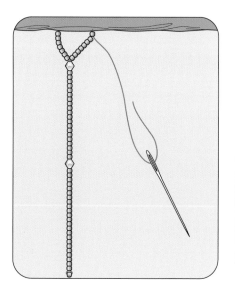

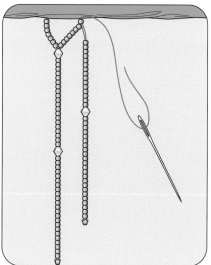

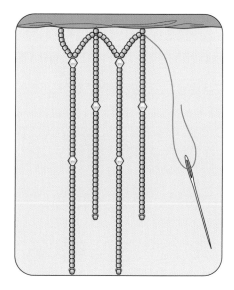

3 Take the needle back through the last bead (bead eight), ready to begin the next section of fringe.

4 Pick up 15 seed beads, one crystal bead and 24 seed beads. Skipping the last bead, take the needle back through all the beads and bring it out above bead eight from step 3.

5 Make a tiny stitch through the hem in the same place as the stitch made in step 2. Take the needle back through the last bead (bead eight), ready to begin the next section of fringe. Repeat the steps along the entire hem and then secure the thread end (see page 249).

beaded motifs

Beaded motifs can be created by adding beads to printed or woven motifs that are already on the fabric, or by creating a new motif from scratch on plain fabric.

Beaded fabric pattern

Damask fabric lends itself to embroidery as you have a pattern already there that you can enhance, using assorted small beads to greater effect.

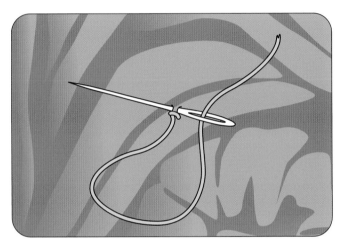

1 Look at the material and decide what motifs will be best enhanced by bead work – choose large distinct areas such as big flowers. Thread up a needle with 90cm (1yd) of fine beading thread and make a couple of little stitches to secure.

2 To create angled bugle outlines, which are best used for thick stems and leaves, thread on a bugle, and pass the needle back through the fabric so that it emerges about halfway along the side of the bead.

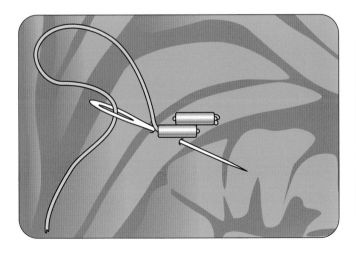

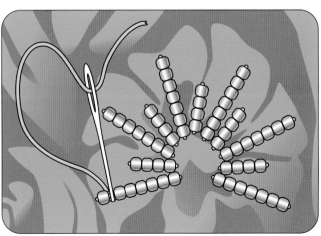

3 Thread on another bugle bead and place it so that it lies parallel to the first. Pass the needle down and up through the fabric again, halfway down the second bugle bead. Repeat as necessary to bead the section of motif.

4 To create seed bursts in the centre of a flower, couch (see page 250) alternate lengths of seven and four seed beads in a star burst pattern.

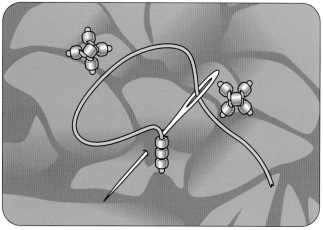

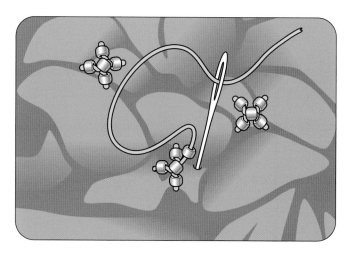

5 To create scattered beaded buds, thread on three seed beads. Pass the needle down through the fabric to emerge at right angles under the row of beads.

6 Thread a seed then pass the needle through the centre bead of the three, pulling it at an angle. Add on another seed opposite, then pass the needle down through the fabric.

Beaded motif on a brocade scarf.

7 Continue embellishing until you are happy. It is better to embellish fewer motifs in a denser way than to spread beads too thinly over a large area. Secure the thread firmly by making a few tiny stitches in an inconspicuous place.

Lazy daisy stitch

The number of beads on each lazy daisy petal will vary depending on how large you want the finished flower to be.

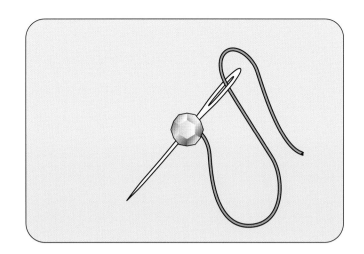

1 Sew on a large bead or crystal, such as a sparkling diamanté gem, to make a centre for the flower.

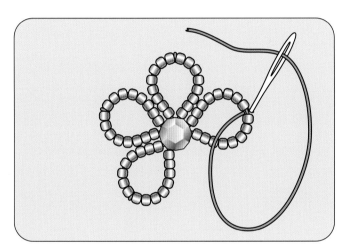

2 Bring the needle up next to the centre bead and thread on about 16 seed beads. Take the needle back down right next to where it came out and then up again a short distance away, catching the centre of the beaded loop under the tip of the needle. Take a tiny stitch over the loop to secure it in place, and then bring the needle back out next to the centre bead to make the next petal.

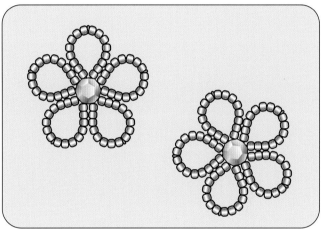

3 Continue working petals around the centre gem in the same way, to create the flower. As many beaded flowers as you like can be scattered at random over the area.

Using purchased trims

Beaded trims can be purchased ready-made, which will save time if you need a fast result or if you want large amounts of beaded trim.

Hand stitching trims

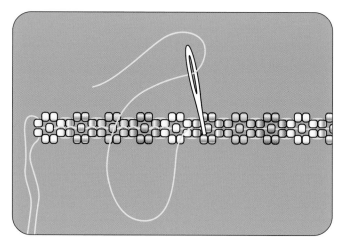

1 Pull a few beads off the end of the trim thread so you begin with a complete pattern repeat, leaving the thread ends hanging free. Use a fine sewing needle and sewing thread to match the trim thread. Bring the needle up beside or between the beads of the trim, take a stitch over it, and pull the thread so it slips between the beads. Bring the needle to the front again further along the trim and repeat.

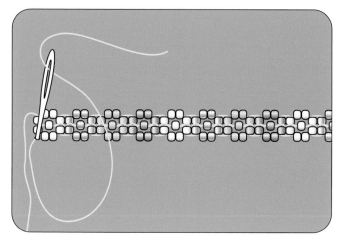

2 When the trim is securely attached, thread a needle with the ends of bead trim thread, take them to the back of the fabric and secure with a couple of small stitches. Beads do not need to be confined to evening wear – even jeans look better with a beaded trim.

Beaded trims are available in many different designs.

Machine stitching a beaded fringe

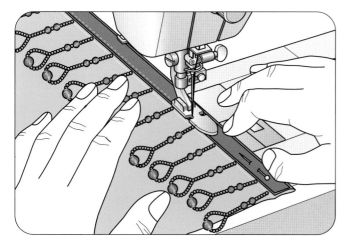

1 Turn under and press a double hem slightly wider than the fabric or ribbon band along the top of the fringe. Open the first fold of the hem and pin the band to it on the right side of the fabric. Using a zip foot, machine stitch the band to the hem, stitching close to the fringed edge.

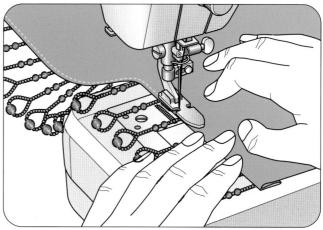

2 Fold the hem up and, working on the right side of the fabric and using the marks on the machine bed to guide you, machine stitch close to the top of the hem position, stitching the top of the band in position at the same time.

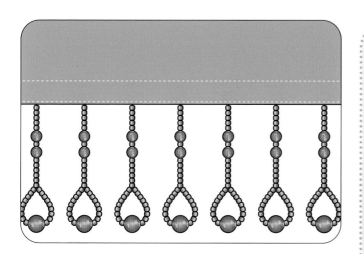

3 Purchased beaded fringe trim works equally well on home furnishing items and on wearable accessories.

Beaded fringing

Fringing with beads is available from good sewing stores or on the Internet. It is worth buying good quality because the cheaper examples may use inferior thread that breaks so the beads fall off. It can be expensive – but even a short length will add a great effect to the right project.

cardmaking with beads

Embroidery combined with beads in different shapes can also be used in cardmaking to add colour and texture in a variety of different ways.

Beaded card edges

Many of the beaded embroidery stitches given in the previous pages will work equally well if stitched on thin card instead of paper. Beading along an edge is a great way to finish most card designs, but make sure the beads are not too large or they may make holes in the envelope.

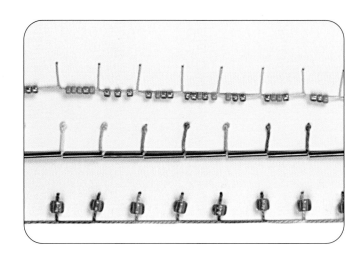

Beaded Christmas tree

The beads on this card are used to create the impression of baubles on the Christmas tree. Use small flat beads or the card will be too bulky.

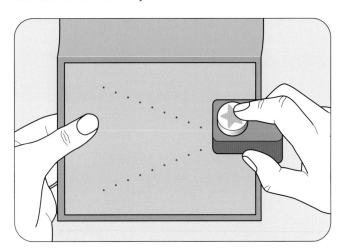

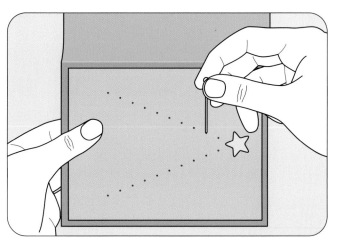

1 Draw a triangle for the Christmas tree shape on a piece of tracing paper and mark the stitching holes evenly spaced down each side. Lay the tracing paper over the front of the card blank as a guide and punch out a star at the top of the tree.

2 Using a pin, pierce holes through the front of the card at each of the stitching holes marked on the sides.

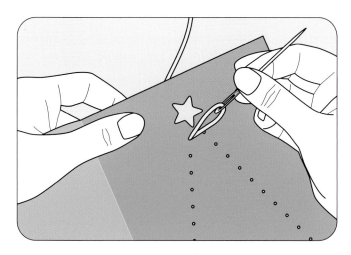

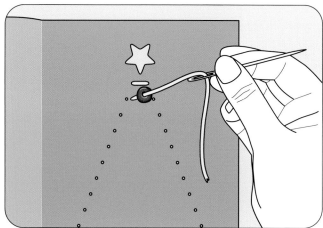

3 Thread a needle with a long length of embroidery thread and tie a knot at one end. Push the needle through the top left-hand hole, from back to front, and pull the thread through right up to the knot.

4 Take the needle down through the top right-hand hole to make the first stitch. Bing it back up through the next left-hand hole, thread on the first bead, then push the needle back down through the parallel right-hand hole.

Finishing inside

The stitching inside may look a bit messy if you are not careful. To cover it you could line the inside of the card just behind the tree.

5 Continue, threading one or more beads onto each stitch until the tree is complete. Fasten off the thread on the back. With the card closed, glue a star sequin through the star aperture to the back inside of the card.

Beaded window card

An open window in a card can be decorated with a string of assorted flat beads on fine wire or coloured thread.

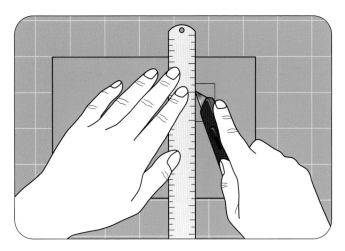

1 Take a 17 x 12cm (6¾ x 4¾in) pre-cut card blank and use a ruler and pencil to measure and lightly mark a rectangle for the aperture 4 x 2cm (1½ x ¾in) in the upper half of the front. Open out the card and place it on a cutting mat. Use a craft knife and steel ruler to cut out the aperture.

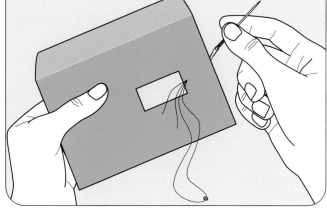

2 Thread a needle with embroidery thread and slide on a bead. Slip the free end of the thread through the eye of the needle as well, so the bead sits in a loop. Align the two thread ends in the needle. Push the needle through the card from front to back just above centre top of the aperture; pull through so the bead sits against the card.

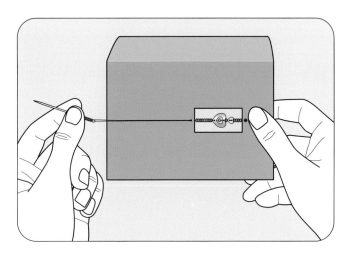

3 Thread a selection of small beads onto the needle, followed by a larger flat bead or shaped sequin as the main focal point. When there are enough beads to run across the aperture from top to bottom, push the needle through the card from back to front at centre bottom of the aperture. Pull the thread taut.

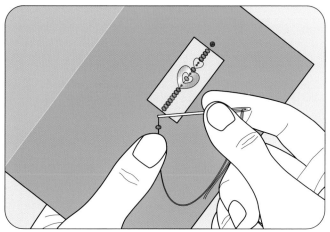

4 Slide another small bead onto the needle and then push the needle back through the hole it came out of. Pull the thread taut so that the bead sits next to the card to match the one at the top of the aperture. Take the needle around the thread on the back of the card to secure and then back out to the front through the same hole.

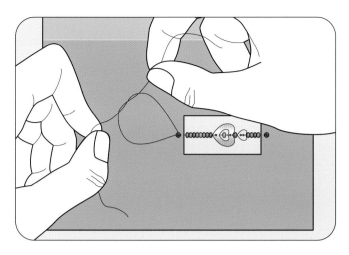

5 Remove the needle from the thread and knot the ends close to the card. Either trim the ends close to the knot, or add a couple more beads and trim the ends to uneven lengths so the beads will dangle at different heights on the front of the card. Knot the ends and secure the dangling beads to the thread with a dab of glue.

Stringing beads

There are many different types and shapes of beads available, but for this technique make sure you select ones that are relatively small and flat in profile to avoid causing too much bulk in the envelope.

There is a wide range of shaped and novelty beads available, so the bead shape for the centre of the stringing can be chosen to fit the occasion.

Valentine card with heart centre sequins on beaded thread.

Beaded line card

This card is a concertina type so the beads can be threaded to hang between the panels when the card is opened out.

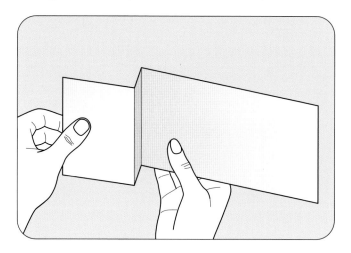

1 Cut a piece of heavy watercolour paper 10 x 35cm (4 x 14in) and mark two panels 7cm (2¾in) wide at the left-hand end. Score along the lines and fold one panel one way and the next the other way to create a concertina.

2 Decorate the panels in the chosen theme, here a fish motif is being used. Thread several tiny fish-shape beads onto a length of transparent elastic cord.

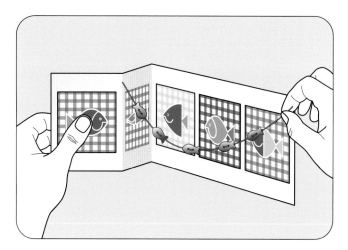

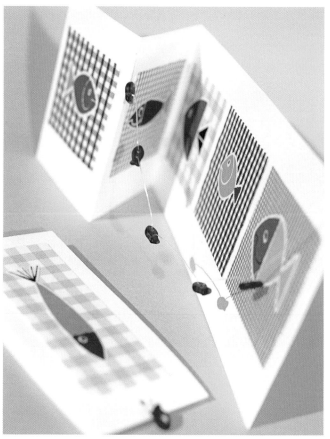

3 Pierce two holes in the card, one 1cm (½in) from the top on the fold between the two small panels and the other 1cm (½in) in from the top right corner of the long panel. Thread an end of the elastic through each hole and adjust so it does not hang below the bottom of the card when it is closed. Knot the ends and trim the excess.

Beaded daisy card

This card uses beaded Blanket stitch (see page 260) with the beads sitting on the face of the card.

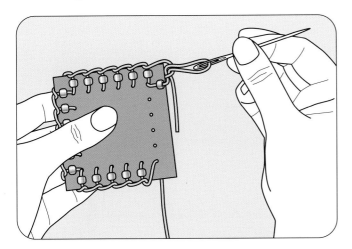

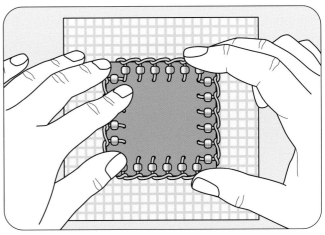

1 Mark the position of the stitches along the edges of a square of card smaller than the card blank. Hand stitch around the edge with beaded Blanket stitch (see page 260), with the beads as in step 3. To turn the corners neatly, loop the thread behind the corner of the card.

2 Add strips of double-sided tape around the decorated square and remove the backing paper. Position the decorated square in the centre of the card blank and press down firmly. If you prefer, stick on the square with double-sided foam pads, which will lift it off the surface of the card for a three-dimensional effect.

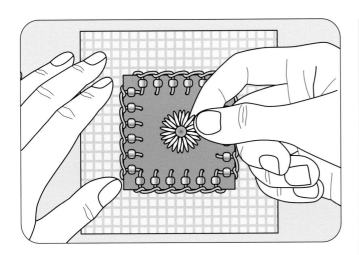

3 For an added decorative touch, stick a pressed flower in the centre of the decorated square – pick one that coordinates with the beads.

glossary

abbreviations Short versions of words and phrases used in knitting and crochet.

air-erasable marker A marker used to mark beaded embroidery designs onto fabric before beading. The lines will disappear within a few days on exposure to the air. See also water-erasable marker.

anchor bead The last bead in a string, the thread is taken through and then over it and up some or all the other beads in the string so the last bead will hold the other beads in place.

appliqué A method of attaching pieces of material or bought motifs onto a project.

awl A small, sharp pointed tool used to hold a thread loop tight while making a knot close to a bead or to punch holes in fabric.

B

back stitch An embroidery stitch, see page 252.

ball band The paper wrapper around a ball of yarn, which gives the manufacturer's details, colour and dye lot number and also information about the fibre content, metres/yards in the ball and the optimum tension and needle/crochet hook sizes.

base chain *See* Foundation chain.

bead crochet Technique of adding beads as the fabric is made.

bead loom A small loom use to weave beaded strips.

bead spinner A round bowl that spins, used to thread many seed beads onto the thread quickly.

beading The craft of making an item with beads; adding beads to the surface of a piece of fabric.

beading board A board with parallel slots in a U-shape used to design stringing patterns for necklaces and bracelets.

beading needle Very fine, long straight needles with long narrow eyes used for threading or sewing on beads. The long shaft means they can hold several beads at a time. The type used for sewing has a sharp tip to pierce the fabric.

bell caps Also known as end caps, these sit over the knot in beading thread to conceal it and are used at the end of necklaces, bracelets or earrings.

border A finishing of some description added to the edge of a fabric or project.

braid A decorative edging that may be made or purchased.

blocking The process of pinning out and finishing knitted or crochet fabric.

bugle beads Long thin tubular beads.

button band The band down the centre front of a cardigan or jacket to which the buttons are sewn.

buttonhole A hole in the buttonhole band through which buttons are put to fasten a cardigan or jacket.

buttonhole band The band down the centre front of a cardigan or jacket into which the buttonholes are worked.

C

calotte crimp A metal finishing end for beading wire/thread that consists of two small hinged cups with a loop attached. The thread or wire end is enclosed in the cups and the loop is attached to a clasp.

casting (binding) off The process of securing the stitches at the end of a piece of knitting to prevent the fabric from unravelling.

casting on The process of making the first row of stitches of a knitted project.

chain The loops created by passing one loop of yarn through another using a crochet hook.

chart A drawing on graph paper that replaces all or part of written pattern instructions with coloured blocks or symbols denoting which bead, stitches or colours of yarn are to be used where.

chevron A zigzag design.

clasp The part of a necklace or bracelet that holds the ends together.

cloisonné A type of enamel work in which outlines in decorative wire are soldered onto a metal base bead and then the different areas of the design are filled with coloured glass enamel.

collar A style of neckband.

colour knitting Knitting with more than one colour of yarn.

colourway The range of colours used in a project design.

conditioner A substance to run the thread through before beading to strengthen it and help it to resist tangles. Traditionally beeswax or paraffin wax was used, but these can make the thread quite stiff – modern synthetic alternatives are now available.

contrast colour A secondary colour in a project that is very different colour to the main colour.

cord A long thin length of material, either leather or woven threads, on which beads can be threaded. It can also be made of crocheted or knitted yarn.

couching A method that involves laying a beaded thread onto the surface of the fabric and then overcasting it in position with a second thread.

crochet A fabric made by intertwining loops of yarn or thread with a crochet hook; the action of making this fabric.

crochet hook A small hook used to make crochet fabric.

cross stitches A type of embroidery stitch made by crossing individual straight stitches over one another.

crystal beads Beads made from glass with a high lead content, which increases the sparkle when the facets are cut.

D

decreasing The process of reducing the number of stitches on the knitting needle.

delica *See* Miyuki delicas.

double-pointed needles Knitting needles with a point at both ends; used for circular knitting.

dye lot The number/reference that indicates which batch of dye was used for the yarn. The same colour yarn will vary across different dye batches, so buy all the yarn for a project at one time and check all balls are from the same batch.

E

ear studs A type of earring for pierced ears with a bar that pushes through the ear, with a butterfly or plastic disk that goes onto the back to hold it secure.

earring wires The fishhook shape part of an earring for pierced ears that hook through the ear.

edge stitches The first and last stitches of a row of knitting; stitches worked to make a selvedge.

end cap *See* Bell caps.

end clamp A metal finding used to finish off the end of leather cord or ribbon so it's possible to attach a clasp.

eye pin Metal pin with an eye at the top and no point, available in an assortment of thicknesses and lengths and in different metals. Eye pins are used in jewellery making.

F

fabric dye pens Similar to ordinary felt-tip pens, these contain fabric dye instead of ink and are used to draw on fabric or felt.

fasten off Finishing off the last stitch or a piece of crochet in a way that prevents stitches from unravelling.

felting The process of applying friction and heat to wool fleece so the fibres matt together into a solid fabric; washing knitted fabric made from wool yarn to turn it into felt fabric.

fibres Filaments of animal, vegetable or man-made material that are spun to make yarn.

findings A general term to describe the metal odds and ends that finish off a piece of jewellery – many of them can also be used in other ways.

formers Base beads to decorate in many different ways.

foundation chain Also sometimes called the base chain. The length of chain made at the beginning of a piece of crochet as a basis for constructing the fabric.

frill A wavy edge, also known as a ruffle.

front loop The loop of a stitch that lies in front of the knitting needle as you look at it.

G

garter stitch A knitted fabric made by knitting every stitch and every row.

graphing The process of drawing out a beading design on graph paper.

group Several beads worked into the same place.

H

head pin Metal pin that looks like a dressmaking pin with no point, available in an assortment of thicknesses and lengths and in different metals. Head pins are used in jewellery making.

hem The edge (usually the lower edge) of an item, which is usually folded over and sewn for a neat finish.

I

i-cord A yarn cord made by knitting in a specific way.

incomplete stitch A knit or purl stitch that was not worked properly and has left two loops of yarn over the knitting needle instead of one.

increasing The process of adding to the number of stitches on the knitting needle.

J

joining in yarn The process of attaching a new or different-coloured ball of yarn to a piece of knitting or crochet being worked.

jump rings Tiny circles of wire with two unconnected ends used in jewellery making to join components together.

K

knit The most basic of the stitches used in knitting; the generic term used to describe the action of making knitted fabric.

knitted fabric A fabric made from only knit stitches, only purl stitches (very rarely), or any combination of the two; a fabric made by knitting.

knitting needle A stick in wood, metal or bamboo used for knotting.

knitting A generic term for a knitted fabric and the action of making it, whether the stitches used are knit or purl.

knitting needle The needles used in hand knitting, which are available in many different materials including wood, plastic and metal.

L

left-hand needle The knitting needle held in the knitter's left hand.

M

main colour The primary colour in a project.

mattress stitch A sewing stitch used to sew pieces of knitted fabric together, producing a very neat and often undetectable seam.

measure The size or extent of something; to find the size or quantity of something by using an instrument such as a ruler.

memory wire Steel wire that has been treated by heat so that it returns to its original rounded coil even when pulled out of shape.

metal threads Threads made from finely spun lengths of thin metal fibres, including gold, silver, copper and aluminium.

metallic/metallic effect threads Fine synthetic threads with a metallic finish.

metallized threads Synthetic thread with a thin layer of real metal over the top; the synthetic core gives the thread strength and flexibility.

metreage (yardage) The length of yarn in a ball in metres (yards).

mitre A neat corner produced by working angles on the two pieces to be joined so that they lie flat against one another.

Miyuki delicas A more tubular version of a seed bead, these come from Japan and are almost perfectly identical in shape and size.

monofilament Single filament synthetic thread.

moss (seed) stitch A knitted stitch pattern made by alternating knit and purl stitches.

motif A complete decorative design that can be a standalone piece or repeated several times to make up a bigger design.

N

needle *See* Beading needle, Knitting needle, Sewing needle, Tapestry needle, Yarn needle.

needle tool A tool with a wooden handle and long metal tip that is used to draw fine designs on soft materials, to sculpt with and to make holes in beads.

needle threader A small piece of metal with a fine metal wire loop at the tip used to make threading most types of needles much easier and faster.

P

pattern The written instructions for making a knitted or crochet project; the design made by a combination of knit and purl stitches or by using different-coloured yarns.

pattern repeat A small section of a design that is repeated several times to make up the full design.

pattern terminology Standard phrases that are used to describe specific actions or sequences in written patterns.

picot edge A series of small points that make a decorative edging.

pressed glass A form of glass made using a plunger to press molten glass into a mould.

ply/plies Thin strands that are twisted together to make knitting/crochet yarn.

purl The other stitch (other than knit stitch) used in knitting.

R

reconstituted beads Beads made from the dust and chips from expensive stone glued together with resin and reshaped.

reverse stocking (stockinette) stitch A knitted fabric made by working alternate rows of knit stitches and purl stitches; the reverse side of stocking (stockinette) stitch fabric.

rib A knitted stitch pattern made by alternating knit and purl stitches.

right-hand needle The knitting needle held in the knitter's right hand.

right side The side of any type of fabric that will be outermost when the project is complete.

round Circular in shape; a row of crochet worked in a seamless piece to create a tube or cylinder.

row/s The lines of stitches running horizontally across a piece of knitted or crochet fabric.

S

seam The join between two (or more) fabrics.

seed beads Tiny round beads in glass or plastic, available in a range or colours and sizes, usually sold by weight.

semi-precious stones Natural stones that are more available and less expensive than precious gems such as diamonds and rubies. Semi-precious stones include malachite, rose quartz, tiger's eye and marble.

sewing in ends The process of stitching any loose ends of yarn into the back of the knitted or crochet fabric to secure and neaten them.

sewing needles Needles used for hand stitching. Sharps, of medium length with a sharp point and round eye, are used for general hand sewing. See also Beading needles.

slip knot The knot used to start almost every piece of knitting or crochet.

slipped stitch A stitch that is transferred from the left-hand needle to the right-hand needle without being knitted or purled.

spacer bar A metal bar with holes that keeps different rows of beads separate from each other around a multi-strand necklace or bracelet.

starting chain *See* Turning chain.

stitch/es The individual loops of yarn that make up the rows of a piece of knitted fabric, or the rows/rounds of a piece of crochet fabric.

stitch pattern The design made by a combination of knit and purl stitches.

stocking (stockinette) stitch A knitted fabric made by working alternate rows of knit and purl stitches.

swatch A small sample of a piece of knitted or crochet fabric.

Swiss darning An embroidery stitch that duplicates the look of knitted stitches.

symbol A drawn design used to represent an instruction, either in a pattern or on a chart.

T

tapestry needle The large eye on these needles lets them carry a heavier weight yarn than other needles. See also Sewing needle, Beading needle.

tension (gauge) The tightness or looseness of the stitches in a piece of knitted or crochet fabric.

tracing wheel A spiked wheel on a handle that is run along the lines of a pattern to make perforations that transfer designs from paper to fabric. It is sometimes used with dressmaker's carbon to make a row of little dots along each line instead.

texture The structure, feel and appearance of the surface of the fabric.

through the back loop Through the loop of a stitch that lies behind the knitting needle as you look at it.

tucks Pleats that run horizontally across a fabric.

turn/turning Moving the work around so that the other side is facing you.

turning chain Also known as a starting chain when working crochet in the round. One or more chains, depending on the length of the stitch being worked, made at the beginning or end of a row or round to take the yarn to the correct height in preparation for the new row or round. Sometimes counts as the first stitch in the row or round.

W

water-erasable marker A marker used to mark beaded embroidery designs onto fabric before beading. The lines will disappear when sponged with water. See also air-erasable marker.

warp The vertical threads of a piece of beadweaving, or fabric, that run parallel to the side edges or selvage.

weft The horizontal threads of a piece of beadweaving, or fabric, that run across at right angles to the warp.

weight A term used to describe the thickness of a knitting/crochet yarn.

wool Yarn made from the fleece of sheep primarily, though some breeds of goats, llamas, camels and rabbits have hair that is spun into yarn that can be described as wool; a term used generically (and inaccurately) to describe all yarns.

working end of yarn The end of the yarn that is coming from the ball.

working from a chart To knit or crochet following a chart rather than a written pattern.

wrong side The side of any type of fabric that will be innermost when the project is complete.

Y

yarn The correct term to use to describe knitting/crochet material.

yarn needle A sewing needle with a blunt tip and a large eye used for sewing knitted and crochet pieces together.

yarn over A technique for creating a hole in a knitted fabric by looping the yarn over the needle before working the next stitch.

suppliers and
useful websites

UK

The Bead Society of Great Britain
www.beadsociety.org.uk

The Bead and Jewellery Shop
Beads, threading materials, findings, tools
95 Crown Road, East Twickenham
TW1 3EX Tel: 020 8891 4920
www.thebeadandjewelleryshop.com

Beads Direct
Online bead retailer Tel: 01509 218028
Email: service@beadsdirect.co.uk
www.beadsdirect.co.uk

The Bead Shop
Beads, threading materials, findings, tools,
jewellery making kits
Afflecks, First Floor 52 Church Street
City Centre, Manchester M4 1PW
Tel: 0161 274 4040
www.the-beadshop.co.uk

Staedtler
Polymer clay and modelling tools
www.staedtler.co.uk

Fred Aldous
Beads, threading materials, findings, tools,
bead looms
37 Lever Street, Manchester M1 1LW
Tel: 0161 236 4224
Email: sales@fredaldous.net
www.fredaldous.co.uk

Bead Flowers
Online retailer for French beading kits,
jewellery, bead flowers, bead spinners
Tel: 07740 706484
Email: contact@beadflowers.co.uk
Website: beadflowers.co.uk

John Lewis
General craft supplies
Online and stores nationwide
www.johnlewis.com

Hobbycraft
General craft supplies
Online and stores nationwide
Tel: 0330 026 1400
www.hobbycraft.co.uk

Laughing Hens
Wool, knitting needles, crochet hooks
The Croft Stables, Station Lane
Great Barrow, Cheshire CH3 7JN
Tel: 01829 740903
www.laughinghens.com

Debbie Abrahams Beads
Beads for knitting and crochet
26 Church Drive, Nottingham NG5 2BA
Tel: 0115 855 1799
Email: beads@debbieabrahams.com
www.debbieabrahamsbeads.co.uk

Beads Unlimited
Beads, jewellery findings, threading
materials, tools
PO Box 1, Hove, East Sussex BN3 3SG
Tel: 01273 740777
Email: mailbox@beadsunlimited.co.uk
www.beadsunlimited.co.uk

Bramwell Crafts
Friendly Plastic®, air-dry clay, papier
mâché, modelling tools, moulds,
Rub-N-Buff®
Email: sales@potterycrafts.co.uk
www.bramwellcrafts.co.uk

US

The Bead Chest
African bead superstore
Tel: 1-877-655-BEAD
Email: store@thebeadchest.com
www.thebeadchest.com

Beadalon, Inc
Basic jewelry findings, jewelry making
tools, threading materials
www.beadalon.com

Staedtler
Polymer clay and modelling tools
www.staedtler.com

Ranger Inc
Inks, color wash
www.rangerink.com

Hobby Lobby Stores
General craft supplies, seashells,
stringing materials
Online and stores nationwide
www.hobbylobby.com

Michaels Stores
Beads, threading materials, findings, tools
Tel: 1-800-642-4235
www.michaels.com

Jo-Ann Fabric and Craft Store
Yarn, knitting needles, crochet hooks
Tel: 1-888-739-4120
www.joann.com

Amaco., Inc.
Friendly Plastic®, Air-dry clay,
Rub-N-Buff®
www.amaco.com

index

acknowledgements

Many of the instructions in this book were created by beaders Jema Hewitt and Cheryl Owen with contributions from crafter Mary Maguire, stitching expert Sara Beaman, knitter Sharon Brant and crocheter Jane Crowfoot. Many thanks also to Katie Dean, Linda Peterson, Debbie Abrahams, Sarah Hazell, Emma King, Carole Meldrum and Alison Nash, whose work is also featured in this book. Special thanks to Katie Dean (www.beadflowers.co.uk) for supplying the beaded flower for the front cover.

The publishers would also like to thank Louise Leffler for the wonderfully clear design, Kuo Kang Chen for his usual fantastic illustrations, Martin Norris for his great photography and Laura Russell for the sympathetic styling. Additional thanks to The Bead and Jewellery Shop in St Margaret's for loaning tools and beads for photography.

Whatever the craft, we have the book for you – just head straight to Collins & Brown crafty HeadQuarters!

LoveCrafts is the one-stop destination for all things crafty, with the very latest news and information about all our books and authors. It doesn't stop there...

Enter our fabulous competitions and win great prizes
Download free patterns from our talented authors
Collect LoveCrafts loyalty points and receive special offers on all our books

Join our crafting community at LoveCrafts – we look forward to meeting you!

the ultimates

978-1-84340-411-8   978-1-84340-450-7   978-1-84340-502-3

978-1-84340-563-4   978-1-84340-574-0   978-1-84340-672-3

This latest volume in Collins & Brown's bestselling Ultimate series reveals everything you need to know about beads and beading in an easy-to-understand format, with detailed step-by-step instructions.

The Ultimates are a growing series of comprehensive reference guides, with everything you could possibly want to know about a wide variety of craft subjects. Each title contains clear, concise text and step-by-step illustrations, making these books the perfect companion for both beginners and experts.

All titles retail at £25 and are available direct from the Collins & Brown website: www.lovecrafts.co.uk.